A Golden Thread: An Unofficial Critical History of Wonder Woman

Philip Sandifer

Copyright © 2013 Philip Sandifer

Published by Eruditorum Press

All rights reserved.

Wonder Woman and all related concepts are copyright DC Comics and are used under the principle of fair use

ISBN: 1493566725
ISBN-13: 978-1493566723

This book is not dedicated to anybody

Philip Sandifer

Acknowledgments

First and foremost, to the book's Kickstarter patrons, without whom the book would not have happened. Anna Wiggins, Alison Flynn, Eric Burns-White, Cara Milne Gee, and Becky Bolton. You are the very definition of wondrous.

Next up, James Taylor for his typically gorgeous cover art, and Allison J. Campbell for her diligent copyediting. As ever, all bits of the book that are recognizable as English language sentences are entirely due to her hard work, and all errors are entirely due to my incompetence. Thanks also to Meredith Collins for her excellent work promoting the book, and for her insights on Chapter Six.

Thanks to my long-suffering wife, whose relationship with me and this book's excessive gestation period coincide almost exactly.

Finally, thanks to the readers and commenters whose insights have shaped the book's development, both those who read it as it was being drafted due to supporting it on Kickstarter and those who commented on various preview chapters on my website at philipsandifer.com

Table of Contents

Introduction: The Last Utopia 1

Chapter 1: Man's World (December 1941) 6

Chapter 2: Clay (1942) 15

Chapter 3: God of War (1943-45) 23

Chapter 4: William Moulton Marston 39

Chapter 5: The First Transition (1946-48) 54

Chapter 6: Harry G. Peter 63

Chapter 7: Robert Kanigher (1948-1958) 74

Chapter 8: The Silver Age (1958-68) 85

Chapter 9: The "I Ching" Era (1968-72) 102

Chapter 10: Gloria Steinem, Wonder Woman, and Feminism
.... 116

Chapter 11: Julius Schwartz (1973-76) 131

Chapter 12: Lynda Carter 141

Chapter 13: Return to World War II (1977-78) 153

Chapter 14: Repeated Turmoil (1978-85) 162

Chapter 15: Crisis on Infinite Earths (1985-86) 174

Chapter 16: George Pérez (1987-92) 181

Chapter 17: William Messner-Loebs (1992-95) 192

Chapter 18: The Second Wilderness (1995-2002) 203

Chapter 19: Greg Rucka (2002-05) 214

Chapter 20: *Infinite Crisis* (2005-07) 230

Chapter 21: Gail Simone (2008-10) 244

Chapter 22: Movies and TV Projects 253

Chapter 23: Brian Azzarello (2011-13) 263

Oh had I a golden thread
And a needle so fine
I would weave a magic strang
Of rainbow design

In it I'd weave the bravery
Of women giving birth
In it I would weave the innocence
Of children over all the earth

-Pete Seeger, "Oh Had I a Golden Thread"

Introduction: The Last Utopia

Nobody indulges in utopian visions anymore. On the rare occasions when people do – the playing at classless society offered by the Occupy movements in late 2011, for example – the general reaction is one of condescending pity. Utopians, in our culture, aspire towards harmlessness. The best of them are charmingly naive people you might want to invite over for dinner, but you'd never actually put them in charge of anything.

Too often, though, utopianism is viewed as outwardly sinister. You can see it in the lines of political attack taken against Barack Obama – not just the outright lie he's a socialist (a political view that's produced a disproportionate amount of utopian literature), but the basic claim that he wants to transform America. That the desire to engage in radical change to improve things is self-evidently terrible shows just how far utopianism has fallen.

Sadly, the most common utopian visions today are eschatological. If there's to be Utopia, it can only come after a cathartic purging of society, whether at the hands of the gods or at the hands of humanity's own folly run amok. The idea we can make this world a better one, as opposed to simply leveling it and starting over, is all but completely gone.

It wasn't always like this. Our cultural landscape is littered with the debris of abandoned utopias. Many, though not all, emerged from the years following World War II, a golden age of utopian thinking where gleaming space colonies and cute robotic servants would give everyone a life of perpetual leisure. Entire popular genres emerged from such dreams. By the late 1970's they became shell-shocked survivors: a set of images without a purpose. The idea we'd yet to colonize Mars by 2012, let alone possess a clear vision of how to get there someday soon, would be unthinkable to the world of the 1960s.

Some years ago, a briefly popular book called *Where's My Jetpack?* revisited various futuristic technologies with jaded longing, an implicit sense that the future we were promised never arrived. This is, on the face of it, strange. The machine I'm using to write this book is more advanced and sophisticated than the wildest dreams of post-war science fiction. I have a mobile phone better than any "communicator" *Star Trek* imagined for the 23rd Century. Clearly the future *has* arrived, and from a purely technological standpoint it's pretty impressive, though markedly different from what post-war futurists imagined. But it's not utopian. The longing for the jetpack is less a longing for individual human flight than it is for the lost utopian vision it represented.

Wonder Woman was not the last of the utopian visions that followed the Second World War. If anything, she was one of the first, created during the war itself both to serve as anti-German propaganda and to envision what post-war society might look like. But she is the last one standing. The reason why isn't terribly complex: she avoided the typical utopian iconography. Her utopianism was not one of rocket ships and gleaming cities, so when the steam went out of such technologies, she was not as straightforwardly discredited. She escaped the purge of utopias by disguising herself as a silly comic-book superhero.

In another sense, however, she survived because her utopia was discredited so early on it never had time to negatively impact her. Her creator, William Moulton Marston, envisioned her as an avatar for a female-supremacist utopia characterized by sexual liberation that was so lacking in any real-world credibility it was unceremoniously abandoned before the end of Wonder Woman's first decade. Having learned to suppress her utopian zeal so early, Wonder Woman had fewer problems enduring the wave of cynicism that felled her contemporaries. She was already used to playing down her own radicalism.

Either way, she survived. And while only a handful of moments in her history lay out an explicitly utopian manifesto, she's survived as an essentially utopian character in a world that has little if any use for utopianism. It has not, however, been a smooth ride. Wonder Woman is extremely well-known and well-liked, but with few exceptions her comic sales have historically been mediocre at best, and she's never done as well as Superman or Batman when adapted into other media. She is at once a universally recognized media icon and an arcane, niche character.

Nor does her history track well with any larger political movement. It would be convenient if a history of Wonder Woman paralleled a history of feminism neatly, but it doesn't. At her debut she was far more radical than the feminism of the time. But at the political height of feminism in the late 1960s and early 1970s, Wonder Woman and feminism were cast on opposite sides of the debate, and even though Wonder Woman adorned the first issue of *Ms.*, Gloria Steinem's feminist magazine, the actual relationship between the two was tense. In the early 2000s she was ahead of the curve as far as the emerging strands of feminist geek/sci-fi fandom were concerned; today, that fandom is considerably more advanced, and she's suffered more than a few setbacks.

However, it would be foolish to suggest that Wonder Woman's history is somehow insulated from larger social movements. Wonder Woman has changed with the times, but she neither follows the trends of social change nor establishes them. She is something else: a persistent thorn in the side of cultural progress, the ghost of an abandoned and "childish" utopianism who stubbornly refuses to sit quietly in the corner while the grown-ups are talking.

As such, her history is unique. Not infrequently, she's marginalized and silenced by her writers and artists, who are almost exclusively male and often hostile to what she represents. Equally, she finds odd perspectives on the margins that subvert and undermine mainstream assumptions, giving a voice to viewpoints that would otherwise be overlooked. Often, in fact, she does both at once, finding new ways to reassert her concept in the face of overt attempts to diminish it.

This book traces that history, telling the story of Wonder Woman's evolution in her primary medium: the comic books published by DC Comics since 1941. Though her comics form the main spine of the book, there are frequent excursions to her other media appearances and the larger context in which the comics exist. The book does not endeavor to explain the plots of every Wonder Woman comic it covers; it's not a guide to her continuity or character history, but to the history of her publication and the approaches taken to her.

(A brief note on terminology – DC Comics as it exists today is a subsidiary of Time Warner, the product of a series of mergers and acquisitions. At its start Wonder Woman was published by All-American Publications, which was absorbed into DC, itself then called National Comics, in the mid-1940s. For the sake of simplicity, I've opted to use "DC Comics" to refer to Wonder Woman's corporate owners regardless of the time period.)

That said, it's not written with the assumption the reader will have read all or indeed any of the comics discussed. I've tried to provide enough context to follow the argument, but anyone seeking to consult the original sources will no doubt find plenty of surprises and details I didn't mention. Many of the comics discussed have been reprinted by DC in various collections, which I recommend. For the ones not in print, Chris Hayes has a phenomenally detailed website called

Amazon Archives at amazonarchives.com, which provides rough summaries of most Wonder Woman stories, and which was an invaluable aid – I've read hundreds of Wonder Woman comics, and don't always recall in which issue a given story appears. Also essential is the Grand Comics Database at comics.org, which provides detailed information not only on Wonder Woman but on nearly a million other comics.

This thorough and completist approach to Wonder Woman's history risks losing the forest for the trees. I've focused on periods of historical importance, but the nature of Wonder Woman's history is messy and disorganized. She isn't the product of any sort of ordered process, but of dozens of writers and artists covering a span of nearly seventy-five years. Consequentially, substantial focus is often given to periods of Wonder Woman's history that had little influence on the whole. In many cases it is precisely this lack of influence that's interesting, as it reveals the various secret histories and alternative visions of what Wonder Woman could have been.

So when it comes to Wonder Woman, the idiosyncrasies of the trees are more illuminating than the homogeny of the forest. Various themes and motifs will recur throughout the history, but they don't march towards some grand and unifying conclusion. Nor could they possibly – Wonder Woman's history is ongoing, and this book will be outdated by the time it's in your hands. This is appropriate. More to the point, this messy and unfinished process is, I think, an accurate portrayal of material social progress.

Wonder Woman's history is the history of a discredited utopia that refused to lie down or go away. Her story is neither triumphant nor tragic; it's a demonstration of how the determination to make the world a better place plays out in the world. And in that regard it is, at least, a story brimming with wonder.

Chapter 1: Man's World (December 1941)

The first thing we have to admit is she doesn't get a glorious debut. Batman and Superman, the two better-selling members of DC's supposed "Trinity" of characters, got famous debuts. *Action Comics* #1 and *Detective Comics* #27 are two of the most valuable comics in the world, introducing their characters with splashy, iconic covers. Wonder Woman, on the other hand, debuted as a backup feature in *All-Star Comics* #8 in what is best described as an advertisement.

It's not as bad as it sounds. *All-Star Comics* was in general an advertisement. To understand this, we need explain what DC Comics looked like in 1941. The bulk of DC's line was not composed of single-character comics like *Batman* or *Superman*, but of anthologies featuring a lead story and several backups. So, for instance, *Action Comics* #43, which came out the same month as *All-Star Comics* #8, featured a thirteen-page Superman story followed by five stories with more obscure superheroes (The Vigilante, Three Aces, Mr. America, Congo Bill, and Zatara) ranging from six to thirteen pages apiece.

All-Star Comics is a comic that only makes sense in this context. Its main feature is the Justice Society of America – the first real team of superheroes. The Justice Society was a simple idea: take a bunch of characters, none of whom can support their own comic, and put them in a single book. Crucially, the typical Justice Society story is not about a team working together, but a team-based frame story wrapped around solo stories featuring the individual heroes themselves, each of which ends with a reminder that the reader can follow the adventures of the character in another book. It is, in other words, a book that exists to get fans of one character to try the stories of another in the hope they'll buy more comics.

Wonder Woman was introduced in the final nine pages of *All-Star Comics* #8, after the conclusion of that month's installment of the Justice Society. Not only is her debut, unlike that of Batman or Superman, not the lead feature of the issue, it's not even treated as a highlight; she doesn't merit mention on the cover, little yet a big, iconic image like that of Superman on *Action Comics* #1. Her debut is an advertisement for the upcoming *Sensation Comics* that's been shoved to the back of a book consisting of ads for other books.

There's more than one way to look at this. Pessimistically, the history of Wonder Woman is going to be characterized, in part, by having a harder time in the market than her male counterparts. Batman and Superman both anchor entire lines of comics, with at least two solo books apiece running alongside a host of spinoffs. Wonder Woman hasn't starred in a second book since 1952. She may be one of DC's best-known characters, but she's rarely been a best-selling one, and she's never treated with the same respect as Superman or Batman. In this context, to launch Wonder Woman with an unheralded advertisement in another book is merely the first of a thousand slights.

This can also be read as sickly fitting. If Wonder Woman has never managed to be unambiguously successful and equal to her male colleagues, this is surely no worse a fate than that suffered by feminism, itself an unfinished project. Wonder Woman – as an unspoken second-class citizen – mirrors the basic struggle she represents.

But it behooves us to consider the actual content of her debut story. We're told explicitly that Wonder Woman is "giving up her heritage and her right to eternal life" to come to Man's World. For all that is made of the messianic themes in Superman, fleeing the dying world of Krypton is not half as drenched in Christ imagery as this. Wonder Woman departs the world of the gods for the world of man, giving up her divinity to become mortal.

Looking at Wonder Woman's first appearance through this lens, the frustrating aspects of it make an odd sort of sense. Central to the Christ story is the image of the divine incarnating not just into the mortal world, but into the most degrading and humiliating of conditions: not only does he walk the Earth, he's born in a manger, dies in agony nailed to a tree, and spends the time in between amidst the sick, the poor, and the outcast. Likewise, Wonder Woman descends from Paradise Island to Man's World, to incarnate in comics' most crassly materialist form, an advertisement in the back of a book that only exists to sell other books.

Yet reading *All-Star Comics* #8 seventy years later, the first page of Wonder Woman still bristles with uncanny power. This power is not merely the weight of history and the realization that one is about to read nine of the most important pages in comics history, although that's certainly there – rather, the entire tone of the comic changes. The artists over the first sixty-nine pages of the issue fall into fairly predictable comic styles: the cartoonish approach of Stan Aschmeier; the photorealism of Jack Burnley; the frenetic, noir layouts of Bernard Baily; and the scratchy angularity of Everett E. Hibbard. All of these men (and especially Baily, whose command of the page is miles ahead of his contemporaries) are skilled artists who compellingly execute the sorts of styles that fit the comics they're writing.

Despite all this, one is utterly unprepared for the sight of Harry G. Peter's art. The opening splash of Wonder Woman – a pose recycled for the cover of *Sensation Comics* #1 a month later – is striking. The image is almost completely devoid of straight lines; even the stars on Wonder Woman's billowing skirt are bent and lumpy compared to the stars adorning the ad on the previous page for the next Justice Society story.

The lettering strives for the tight regularity of type instead of the more natural and hand-written feel of the issue's other artists. The entire thing has a posed, almost tableau-like feel, unlike the action-packed dynamism of Peter's contemporaries.

But the most compelling difference is how Peter draws the face. We'll talk at length about his art in a later chapter, but for now let's look simply at Wonder Woman's face. Her nose consists of little more than two dots for nostrils. Her eyes are widely spaced, and misaligned to boot. Her lips are pursed and unexpressive. Her jaw is statuesque. As a result, attention is drawn away from her face and towards the rest of her body, a technique similarly employed in the Decadent-era erotica of Aubrey Beardsley and Franz von Bayros – and a far cry from the anatomical referencing found in other comics.

Peter's initial depiction of the character is a fascinating mixture of the severe and the libidinous. As we'd expect from art visibly influenced by Victorian erotica, she's unquestionably a sexy woman. Her skirt billows up to reveal one of her thighs, and though tame by modern standards, it falls around her in a way that's tantalizingly close to revealing her undergarments. Her arms and shoulders are bare, and her breastplate is complementary to her cleavage. But her expression is serious, and her eyes are trained not to make eye contact with the reader – instead they look beyond, as if focusing on some larger object behind us. Her build, though sensuous, is strong and muscular. She's erotic, but not in a way that lends itself to being claimed or leered at. She refuses to interact with the reader or to acknowledge their gaze.

But who are these readers? Wonder Woman wasn't even advertised on the cover, so one has to assume the readers of this particular issue were overwhelmingly male, like those of most superhero comics. Given that assumption, the first few pages of this story must have been deeply off-putting. The story opens with a plane crashing onto an island; two women, alarmed at the very prospect of finding a man on Paradise

Figure 1: Harry G. Peter's initial splash page of Wonder Woman, from *All-Star Comics* #8 (1941). copyright DC Comics, used under the principle of fair use.

Island, rescue him and identify him as Captain Steve Trevor of the US Army Intelligence Service. The plot quickly changes to one of forbidden love: one of his rescuers falls for him, and her mother, the Queen, forbids her to see him.

The first two-and-a-half pages push the standard male comic book reader out of the story. Yes, Steve Trevor is the sort of character one expects to see in a superhero comic – both his name and his appearance evoke Captain America, a.k.a. Steve Rogers, another blonde American soldier introduced a little over a year before. But here the character is injured, unconscious, and stuck inside some sort of love story. If one adheres to a theory in which the reader imagines himself as the superhero, this amounts to the antipode of Wonder Woman's fall into Man's World: the fall of a standard-issue superhero (indeed, a thinly veiled parody of DC's competitor's flagship character) onto Paradise Island.

After its first two-and-a-half pages the story breaks into a one-and-a-half page text piece with a couple of illustrations. This is not unheard of in comics from the time, but it's not standard practice either. More importantly, it's not even the first block of text in the story. The very first page of Wonder Woman contains a typically enthused description of her might and power: "As lovely as Aphrodite – as wise as Athena – with the speed of Mercury and the strength of Hercules – she is known only as Wonder Woman, but who she is, or whence she came, nobody knows!" (Such text pieces at the start of comics were and are quite common). But it's the first sentence, describing "a world torn by the hatreds and wars of men" and how, at last, there "appears a *woman* to whom the problems and feats of men are mere child's play!" that sets the tone for what's to come.

The larger text piece beginning on the third page expands upon this idea. It describes the culture of the Amazons, defined first and foremost by their need to remain distant from men after Aphrodite rescued them from enslavement to Hercules, who stole Queen Hippolyte's Magic Girdle. As a reminder of this duty, they all wear the bracelets they'd once worn as slaves. Their culture is overtly utopian: it is said to be free of disease, war, and death, and enjoys advanced technology like the Magic Sphere, which can show any place in the world, see any event in history, and, in some cases, predict the future – all this, just so long as Hippolyte retains the Magic Girdle she recovered from Hercules and is not "again beguiled by men."

There's a clear sexual aspect to this story. The fact that Hercules specifically tricks Hippolyte out of a magical undergarment and that this appears to take place outside of combat strongly hints he stole it during a night of passion, suggesting that the beguilement of men is specifically sexual. This is supported by the way in which the Amazons react to Steve Trevor's presence. It's not the fact that there's a man on the island that's objectionable; indeed, the Amazons act as though they have a duty to help Trevor. No, what makes Trevor dangerous is the possibility that one of the Amazons will fall in love with him, risking the loss of Aphrodite's favor. This might seem strange given that Aphrodite is a love goddess. We'll develop this theme in later chapters, but suffice it to say that Marston is gesturing towards a very, very unusual conception of love here.

Following the backstory of the Amazons, we get the origin of Steve Trevor. Though it's the longest section, taking up a third of the story, it's little more than a generic military action piece, and serves mostly to reinforce the point we've already made: Trevor is a traditional male action hero, albeit one in crisis, and suddenly dependent on these strange female characters.

This is made even more explicit in the final two pages of the story, which begins with Hippolyte consulting Aphrodite and Athena for advice on what to do. Aphrodite informs her that she must help Trevor get back to America, while Athena says she "must send with him your strongest and wisest Amazon – the finest of your wonder women! – For America, the last citadel of democracy, and of equal rights for women, needs your help!" Although this sounds like the standard-issue jingoistic patriotism common in the comics of the era, focusing on that misses the fact that this particular jingoistic portrayal describes America as being in crisis and needing intervention from these female utopians.

This is where the divine half of the imagery comes in. Wonder Woman is cast into the degrading materialism of Man's World, but she brings the power of Athena and Aphrodite – two goddesses – to save it, cutting against the Superman/Christ narrative she tacitly mirrors. She's a Pagan figure, explicitly libidinal, resistant to any personal relationship with the reader, expressly militaristic, and, perhaps most obviously and significant, a woman. A more nuanced look at the mythology would take her not as a Christ analogue but as a callback to the older deity Ishtar, the Babylonian goddess of love and war, a fusion of Aphrodite and Athena with her own famed descent into the underworld.

The remainder of the story is straightforward. In order to find the best Amazon, Hippolyte organizes a competition, which she forbids her daughter to participate in. Her daughter, of course, sneaks in and participates anyway, wins, and is given the familiar Wonder Woman costume for her descent to Man's World.

That's it: a rather unremarkably plotted origin story plugging her next appearance in *Sensation Comics* #1, where she'll presumably get to have an actual adventure instead of being stuck explaining the premise for eight straight pages, several of which are pure text. It's not an inauspicious beginning by any measure – the story is intriguing and gives every reason to check out *Sensation Comics* – but for all its declarations it's not exactly a triumphant clarion call of feminism.

And so begins a barely believable epic of feminism and sexuality, and one of the most radically left-wing agendas ever to be catapulted into the American mainstream. In nine pages we see a towering goddess descending into the ugly viscera of our world, into the crassly commercial and blithely jingoistic world of American superhero comics in all their violent, macho glory.

Now for her seventy-year ascent.

Chapter 2: Clay (1942)

The early years of any major comic book character are always a bit unnerving to read. They establish the iconic elements of the character, but are full of false starts and abandoned alternatives. All of this becomes even more complex because one of the mainstays of Marston's Wonder Woman is a BDSM-inflected feminism that both DC and later creators have been uncomfortable with for decades, so what's established here is not quite the Wonder Woman of popular culture.

But one of the most shocking things to jump out of the first year of Wonder Woman is how frequently Marston and Peter make use of blatant racial stereotypes. These include not just the Japanese as deformed midgets (as they were often caricatured during World War II) but minstrel-style black characters, indolent Mexicans, treacherous Hawaiians, and the treatment of all East Asian nationalities as interchangeable with the Japanese. This is hard to explain without resorting to the harsh but likely accurate truth that Marston and Peter were, in fact, spectacularly racist.

This gets at a larger aspect of Wonder Woman in her original conception: her fundamental association with the United States of America. To some extent this is simply a cultural artifact: all World War II-era American superhero comics were unrelentingly patriotic and jingoistic. Considering that Marston and Peter break from the normal order of superhero comics in so many other ways, in terms of both storytelling and ideology, the fact that strident and unwavering patriotism is one of the things that they retain is significant.

It's doubly true given the extent to which Marston builds an entire theology that promotes a pro-American ideology. In *Wonder Woman* #1 Marston retells and reworks the origin story he'd debuted in *All-Star Comics* #8 some six months previously, presenting the world as "ruled by rival gods – Ares, God of War, and Aphrodite, Goddess of Love and Beauty." In a move that should astonish no one, Marston further associates men with Ares and women with Aphrodite. More important, however, are their nationalistic allegiances. Ares boasts, "Ho! Ho! The whole world's at war – I rule the Earth!" But Aphrodite responds, "Your rule will end when America wins! And America will win! I'll send an Amazon to help her!" America is gendered female, which is a common way to refer to the country, but more to the point, America's specifically allied with Aphrodite. The equating of the Axis Powers with Ares is sensible enough, but this is altogether more surprising.

It is, however, consistent with the larger portrayal of America we get throughout these stories. Wonder Woman is reflexively patriotic, yes, but her patriotism is unusual. In the first twelve issues of *Sensation Comics*, and the first two of *Wonder Woman*, it's repeatedly demonstrated that however noble the square-jawed American masculinity of Steve Trevor may be, it frequently needs help. The American military is unequivocally a force for good, but continually threatened by secret plots of various sorts.

The most common plot hook by far involves Steve Trevor being dispatched on a mission that's actually a trap laid by a Japanese or German villain. These traps have an air of seduction around them: Trevor is led to believe one thing or another, but once he gets there he's to be taken in and interrogated or killed by the leering villains. It's a variation on one of the more common misogynistic images of women:

that of the *vagina dentata*, whereby women seduce men to their ruin – except here it's not the duplicity of women that endangers Steve Trevor, but rather the masculine heroic fantasy; the intervention of a different sort of femininity is what saves him.

Although *Sensation Comics* is less-obviously marketed to boys than *All-Star Comics* (Wonder Woman at least makes the cover here, and the "Black Pirate" story within features an unusually large number of shirtless men) there is little in the comic to suggest that it's looking for a female audience. The remaining backup features – "Mr. Terrific," "The Gay Ghost," "Little Boy Blue," and "Wildcat," – are standard male-focused action strips, and the back cover advertisement for Daisy Air Rifles is second only to Charles Atlas in terms of its adherence to traditional gender roles. By all appearances, this is a comic targeted at boys. And yet within it we find Wonder Woman, upon arriving in Man's World, immediately going clothes shopping, noting that "mother told me so much about styles of American women that I'm dying to see them."

This turn towards shopping and fashion, like the turn in *All-Star Comics* #8 from the crash landing of an American pilot to a love story, must be taken as a refusal to cater to the reader's normal desires. Notably, the previous page of the comic ends with Wonder Woman refusing to confer with the doctors at Walter Reed and running off, leaving Trevor in their hands. Wonder Woman abandons the plot of the issue (in the last panel, bottom right-hand corner, she physically flees the page) to go shopping, in defiance of the narrative conventions the primarily male readers would expect. Taken in this light, her decision to go shopping is less a stereotypically female pursuit and more a stereotypically non-masculine one, and thus actively hostile to the presumptive audience.

This antipathy fuels Wonder Woman's early appearances, which frequently stress the fish-out-of-water nature of her engagement with the world. In *Sensation Comics* #1, after preventing a robbery, she easily fends off the bullets of the crooks with her bracelets, which she likens to a game. But her naiveté about the world is in no way a disadvantage. When a smarmy theater promoter swindles her out of the wages from her "Bullets and Bracelets" act (a job that quietly and unnervingly parallels the more obvious theatrical role available for an attractive, scantily clad woman) she casually turns the tables and recoups her money from him, only to just-as-casually give it all away in exchange for the credentials of a nurse, thus providing her secret identity as Diana Prince. Her lack of knowledge of the world isn't a weakness – it's a license to transgress.

In this context we can also make sense of Wonder Woman's major recurring ally, Etta Candy, introduced in 1942. More than almost any other character in Wonder Woman, Etta challenges the norms of American superhero comics. A solidly plus-sized chocoholic, at first glance she seems a crass stereotype of an overweight woman with an eating disorder. But as one reads on, a curious detail emerges – or rather, an expected detail fails to emerge. Nowhere in these fourteen issues, or indeed anywhere in Marston's tenure on the book, are there any scenes in which Etta is humiliated, looked down on, or shown to be less than capable because of her weight.

Her insistence on bringing candy wherever she goes is regularly played for laughs, but the tone is that of character-based humor about a woman with an excessive fondness for chocolate, not of shameful gluttony. Sure, Wonder Woman tries (and fails) to get Etta to go on a diet, but what's remarkable is the confidence with which Etta bats her concern away, including a delightful scene where Wonder Woman tries to persuade Etta to lose weight so she can get a man; Etta points out that once you get a man there's nothing else to do with him, but you can always eat candy. Compared to Wonder Woman's hopeless fawning over Steve Trevor, Etta's level-headed refusal to change who she is in order to get a man makes her, in this regard at least, even more of a feminist icon than Wonder Woman herself. Like Wonder Woman, her power stems from her refusal to allow herself to be subject to the structures of power within the world.

Etta presides over the Beeta Lamda [sic] sorority at Holliday College, giving Wonder Woman a convenient small army of female characters to call on. This, in turn, helps establish Wonder Woman as a broader social force: she's the de facto leader of a large group of women – indeed, of an entire generation. It's no coincidence that Wonder Woman's allies are all college-age women, approximately the same age as the men fighting World War II.

Wonder Woman is building an army via Beeta Lamda, but it's an army as only Marston would envision it. In their first appearance, Wonder Woman leads a hundred Holliday girls to walk up to the soldiers holding Trevor captive, moving as if to dance with them, only to surprise them by chaining them up. In other words, the sisters of Beeta Lamda don't fight, they beguile and capture. This speaks to the other obvious use of the Beeta Lamda girls: they can engage in acts of bondage and spanking, which are written off as "sorority initiations."

Ah, yes, bondage. It's no secret that Wonder Woman has a lot of bondage and fetish themes; it's a fairly standard hook for any history of the character. Almost every Marston-era story involves Wonder Woman (and often several other characters) being tied up. Wonder Woman's major weakness is that she loses her power if she's bound by her wrist cuffs by a man. And, of course, the girls of Beeta Lamda will take almost any excuse offered to bend someone over and paddle them. Images of bondage and discipline are rife through Marston's work.

It even appears in the basic iconography. The magic lasso (which isn't introduced until *Sensation Comics* #6, although the retelling of Wonder Woman's origin in *Wonder Woman* #1 goes back and gives it to her from the start) is the most obvious example, a rope that forces anyone bound with it to

Philip Sandifer

Figure 2: Etta Candy presides over the Beeta Lamda sorority, from *Sensation Comics* #4 (1942), art by Harry G. Peter, copyright DC Comics, used under the principle of fair use.

obey her. This is often linked to Marston's invention of a form of lie detector, but this is misleading. The modern version of Wonder Woman's lasso, which compels one to tell the truth, post-dates the original conception: in Marston's comics, the lasso is more an instrument of BDSM, compelling obedience in general.

This is probably the point to make the obligatory admission that Marston's own sex life was unconventional – he lived with both his wife and his former student/research assistant, Olive Byrne, and had two children with each of them; Wonder Woman's metal bracelets were modeled off of cuffs worn by Byrne. If you were to assume that his narrative interest in female domination carried over to his personal life, you would not be alone in the assumption (although it is an assumption). But it's a mistake to look at Wonder Woman primarily through the lens of Marston's sexual fetishes. Of far more relevance is what we might call his philosophical fetishes.

We'll talk about Marston's academic work in a later chapter, but the considerable intellectual depth behind his Wonder Woman stories is obvious in reading them. *Sensation Comics* #11 offers a clear example: Wonder Woman, Steve Trevor, and Etta Candy astrally project themselves to the land of Eros, a place where positions of leadership are considered a grave punishment, and imprisonment is a reward. This is not merely an interest in bondage, but an exploration of its philosophical consequences. For Marston, it's quite clear that bondage is of interest in large part because it symbolizes the act of submission, which Marston holds dear. Crucially, it's only submission to loving female authority that's valued – the Eros story is in part a parable about how everything goes wrong when men do the enslaving instead of women, because men don't make slavery fun.

It's easy, seventy years later, to forget how far ahead of his time Marston was. He told stories infused with the ideologies of second-wave feminism and the BDSM community several decades before either of those things actually existed. The first year of Wonder Woman remains deeply problematic, yet in many ways it would feel more at home in the 1970s, when Gloria Steinem would go on to edit a collection of Marston-era Wonder Woman stories, than it does in its birthplace of the 1940s.

This is not true in all regards – the racism, for instance, is as regressive in 1941 as the sexual politics are progressive – but it's broadly true, and the tension by which Marston's Wonder Woman is at once firmly of her time and ahead of her time imbues the character with a confused and deeply tangled ideology full of contradictions and problems. Then again, there's no such thing as a historical ideology without contradictions and problems, and all ideologies eventually become historical.

We can at least say this: nothing else in 1942 had problems quite like Wonder Woman's. Marston was making mistakes none of his contemporaries could even imagine making. Progress is often nothing more than a matter of making new mistakes. By that standard, Wonder Woman is a quantum leap forward.

Chapter 3: God of War (1943-45)

Given everything she's designed to stand for, in some ways it's surprising that the pinnacle of Wonder Woman's popularity came during World War II. The early 1940s were a good period for comics in general – not for nothing is it called the Golden Age – but Wonder Woman's popularity in the early 1940s isn't just out of proportion to her popularity in the rest of her history, it's out of proportion compared to DC's other superheroes. In the most recent sales charts at the time of writing, Wonder Woman is DC's sixth-most popular superhero, with her sole line of books coming in not just behind Batman (who has thirteen different titles) and Superman (four titles) but behind Green Lantern (also four titles), the Flash, and Aquaman (one apiece). Her status as the third of their "big three" is not based on her current popularity at all, but on the fact that she, along with Batman and Superman, are the only superheroes from the Golden Age to be published throughout the 1950s. Her stature is based on the legacy she built in the 1940s and the ability she had to weather the dip in popularity superhero comics suffered the following decade.

In 1944, not only did Wonder Woman anchor her own book and *Sensation Comics*, she was a lead feature in *Comic Cavalcade* and appeared regularly in *All-Star Comics*. (The last of these is difficult to take much pride in given she was stuck as the Justice Society's secretary and only got to participate in one or two adventures, hanging out in the background of the frame stories the rest of the time.) Furthermore, she appeared in a daily newspaper strip between 1944 and 1945. Only Superman, the company's flagship character, appeared in as many titles during this time.

What makes this all the more amazing is that, save for a lone feature in *All-Star Comics* #11 and her background appearances in the Justice Society stories, every Wonder Woman adventure of this time period was written by Marston and drawn by Harry G. Peter. Neither Superman nor Batman maintained a single writer or art team across their stories, whereas Marston and Peter kept up this staggering output on their own. Accounts suggest that Peter was supported by a sizable studio of artists doing backgrounds and inking, as was common for the period, and Marston solicited story ideas from his family; nonetheless, their combined output is impressive, and both stayed more involved than the creators of either Superman or Batman.

However, despite the popularity of Wonder Woman's comics, they are utterly, mind-wrenchingly strange. It is difficult to effectively communicate just how weird these comics are to someone who hasn't read them. To be fair, some of the strange bits are simply products of their time; reading Superman or Batman comics from the same era is jarring too. The comics of the Golden Age were produced quickly and at high volume, which promoted a manic inventiveness. Nothing spurs weirdness quite like a deadline.

But with Wonder Woman there's more to it than this. She flits through the weird and over-the-top inventiveness common to the era, but what really makes reading early Wonder Woman comics strange is the way in which even as the stories engage directly with American culture of the time, they consistently and completely reflect an ideology that is, by any standard, utterly outside the mainstream of that culture, if not more so today. To put it bluntly, it's astoundingly strange to see World War II used as a pretext for actively indoctrinating children into a life of sexual submission to powerful women.

Once Marston made it through the first year of Wonder Woman stories and began to hit his stride, this ideology, which was hardly subtle to begin with, becomes so thoroughly integrated into the comic that it's not a surprise to see Wonder Woman idly contemplate, "If girls want to be slaves there's no harm in that. The bad thing for them is submitting to a master or an evil mistress like Paula! A *good* mistress could do wonders with them!" This sentiment may seem bizarre in the larger context of 1940s America, but for Wonder Woman it's par for the course.

No, what's so incongruous is that this sentiment comes in a story that's also an unmistakable piece of jingoistic American World War II propaganda. The evil mistress Paula is Paula von Gunther, described earlier in the issue (*Wonder Woman* #3) as the "Nazi chief agent in America." A page before Wonder Woman's philosophical musings on consensual slavery, the reader is presented with the contrasting view, described as "the Hitler principle that women must remain men's slaves." Don't forget, in her early days Wonder Woman wasn't catering to the fringe of society, she was massively popular and read by the same male audience who read the rest of DC's output.

With this in mind, the entirety of *Wonder Woman* #3 is worth looking at. Unlike *Sensation Comics*, where Wonder Woman only appears in the first story of a given issue, her solo series, published quarterly for most of the 1940s, consisted of four separate Wonder Woman stories (typically accompanied by short text pieces on subjects like fighter pilots and "Wonder Women of History"). Although each of the four stories had distinct plots of their own, they tended to form larger narratives with varying degrees of coherence. The plots of *Wonder Woman* #3 and #4 are further linked to create an overall account detailing the conversion of Paula von Gunther from Nazi villainess to one of Wonder Woman's allies.

Prior to this storyline, von Gunther is the only major and recurring member of Wonder Woman's rogue's gallery. Admittedly, Wonder Woman's rogue's gallery is infamously subpar. Only three of her villains are well known: Doctor Psycho, The Cheetah, and Giganta. All three make their debut in the three years under discussion, and they're not a particularly inspiring lot. Doctor Psycho and The Cheetah are both interesting inasmuch as they are opposite sides of the same coin. Doctor Psycho is driven to villainy out of abjection over his diminutive and unattractive looks, whereas The Cheetah is the jealous alter-ego of Pricilla Rich, a vain socialite. Marston favors villains whose concepts are based around some sort of psychological imbalance, but villains born of day-to-day neuroses lack the inspiring punch of Batman or Superman's rogue's galleries. Giganta's origin is at least more idiosyncratic – she's an ape who's artificially evolved into a cave woman – but she makes only two appearances in the Golden Age before vanishing until 1966, at which point she gets a revamped origin.

By *Wonder Woman* #3, Paula von Gunther was the only villain to have made a second appearance, so it's striking to see her become an ally when the series is hardly long on antagonists; as mentioned before, her conversion to a heroic character takes up the entire plot of two consecutive issues. Given Marston's concern with issues of domination, submission, and control, and the way in which he clearly sees Wonder Woman as a tool for rehabilitating a flawed world both within the story and without, what amounts to a 102-page storyline about rehabilitating Nazis deserves greater scrutiny. (For context, at 102 pages this two-issue story is equivalent to a five-issue arc in a contemporary comic, and would likely be published as a single trade paperback in the current market.)

Much of the storyline centers on the construction and implementation of an Amazon-run prison on what is called Reform Island. In this prison an Amazon, Mala, supervises the reform first of Paula's henchmen and later von Gunther herself. The problems Marston envisions in this process are probably not you'd expect. The henchmen refuse to accept freedom, demand they be chained, and grow violent in fear of being free. After Paula's capture, Wonder Woman and Mala allow her to attempt a prison revolt. To Paula's astonishment, when she fires a gun at Mala her former slaves rush to Mala's defense. Wonder Woman helpfully explains they've changed allegiance "because you held them captive by fear. Mala made them love her and love is always stronger than fear."

Confronted with concrete evidence of the superiority of Amazonian slavery to Nazi slavery, von Gunther is persuaded by Wonder Woman to confess her own origin. We learn she served the Nazis only to protect her kidnapped daughter Gerta, who Wonder Woman subsequently rescues, thus converting Paula to good. The final story of issue #3 demonstrates the conversion is genuine: Paula sacrifices herself to save Wonder Woman, becoming badly burned in the process. She's then brought to trial for her crimes, but is acquitted after Wonder Woman presents her scarred face to the jury, and she returns to Reform Island, where Queen Hippolyte restores her appearance. Even here there are clear structures of dominance and submission, as Wonder Woman tells Paula that "when you feel naughty look at your new face and it will cure you" before ending the issue by tying herself with her own magic lasso and commanding herself "never to use your influence over Paula for your own selfish purposes or to make yourself feel smart. It's a tremendous responsibility to shape another girl's life and I must do it right!"

In the second half of the storyline, *Wonder Woman* #4, Paula's put through some "Tests of Aphrodite" as Wonder Woman's sidekick in a series of otherwise disconnected adventures. The most interesting of these is the third and final test, which features American capitalists hiding industrial secrets from the government so they can take over the rubber market after the war. It's the most explicit instance yet of Wonder Woman confronting patriarchal power in the United

States. As World War II winds down, it becomes increasingly clear from the comics themselves that Marston has a broader agenda than wartime propaganda. It also marks the first time another one of DC's flagship characters crosses over with Wonder Woman.

But we're getting ahead of ourselves. A conceit of the story is that Paula has invented a machine that reveals the contents of someone's subconscious. On the surface this is simply another variation of Marston's obvious fascination with lie detectors (quite understandable, given his role in inventing one); after all, the Subconscious X-Ray is just another way to use technology to understand people's true thoughts. Looking deeper, though, Marston puts a lot of effort into playing up the machine's legitimacy, with a declaration that "the subconscious is in the fifth dimension – these kappa rays make it visible," and Paula's explanation, "You're looking through an electrical doorway into this girl's inner world. What happens there is just as real as what happens outside." The idea of the Subconscious X-Ray anchors the psychological theories underlying Marston's stories to the material world depicted within them, and oddly echoes Carol Hanisch's famed feminist maxim that the personal is political.

This brings us to the brief one-panel crossover. As one of the arch-capitalist rubber magnates is x-rayed, his subconscious self-image turns out to be Superman with a top hat and cane, resembling Rich Uncle Pennybags from the popular Monopoly game (itself likely drawn from an image of JP Morgan). This equation of Superman with the decadent trappings of wealth and the selfish, destructive urges of capitalism clearly sets Wonder Woman apart from other DC titles. It's a prime example of what's so compelling and powerful about these early Wonder Woman comics: the way in which they take up a position that corrupts and inverts the standards of the genre it ostensibly belongs to.

Marston's stories inevitably point towards a larger social structure, which this story illustrates. After Paula passes her final test, she fully enters into Aphrodite's service by enslaving men. This reflects an essential feature of Marston's worldview, namely that women have a duty to compel men to submit to them, while simultaneously submitting themselves to female authorities of their own. This point is made most blatantly in *Sensation Comics* #19: stripped of her wristbands, Wonder Woman becomes wild and violent, because "the bracelets bound my strength to good purposes – now I'm completely uncontrolled! I'm free to *destroy* like a *man*!" Male power, which is inherently dangerous, must always submit to female power; female power, while fit to dominate, also needs to submit to stay balanced.

This reveals a particularly disturbing aspect of early Wonder Woman, namely her relationship with Steve Trevor. Steve Trevor is not the most immediately galling aspect of Marston-era Wonder Woman – the racial stereotypes stick out more, as does the crass tokenism of making Wonder Woman a secretary to the Justice Society. But the former is ultimately incidental to Marston's intended point, and the latter wasn't actually his decision. The relationship with Steve Trevor, while not overtly offensive, is far more insidious, because it's ultimately concerned with the basic thematic heart of Wonder Woman: the relationships between men and women.

To be fair, we're past the worst of it, which comes in *Sensation Comics* #1. That story ends with Wonder Woman spurned by Steve in her Diana Prince guise, leaving her to reflect, "So I'm my own rival, eh? That's funny... if mother could only see me now... as a very feminine woman... a nurse, no less, in a world full of men, and in love too – with myself for a rival!" While there's nothing inherently bothersome about Wonder Woman being in love with a man – attraction to men is a necessary component of her larger mission to get them to submit to her loving authority – there is something deeply dismaying about how quickly she is shoved into a plotline of unrequited love. It makes her subservient and in perpetual thrall to men in a fashion that threatens to undermine Marston's larger project.

But as early as the next issue Marston complicates the relationship dynamic. In *Sensation Comics* #2 Wonder Woman criticizes Steve's attitude towards her – after bursting in to rescue him, he calls her "my beautiful angel" and she responds, "What's an angel? I think I'd rather be a woman." The relationship is never entirely simple. Diana's in love with Trevor, but he only loves Wonder Woman, largely ignoring Diana Prince; Wonder Woman in turn rejects him for failing to find Diana Prince as attractive as herself. As irritating as the cliché of unrequited love is, it's important to remember Wonder Woman has near-complete agency in this plot. Her love for Steve Trevor isn't wholly unrequited – it's just not requited in a way she finds acceptable.

Two stories within the period add more wrinkles. The first comes from 1944's *Comic Cavalcade* #8. Steve Trevor decides to take Diana out on a date, demanding she go with him over her protests because "since I met Wonder Woman it seems all women tell me what to do! Now you'll do what I say, this time – we're going dancing!" They go on their date, and Steve orders a wealth of rich and heavy food, again over Diana's objections. But after drinking some of Trevor's coffee, which has been drugged by a gangster, she staggers home and falls asleep.

From there the story unfolds curiously, with Wonder Woman waking up and realizing Steve's in danger, only now she's lost her powers. The plot goes pear-shaped when Steve tells her that "you need a man to protect you" and she blurts out, "I love to have you boss me!" This inspires Steve to propose, an offer she readily accepts, along with becoming his secretary and sitting politely as he tells her, "Every woman's place is in the home and girls should not try to do the work of men."

The story continues in a similar vein (Steve even develops superhuman strength and an ability to repel bullets much like Wonder Woman normally does) until it comes to their actual marriage ceremony. When asked to promise to "love and obey" Steve, Diana becomes woozy, passes out, and wakes up in her bed; everything since the end of the dinner date turns out to be a dream sequence. Understanding that she erred in yielding to Steve's domination, she quickly puts on her costume and, over the course of three panels, rescues Steve from danger and resolves the plot. Once again he implores her to marry him, but now, in the real world, she sarcastically replies, "Man's world marriage to a dominant man like you, Steve, must be thrilling – but for an Amazon maiden, it's just – a dream!"

A more explicit version of the same moral appears a year later in *Sensation Comics* #46. The Lawbreakers' League tempts Steven with an "electronic globe" that can give him strength comparable to Wonder Woman's. Delighted, he tells Wonder Woman, "Now I can boss you around." She initially finds this attractive, but when he grabs her wrist and refuses to let go, complaining that she's always brushed off his marriage proposals and that "this time I'll make you listen," she becomes more reluctant and thinks, "Some girls love to have a man stronger than they are make them do things. Do I like it? I don't know – it's sort of thrilling. But – isn't it more fun to make the man obey?"

After this internal monologue she breaks free of his grasp and the two are estranged for the rest of the story until Steve, separated from his globe for too long, loses his strength and gets into trouble. Wonder Woman rescues him, of course, but he immediately tries to regain his strength, in order to get her to marry him. She stops him and declares, "I've discovered that I can never love a dominant man who's stronger than I am." Steve smashes the globe, restoring the status quo. More importantly, this demonstrates his tacit acceptance of Wonder Woman's domination over him.

Both stories make an initial play towards the patriarchal establishment before decisively turning away from it. This is in many ways the signature gesture of Marston's utopian tendencies. He doesn't present an ideal world. Even Paradise

Island is repeatedly invaded by external threats and, more profoundly, undermined by internal conflicts, most obviously in *Comic Cavalcade* #12 when another Amazon, Dalma, becomes jealous of Diana's enjoyment of man's world and stages a rebellion on Paradise Island itself.

Marston's utopianism is better described as a process. His utopia isn't a schematic for an existing society, but a set of behaviors and values that are desirable even in the absence of an outright utopia. There is no endpoint for this view of the world, just repeated acts of dominance and submission; it's the act itself, not the resulting society, that's utopian. This is underscored by the way Marston's female characters are shown to benefit through submission to loving authority. Diana isn't an infallible woman who maintains some kind of ideal stance with the male figures in her life. Rather, she continually makes the decision to have what Marston views as healthier and more ethical relationships with these figures.

An unusual consequence to this is that there's no absolute authority to which one submits – including a theological or metaphysical one. In sharp contrast to the attitudes of the time, Marston's comics depict a pre-Christian sense of the world. Some aspects of this are obvious, the reliance on Greek mythology being the most straightforward example. Others are comparatively subtle. Wonder Woman is repeatedly shown to have an affinity with animals. In *Sensation Comics* #14, she even has an ability to converse with trees. Twice in the first four years of the comic, she wrestles and tames a lion, an image that evokes the Tarot card of Strength.

The most conspicuous Pagan moment of the first few years comes in the previously discussed *Wonder Woman* #3. The first piece in this issue is a Christmas-themed story set on Paradise Island, which necessitates the creation of an equivalent Amazonian holiday. Named Diana's Day, it's explained in (astronomically inaccurate) terms of marking the point when Apollo, the sun, begins his approach to the Earth again, much to the joy of his sister, the Moon Goddess. This overt reversion of the winter solstice to its pre-Christian nature as an astronomical/astrological occasion moves it away from being about a masculine figure and towards a celebration incorporating the divine feminine.

But it would be wrong to suggest that Marston's work is entirely focused on the European pre-Christian tradition. *Sensation Comics* #18 provides an interesting counter-example, as well as one that complicates Marston's use of racial stereotypes. In it, Wonder Woman discovers a "lost tribe" of Incans, described by one character as "wonderful Indians who made houses, temples, and weapons of pure gold!" This description, while distressingly imperialist, is a notable contrast to the hostile stereotypes that make up most of the non-American cultures in Marston's scripts. Harry Peter's art provides reinforcement, avoiding the grotesque faces that mark his racial caricatures and treating the Incan characters with comparative dignity. It's still racist as heck, trading in the banal stereotypes of the noble savage, but it's a departure from much of Marston's other writing, and shows he's more invested in the general idea of a long-lost order of things than a culturally specific vision of how the world should be.

A similar but more fantastical conception of the ancient world appears in *Sensation Comics* #35, where Wonder Woman helps establish a new government in Atlantis. Despite the mythic nature of Atlantis, this is another example of the trope where an ancient pre-Christian civilization has greater moral authority than the contemporary Western-dominated world. Atlantis is, both here and in its first appearance in *Wonder Woman* #8, portrayed with a sense of respect; it is a society with special wisdom and insight lacking in Man's World. But *Sensation Comics* #35 also gives Marston the opportunity to expound an explicit philosophy of government. Wonder Woman suggests Atlantis hold elections, and vote for Queen Octavia, because "she asks only to become the slave of her country! And really – the true stateswoman is no more than a public slave."

It's predictable at this point to see Marston extolling the virtues of consensual slavery; that the view of the world he holds in all other regards should apply to the state as well cannot be taken as a particular shock. But look at the way in which the notions of slavery and government run together. Wonder Woman doesn't have a particularly strong commitment to democracy. While she visibly prefers it to monarchy, it's not as though demands Octavia be elected instead of serving the hereditary queen. Don't forget, Paradise Island is a monarchy, and Diana is heir to the throne. However, she doesn't believe that government ought to have clear and unambiguous dominion over the people; rather, government should be in service to a greater good as defined by the people.

This is notably different from the relatively authoritarian propaganda found throughout the comics regarding World War II. In late 1944, every page of *Sensation Comics* touts war propaganda framed in catchy rhymes like "Tin cans in the garbage pile are just a way of saying 'Heil!'," "If you have an extra quarter, buy a stamp to make war shorter," or "If you still have metal scrap, turn it in to beat the Jap." The comics as a whole unambiguously contribute towards a patriotic model in which the citizen is expected to serve the state in the war effort. But within them Wonder Woman carves out space for a clear alternative that inverts the standard model, demanding that the state submit to its citizens.

This is not the only way Wonder Woman inverts the normal wartime order. A two-issue story arc in *Sensation Comics* #27-28 deals with Wonder Woman's "pet project, the Fun Foundation," which is based on the premise that "America's greatest need today is more fun, recreation, and health giving amusement," a state of affairs blamed on the war. Although such a view isn't unheard of, it differs sharply with the prevailing spirit of militarism, even when couched in the idea of "national morale," further emphasizing the strange space Marston found within the mainstream.

But while the Fun Foundation is strange in the context of World War II propaganda, it's quite in line with Marston's more general moral message, which also stresses the importance of childlike imagination, of listening to and believing in children. One of his more memorable stories, in *Sensation Comics* #31, even presents the spectacle of Grown-Down Land, an inverted world where young children rule over adults.

Two things stand out about Grown-Down Land. First, it's closer to Marston's general principles than the adult world. It has a matriarchal component: women run the penal system, a direct echo of Reform Island. This is further reinforced by Wonder Woman's reactions to Grown-Down Land, which are wholly approving. Although it's hardly unusual to see Wonder Woman willingly surrender herself to bondage, usually because her friends are threatened, in Grown-Down land she reacts with positive cheer to being arrested, tied up, and imprisoned. Even when she's bound with her magic lasso she remains cheerful. She happily says, "That's right – so long as you keep me tied up with this lasso I'm your slave."

And then there's the manner in which the bondage of Grown-Down Land is presented. The opening splash page of the story is one of the strangest panels that Peter ever drew for the comic, consisting of a child bending Wonder Woman over her knee and spanking her while a crowd of babies laughs and applauds. Wonder Woman's buttocks and breasts are both prominent in the picture, much of her back is visible, and she turns her head towards the reader and gives a knowing wink as if to acknowledge the strange situation, reassuring them that it's OK.

This gets at something that we've been dancing around, which is the degree of eroticism in Marston's Wonder Woman. Again, *Wonder Woman* #3 proves particularly illustrative. In the opening story, Wonder Woman gives the other Amazons presents for Diana's Day. One of them gets a tennis racket, but misunderstands the nature of the gift, bending over another Amazon to spank her with it while the receiver of the beating exclaims, "Pooh! It doesn't hurt – it's a sissy spanker from the man's world."

Figure 3: Wonder Woman in Grown-Down Land from *Sensation Comics* #31 (1944), art by Harry G. Peter, copyright DC Comics, used under the principle of fair use.

Later, a number of girls Wonder Woman has bested in wrestling matches are dressed up as deer and hunted by Wonder Woman and the other Amazons. Once they're captured, their doe costumes are removed and they are "cooked," leading to a scene where one Amazon tells a bound captive, "You'll make a lovely chicken, darling! Wait until I give you a crisp skin!" Her captive replies with enthusiasm, "You make my mouth water – how about feeding me to myself?" These are just two instances of BDSM-inflected encounters in a several-page sequence that rapidly comes to resemble Victorian pornography in its sheer zeal for putting characters in contrived erotic situations.

This is more than a side-effect of Marston's own peccadilloes. The larger theoretical significance to Marston's eroticism emerges when taken in context with his tendency to treat utopianism not as a material system, but as a continually expressed submission to loving feminine authority. This splits neatly along the same lines as the Freudian dualism of sex and death. A utopian view of the world based on war – and let's remember that, as far from normal utopian thought as this sounds, it's basically the thought behind a phrase like "making the world safe for democracy" – is necessarily based on the belief in a desired end state that war can bring about, not on the idea of continual war.

However, a utopia based on sex is necessarily one of continual action. Sex does not produce a definable end state – or, at least, that's not its primary goal. Even procreative sex, which at least has a definite outcome in mind, can hardly be said to create a stable state of affairs. But for the most part, sex is pursued for the sake of pleasure, not for the outcome. In this regard the eroticism of Marston's utopianism isn't just an incidental moment of his own fetishes spilling into his work, but a fundamental part of his theory of utopia. Marston isn't just imagining a heavily sexualized utopia, but a utopia built out of sexual acts in which erotic and sexual submission to loving authority is practiced continually for the sake of the pleasure it gives. Marston's own fetishes come into play only inasmuch as they're behind his belief that this sort of submission is the highest form of pleasure there is.

At the end of World War II, Marston has accomplished something staggering in its reach. He's created an inordinately popular franchise that doubles as the presentation of a vivid and thoroughly defined worldview. His message, despite contradicting the mainstream focus of American society, is out in the mainstream; more astonishingly, it's printed by a company and in a venue normally devoted to the straightforward and unambiguous affirmation of America's martial culture in the early 1940s. Now, with the war over, Marston can shape his propaganda without having to fight against the grain of the culture quite so actively. It seems, at least, that Wonder Woman's future is one of near-limitless potential.

Chapter 4: William Moulton Marston

It's impossible to understand Marston's vision of Wonder Woman without looking at the broader context of his work and life. Marston was a complex figure with a wide variety of interests. His decision to write a comic book, and the goals he had in doing so, make sense only in terms of his sprawling ambition.

Marston wore many hats, but it was his academic work that occupied the largest portion of his career. His two major scholarly books are *Emotions of Normal People*, published in 1928, and *Integrative Psychology*, published in 1931. Both had a reasonably good reputation, and have been kept in print by Routledge for their historical importance, but calling either a major work in the field of psychology would be a stretch. He also published *The Art of Sound Pictures*, a book about filmmaking that's more remarkable for the fact that neither he nor his coauthor (a journalism professor at Columbia University) had actually made a film.

This gets at an uncomfortable truth about Marston. For all his brilliance, and he had no shortage of it, he was an inveterate impresario with an obsessive zeal for self-promotion. After publishing *Integrative Psychology* he tried his hand at writing a pulp novel: *The Private Life of Julius Caesar,* which was almost universally reviled. He went on to write a series of self-help books before finally moving into comics, where he finally found the popular success he craved.

Throughout this time, he also promoted his invention of the lie detector, both through sensible means (sending copies of his books to the FBI and volunteering to help them) and absurd ones (running an advertising campaign for Gillette that used the lie detector to show how Gillette blades were better for your psychological well being).

Marston, in other words, occupied a strange place between huckster and genius. Most treatments of his life tend to treat his work on Wonder Woman separately from his earlier work, save for superficial observations about specific points of interest. For instance, almost everyone remarks upon the similarity between the golden lasso and the lie detector, or how his case studies on sorority initiations seem to inform the Beeta Lamda girls. This is all true, but it wrongly implies that the only noteworthy factors of Marston's earlier work are in such minor details. In reality there's a distinct arc and unity of focus to Marston's entire career. Wonder Woman is not merely something that the inventor of the lie detector created in his spare time, but a clear part of a larger philosophical system.

To understand this system, one ought to start with Marston's 1928 intellectual magnum opus, *Emotions of Normal People*. *Emotions of Normal People* bristles with the manic energy of someone who is convinced that he has solved everything. In practice, of course, he has not – Marston's theories enjoy little to no currency in mainstream psychology today. But this doesn't mean the book isn't worth taking seriously. On the contrary, the fact that its worldview influenced one of the most important creations of pop culture in the mid-20th Century demands that we do take it seriously.

Marston sets up four concepts – in his later *Integrative Psychology* he defines them as "elementary unit responses" that a human has to external and particularly social stimuli: dominance, compliance, submission, and inducement. This is the only part of Marston's psychological work that anybody other than Marston ever really picked up on, and even then it was mostly as a self-help/management consulting tool called

"DISC Theory" in which the responses are turned into behavioral factors that can then be used to categorize people. For relatively obvious marketing reasons, inducement is changed to the more palatable "influence," and submission is changed to "steadiness," an alteration that marginalizes the sexuality implicit in Marston's work and corrupts the actual concept. "Steadiness" in no way describes what Marston is talking about when he talks about submission. In *Integrative Psychology*, he specifically defines submission as "the active, willing obedience to the commands or stimulations of another person," which has nothing to do with reliable steadiness and everything to do with the active willingness to surrender control to someone else.

Furthermore, the reduction of Marston's theories to a doctrine for self-help workshops renders Marston a far less radical figure than he was. For example, the DISC appropriation of Marston's work reorders his concepts into a convenient acronym. In *Emotions of Normal People*, Marston approaches them in a completely different order: dominance, compliance, submission, and inducement. He maintains this order in *Integrative Psychology*, and makes it clear he prefers it for specific reasons – reasons that are wholly erased in the DISC version. Each response is defined by whether the subject becomes more active or more passive in response to the stimulus and by whether they are opposed to the stimulus or allied to it. The first two responses – dominance and compliance – are the ones in which the stimulus is opposed, whereas the latter two are not.

Marston opens *Emotions of Normal People* by talking about dominance, which he never goes so far as to condemn, but he's clearly interested in curbing it. Most of his case studies in the dominance chapter focus on young and adolescent boys who display violent or destructive behavior and the problems caused by this. He goes on from dominance to compliance, which can be defined roughly as "forced obedience." Compliance is treated as functional, but Marston repeatedly stresses its tendency to involve fear or unpleasantness. In a subsequent chapter he brings the two concepts together and gets at the crux of the problem, namely that "active compliance is normally followed by active dominance." Compliance may stifle a problematic dominant response in the short term, but it doesn't work over the long term.

After setting up this dualism, Marston moves on to his second dyad: submission and inducement. Notice how the order of these is switched from the first dyad. In the first dyad the response in which activity increases – dominance – is put first. By this standard one would expect inducement, which an *active* response focused on getting one's way instead of on acceding to external demands, to come first, so that the second dyad mirrors the first. Instead, however, submission comes first, and inducement second. This highlights Marston's interest, which is not in creating an alternative dualism to dominance/compliance, but in solving the problem of dominance. Submission comes first because it is the next obvious thing to try after compliance. This is confirmed by the frequency with which the submission chapter describes how much better submission is than compliance, a key declaration being that the "submission response, according to unanimous introspective agreement, is pleasant from beginning to end." (The submission section also raises a number of points directly related to what he later did with Wonder Woman, most obviously a section in which he discusses the problem that adolescent males rarely want to submit to women.)

Only has after he's set up submission does he circle around to inducement. At the end of that chapter he lists "popular terms for emotional behavior characterized primarily by inducement," including captivation, seduction, charm, and allure. Inducement, in other words, is presented as a superior version of dominance that is more suitable to invoking submission. The follow-up chapter talks about how inducement and submission are more appropriate for teaching people, and how the use of dominance is often illegal. Again, Marston shapes a clear narrative, setting up what he views as a destructive response – dominance – and then spending several chapters working through the potential solutions to it. The self-help version, in which the chain starts with dominance and ends with compliance, completely erases this structure from Marston's work. While Marston goes to great lengths to stress the empirical backing of this model, it's clearly a narrative based on philosophical appeal. He's building a theory of psychology around the problems he's identified with dominant behavior.

This becomes even clearer when he gets around to talking about sex. As early as Chapter 11 in *Emotions of Normal People*, the chapter on submission, he asserts that the male erection is a submission response, and in Chapter 15, euphemistically titled "Love Mechanisms," he goes all the way down this particular rabbit hole. He blithely declares, "Since the internal genitals of the male can at no time be directly stimulated by contact with the female, the male's overt response throughout the sex relationship is one of *active submission* evoked by cumulatively increased stimulation of his *external* genital organ, which is completely surrounded (captured?) by the woman's internal genital organ, the vagina." There are many ways in which this is an incredibly strange quote. It involves a very unusual sort of biological essentialism that blends empiricist and vitalistic impulses. He grounds his claims in biological processes, but instead of gathering data to support those claims he engages in a sort of aesthetic analysis of vaginal intercourse. His description of how the penis is "captured" by the vagina is in no way a scientific observation, but rather a strange inversion of the *vagina dentata* reimagined as a pleasurable fantasy of light bondage.

Marston reiterates the point in *Integrative Psychology*, saying that "man is so constituted that he must play the role of love captive from the very beginning until, literally, the last moment," and that woman is "by virtue of her menstrual stimulus mechanism, her resulting erotic drive, and double genital mechanisms capable of direct love stimulation, to act as love leader." He pushes the point even further with a lengthy critique of Victorian patriarchy, and then celebrates how women have become more independent since World War I. All of this makes it clear that Marston's views on sexual submission, as advanced through Wonder Woman, had their roots in the heyday of his academic work.

The decade between the publication of *Integrative Psychology* and the creation of Wonder Woman was something of an off period for Marston. He published *The Private Life of Julius Caesar*, a duo of self-help books with the uninspiring titles of *You Can Be Popular* and *Try Living*, and little else. Then he popped up in the October 25, 1940 issue of *Family Circle* with a piece called "Don't Laugh at the Comics."

The piece is written by "Olive Richard," a detail that necessitates some digression. It's implied the author is a Family Circle staffer of some sort who has gone to interview Marston. In truth, Olive Richard is a pen name for Olive Byrne, Marston's research assistant since the 1920s. Byrne lived with Marston and his wife Elizabeth, and two of Marston's four children were with Byrne. After Marston's death, Byrne played the stay-at-home role while Elizabeth Marston, with a Master's degree in psychology, served as breadwinner for the family.

It's around here that most histories of Wonder Woman begin discussing with obvious relish the implications of Marston's clearly unorthodox sex life. The typical insinuation treats Wonder Woman as little more than an outlet for Marston's fetishes, a speculation bolstered by the fact that Byrne wore two metal bracelets much like Wonder Woman's, and served as the visual model for the character.

This is unfair on a number of levels. First and foremost, it amounts to a lazy sort of Freudianism whereby it's assumed that an interesting sex life must control and dominate everything else someone does. More importantly, there's an unsettlingly prurient tone to the entire line of argument. While the unusual nature of Marston's family life is documented in the general case, the details of his private life remain oblique. Building an entire interpretation of Wonder

Woman out of the vague knowledge that its creator was in some sense sexually transgressive isn't just intellectually sloppy, it's ethically dubious. It suffices to say that Marston's personal life was as unique as his intellectual and creative lives, and that the involvement of his family in Wonder Woman's creation was substantial – both Olive and Elizabeth contributed to the original design of the character, and all four children occasionally chipped in plot ideas.

So let's go back to "Don't Laugh at the Comics." First of all, one must acknowledge the bemused and leading tone with which "Olive Richard" approaches her "interview subject." The flagrant artifice of the piece is visible throughout, beginning with Olive's first question, "Do you know anything about comics magazines?" which Marston answers at length with detailed sales figures. Her claim to have "professed amazement at the Doctor's detailed knowledge of the subject" is delightfully, if perhaps unintentionally, hilarious.

Clearly, the piece is carefully calculated and constructed, but complicated in part by the fact that the piece has multiple audiences. Marston is obviously writing for the general *Family Circle* audience, but he's also writing for a more specific purpose: to get a job in the comic book industry. And in this regard, "Don't Laugh at the Comics" was a rousing success. It's quite in character for Marston, who previously published a book in part to break into the movies, an attempt that failed. This time his pandering worked. He was hired by M.C. Gaines, first to serve on the "Editorial Advisory Board," and then to create Wonder Woman. It's telling that about a third of the piece is turned over to praising Superman, and that Gaines is mentioned by name for his foresight in giving Jerry Siegel his big break. (Curiously, the piece omits mention of Joe Shuster.)

However, the article is not merely a letter to M.C. Gaines; if it were, Marston would have just sent it to him. Given that it appears in a supermarket-distributed women's magazine, it's also targeted at mothers: "Olive Richard" plays up her status as a mother who has seen "in my own household that children read the so-called funnies morning, noon, and – unfortunately – night," while omitting the detail that Dr. Marston is the father of those children. Olive, playing the dutiful interlocutor, brings up the specific concerns of mothers that Marston wants to shoot down.

The biggest of these concerns is the violence in comics. Starting in the third paragraph, Olive frets about whether comics are "poisonous mental pacifiers" and goes on to cite an article in *The Chicago Daily News* that proclaimed comics to be "lurid publications" featuring "mayhem, murder, torture, abduction, superman heroics, voluptuous females, blazing machine guns, and hooded justice." The piece returns to this theme at the end as Olive agrees that some comics "are full of torture, kidnapping, sadism, and other cruel business." Marston concedes the point, critiquing a particularly violent bit of *Dick Tracy*. But then he goes on to say that "when a lovely heroine is bound to the stake, comics followers are sure that rescue will arrive in the nick of time. The reader's wish is to save the girl, not to see her suffer. A bound or chained person does not suffer even embarrassment in the comics, and the reader, therefore, is not being taught to enjoy suffering." He suggests that the most sensible thing to do when confronted with a sadistic or ill-advised comic is to write in and complain, and to restrict one's purchases to more positive materials.

This defense, particularly of the endless imperilment of female characters, is certainly problematic. The underlying principle, however, is interesting. Marston is countering a specific set of objections to comics, the most famous of which is Frederic Wertham's 1954 *Seduction of the Innocent*. It post-dates Marston by several years, but as it represents the high-water mark of this particular ongoing critique, it's quite apt to put them in direct conversation.

Wertham's notions of what constitutes appropriate gender roles are hopelessly reactionary and outdated. He references Wonder Woman several times in *Seduction of the Innocent*, singling her out as "a horror type" who "is physically very powerful, tortures men, has her own female following [and] is the cruel, 'phallic' woman. While she is a frightening figure for boys, she is an undesirable ideal for girls, being the exact opposite of what girls are supposed to want to be." He considers Wonder Woman not just one of the worst comics out there, but a lesbian recruitment tool. He even calls out Marston himself, though not by name, describing him as "a psychologist retained by the industry" and quoting him on how men want to submit to women. Wertham derisively declares that if Wonder Woman were real, "Every normal-minded young man would know there is something wrong with her."

Wertham's few defenders are similarly dismissive of Marston. Bart Beaty makes a quite spectacular defense in *Frederic Wertham and the Critique of Mass Culture*, where he rather politely refers to Marston's arguments regarding comics as "unusual" before suggesting that his views were "not widely shared." But given that Marston was clearly in favor of a matriarchal bondage utopia, this snub really can't be taken as surprising.

Beaty points out that Wertham was very much a Freudian who sought to return to the characteristics of Freud's early work, viewing his later work as a wrong turn that had empowered conservative and repressive psychologists. Beaty spends several pages on a 1949 article by Wertham entitled "Freud Now" in which Wertham self-identifies as one of those "who wish to guard the true heritage of Freud and develop in a truly progressive manner."

Seduction of the Innocent bears that out. Wertham describes children playing with marionettes and analyzes their daydreaming in a manner that's straight out of *The Interpretation of Dreams*. He suggests that if children "have a subconscious liking for [brutality], comic books will reinforce it," and worries about boys who "become addicted to the homoerotically tinged type of comic book. During and after comic-book reading they indulged in fantasies which became severely repressed." This sort of thinking is almost classically Freudian.

Here, then, we can find room for Marston to mount a response. As we've already seen, *Emotions of Normal People* seeks out a middle ground between the empiricism that was coming into vogue in the early 20th century and the more sweeping grandeur of the psychoanalytic approach. Marston mentions the subconscious only three times in *Emotions of Normal People*, always in scare quotes; the word "repressed" appears nowhere in the book, and "repression" only once. It's worth quoting the following passage in full, as it shows exactly how far Marston is from Wertham's more Freudian perspective:

> "Removing the mystery from fear is nine-tenths of the battle. So long as any person thinks of fear as some great, hidden, cosmic force that is ready to jump down his throat anytime, from the great beyond, from the 'libido,' from the evolutionary history of the race, or even from his own childhood 'complexes' and 'repressions,' the clinical psychologist hasn't one chance in a million to get rid of it for him."

Marston clearly opposes the Freudian perspective that informs Wertham and that underlies much of the criticism depicting comics as overly gruesome or sadistic. It's that perspective he takes on in "Don't Laugh at the Comics." Equally, it's a perspective that M.C. Gaines was already fighting at DC, hence the addition of sections that endorsed reading "proper" books (cited approvingly by Marston in "Don't Laugh at the Comics") and the creation of titles like *Picture Stories from the Bible*. It is hardly a surprise that the job application portion of Marston's article succeeded and that he found himself writing Wonder Woman.

More puzzling is his second *Family Circle* piece on comics, "Our Women Are Our Future." Once again penned by

"Olive Richard," this article came out in the August 14, 1942 issue, not long into Wonder Woman's run. Given that Marston wrote Wonder Woman under the pseudonym of "Charles Moulton" and that "Olive Richard" was ostensibly meant to be a *Family Circle* staffer, this piece is surprising in several regards. For one thing, it overtly outs Marston as the creator of Wonder Woman. Conversely, Marston credits Olive as the inspiration for Wonder Woman's bracelets, and hints that "Olive Richards" may not be the detached Family Circle staffer she seems. The mask is allowed to slip just a little bit here, and perhaps it was not as firmly fixed in "Don't Laugh at the Comics" as one may have assumed.

"Our Women Are Our Future" is also a much more public admission of Marston's sexual politics than anything else he'd published up to this point. It begins with "Olive Richards" bemoaning the sad state of wartime America before "dropping in" on Marston. When she asks, "Will war ever end in this world; will men ever stop fighting?" Marston replies ("mildly") that it will happen when "women control men." With characteristic manipulative panache, Marston presents another version of his argument from *Emotions of Normal People* and *Integrative Psychology* about the natural submissiveness of men towards women. This time he targets it more overtly at the *Family Circle* audience by framing the "desire of males to be mastered by a woman who loves them" in terms of "their childish longing for a woman to mother them." With the aid of Olive's leading questions he shoots down counter-arguments – such as the notion that Wonder Woman is popular in spite of her gender.

He also makes a longer version of his argument from *Integrative Psychology* about how World War I led to the end of Victorian repression of women, because women assumed a greater share of manual labor. Wonder Woman, Marston argues, is "a dramatized symbol of her sex. She's true to life – true to the universal characteristics of women everywhere. Her magic lasso is merely a symbol of feminine charm, allure, oomph, attraction." When Olive expresses doubt that women's strength is all that, Marston presses on: "Woman's charm is the one bond that can be made strong enough to hold a man against all logic, common sense, or counterattack." He claims that female allure is an even stronger bond than Nazi oppression, noting that Hitler's rise to power was not based on force but on charisma, the very trait he asserts that women are better at.

Marston clearly believes it's inevitable that women will rise into positions of power over men, and that they will be a utopian force: "When women rule, there won't be any more [war] because the girls won't want to waste time killing men. They'd rather have them alive; it's more fun from the feminine point of view." The piece ends with him extolling the virtues of women and how men will love submitting to them. Olive concludes, in a line that's impossible to read without some thought of their domestic situation, "I took wing and flew over the housetops to my little nest to spread joy among all the lucky males I could rope in with my magic-lariat charm."

Two things should be apparent from this piece. First, it confirms that Marston's focus on female domination in Wonder Woman was not merely a reflection of his own sexuality, but a full-fledged ideological viewpoint. He didn't just write Wonder Woman because he was turned on by dominant women (though it seems clear he was), but because he had a broader belief that dominant women were a political necessity. Second, Marston's arguments in 1942 are clearly recognizable as variations on the arguments he'd been making since 1928. Wonder Woman was not merely what Marston did after abandoning traditional academia, but a logical extension of that career.

This brings us around to his third populist article regarding Wonder Woman, "Why 100,000,000 Americans Read Comics," in *The American Scholar* (Winter 1943-44). *The American Scholar* is a very different title from *Family Circle*. It's the quarterly of Phi Beta Kappa – an academic publication aimed at a more general audience – and much of the issue reflects a sense that the war was coming to an end, prompting deliberation about the nature of the world to follow.

The article itself draws on Marston's two *Family Circle* pieces and expands on them. Instead of just arguing for their popularity and potential good will, Marston argues that comics "rouse the most primitive, but also the most powerful, reverberations in the noisy cranial sound-box of consciousness," tracing a history of pictorial storytelling similar to the historical arguments advanced by contemporary comics evangelists like Scott McCloud. As in "Don't Laugh at the Comics," the main thrust of his argument is that "if children will read comics, come Hail Columbia or literary devastation, why isn't it advisable to give them some constructive comics to read?"

This time he continues the argument straight into the benefits of Wonder Woman. Marston complains, "It seemed to me, from a psychological angle, that the comics' worst offense was their blood-curdling masculinity," and counters with "a feminine character with all the strength of Superman." The same arguments that "Olive Richard" raised are reiterated: "Girl heroines had been tried in pulps and comics and, without exception, found failures," but Marston tells the story of his own perseverance, declaring in one of his most quoted lines, "Men actually submit to women now, they do it on the sly and with a sheepish grin because they're ashamed of being ruled by weaklings. Give them an alluring woman stronger than themselves to submit to and they'll be *proud* to become her willing slaves!"

Given the relative lack of change from his two previous articles on the subject, one might ask why Marston published this piece in the first place. By 1944 Wonder Woman was a massive success, and his theories were getting considerable attention, albeit in a covert manner. What more did he have to prove? But here the specific context of the tail end of World War II plays in. Broadly speaking, this period was a heyday for scientific technocracy. With both sides of the war investing massively in scientific research, there was a flurry of popular commentary in which public intellectuals sought to map out various futures for the world based on emerging technological and social changes. This time period was the heart of the so-called Golden Age of science fiction, dominated by writers like Isaac Asimov and Arthur C. Clarke who explored the possible social consequences of scientific developments, and marked by scientists like Vannevar Bush (a key figure in the development of the atomic bomb) who published articles in middlebrow magazines like *Life* on how technology would shape the future.

This context makes it much more clear what's going on with Marston's work. The genre of scientists writing popular texts about a scientifically designed future is well known. Marston is not a scientist – not quite, at least – but he certainly has strong scientific leanings, a product of the field of psychology at a time when both the empiricism of then-contemporary science and the more literary approach of the psychoanalysts held sway. It's no wonder that his forays into utopianism look unusual compared to most of the genre. After all, he's not your everyday technocrat. He has one foot in the technocracy of the 1940s, but another in the still-receding Victorian era.

This is crucial to understanding the nature of Wonder Woman. She's not just a popular response to Marston's psychological theories, nor is she just the product of his fetishes. Rather, she's part of a concentrated effort to advance a technocratic worldview that comes not from the hard sciences but from the field of psychology at a point when it was caught between two competing approaches. She's more than propaganda; she's the most populist edge of a broad and thoroughly considered philosophical system.

Yes, the system is a strange one. To modern standards the mixture of empiricism and speculation underlying Marston's psychology is problematic, and his female-supremacist vision of feminism has flaws as well. His attempt to reconcile two competing approaches of psychology ends up failing both – he's too much an empiricist to be beloved by psychoanalysts, and too prone to flights of fancy to be championed by the increasingly empirical field in which he wrote. His more ecstatically emphatic moments were mocked not just by people like Wertham but also by people like the famed literary critic Cleanth Brooks, who wrote a scathing response to "Why 100,000,000 Americans Read Comics" that belittled Marston's writing style and took *American Scholar* to task for publishing his piece. Brooks's response is embarrassingly petty, based mostly on a sense of snobbery that comics were an unworthy topic for the journal, but goes a long way towards showing the somewhat marginal status that Marston's ideas enjoyed.

But if much of the foundation of Marston's intellectual vision was ignored or rejected, the apex of it was unquestionably successful. His ideas garnered little support, but their execution created one of the most popular fictional characters in history. Without ever gaining widespread acceptance of his ideas, Marston embedded his vast and mad worldview deep in the fabric of American popular culture.

And he did it in a way that put his core ideas and premises beyond debate. Ideas are the subject of argument and discussion, but a fictional character like Wonder Woman can present ideas in a form where instead of persuading they need only allure. She is, in this regard, a logical conclusion to Marston's ideas. Given his belief in inducement as the ideal means to teach and evoke submission, the realm of fiction, where an idea presents itself not on its intellectual merits but on its ability to charm and seduce, is the perfect place to express his philosophy. Far from being the lowbrow mass-culture version of his ideas, Wonder Woman represents their natural endpoint: an argument that persuades through no means other than its own captivating nature.

Chapter 5: The First Transition (1946-48)

In May of 1947, William Moulton Marston succumbed to cancer. Early in 1948 the backlog of stories he had written ran out, and Robert Kanigher took over as Wonder Woman's writer. Any attempt to divide Wonder Woman into distinct periods and eras must necessarily draw a line here, and thus this chapter concludes our examination of Marston and his goals for the character.

Given the inevitability of this endpoint, two competing perspectives have emerged. The first treats Marston as an odd little historical fluke, which amounts to the quasi-official position of DC Comics. While Les Daniels's authorized history of Wonder Woman is far too polite to actually criticize Marston, he makes him sound like a brilliant huckster who managed to fool DC Comics into letting him slip his kinky propaganda into their comics. Marston's success and the early popularity of his Wonder Woman are treated as odd artifacts of the 1940s, a slightly embarrassing footnote to DC's later success with her. His book practically sighs with relief when Marston and all this weird bondage stuff are finally gone.

The alternative perspective treats the original Wonder Woman as the shining version of the character, and all future depictions as poor shadows. This is the view taken by Grant Morrison, who declares that after Marston, "The erotic charge left the Wonder Woman strip, and sales declined, never to recover... Once the lush, pervy undercurrents were purged, the character foundered." In this view, Marston created an iconoclastic work of genius that's been screwed up in a variety of ways ever since. Either way, following *Wonder Woman* #28 (generally regarded as the last issue penned by Marston) the character is seen as undergoing a fundamental transformation.

However, the transition is hazier than it's typically painted. The positioning of *Wonder Woman* #28 as Marston's final work has more to do with the fact that it's a backward looking nostalgia piece that dusts off a bunch of past villains than anything else. Yes, it appears to be the last Wonder Woman story he wrote, but it's far from clear that it's the last one DC published. In fact, the exact transition point where Marston's stories left off and Kanigher took over is ambiguous; DC's record-keeping of writing credits is extremely spotty, and while it's relatively easy to identify artists by their style, identifying the writer of any given comic is a greater challenge.

Furthermore, the transition from Marston to Kanigher was gradual, with different titles switching at different times. The switch began as early as the October-November 1947 issue of *Comic Cavalcade*, and may have taken as long as the July-August 1948 issue of *Wonder Woman* to be completed. The positioning of *Wonder Woman* #28 as Marston's final issue is in many ways arbitrary – there's reason to think that *Wonder Woman* #27 featured stories by Kanigher and, potentially, a third writer. (However, it's undisputed that *Wonder Woman* #28 was written by Marston: Les Daniels has quotes from Marston's family supporting the contention that he wrote it.)

Reading the issues in question, it's easy to see why there's doubt about the transition point. The stories commonly attributed to Marston from the period are not significantly different from those attributed to Kanigher. Kanigher, for instance, is the presumptive author of *Wonder Woman* #29, but the first story of that issue presents Princess Snowina,

Ruler of Iceberg-Land, a character who could easily have been Marston's creation, of whom Wonder Woman proclaims, "You're a loving woman, Princess! We've nothing to fear from the Icicle Men while you rule them," and which features no shortage of bondage. Even up to issue #31 (an issue everyone agrees Kanigher wrote) the plots are full of bondage and soliloquies on the importance of loving authority. Yes, Wonder Woman changed rapidly in the years after Marston's death, but the idea that his death marks some sort of bright line where the strips became less strange and sexualized is simply untrue.

To be honest, Marston's writing was in decline over his last two years on the comic. Far from being galvanized by the end of World War II, all the energy in his work seems to trickle away. During the war itself, Marston concocted a plethora of gorgeously bizarre alternate worlds and magical realms for Wonder Woman to explore, but his post-war output grows progressively tamer. It seems as though Marston's iconoclasm needed the contrasting social backdrop of World War II to function. Without anything to wholeheartedly oppose following the war, the vibrancy of Marston's vision withered.

He begins 1946 with an exploration of Pluto's kingdom in *Wonder Woman* #16 – an inventive romp in which Wonder Woman and the Holliday Girls are all split into two selves, their physical bodies separated from their "color bodies," which are dragged down to the underworld beneath the surface of the planet. *Sensation Comics* also has a smattering of bizarre and inventive situations – the threatening Bughumans who live on the Cloud Mold in the stratosphere from *Sensation Comics* #55 is as weird as anything Marston ever came up with.

And then there's *Comic Cavalcade* #16, which features what may be most direct reference of Marston's psychological work. Wonder Woman attempts to reform Don, a "mischievous and high-spirited" boy with too much desire for dominance. Thanks to Paula's new Introspection

Machine, Don is confronted with a battle between the giant, ogreish personification of his dominance and the delicate but beautiful personification of love. When dominance ends up nearly destroying love and cutting her wings off, Don begs Wonder Woman to help. Via Paula's machine, Wonder Woman enters his mind and she teaches dominance to submit to love. Aside from being one of the most inventive of Marston's later stories, it's nearly a direct recitation of the central argument of *The Emotions of Normal People*.

But these stories become scarce as the post-war years advance. One issue after Pluto's kingdom, Marston finds a new obsession that frequently crops up in his late work: time travel. *Wonder Woman* #17 introduces "The Winds of Time" and updates Paula's "Space Transformation Machine" to serve as a time machine as well. The Winds of Time blow in four directions simultaneously from Fate Mountain, and they can apparently cause past life regressions, as in the case of Dr. Lana Kurree, a former Holliday Girl who's been framed for murder, and with the current Holliday girls, who regress into a "lifetime they all had lived together in ancient Rome." Paula's machine conveniently allows Wonder Woman to follow them there.

This kind of story gets used repeatedly in Marston's last few years. *Wonder Woman* #17 visits ancient Rome and the Wild West, while later stories go to the Salem witch trials, a pirate adventure in the 18th century, ancient Rome again, the time of Boadicea, and Incan South America in 1812. While ancient civilizations of various sorts are not a new trope for Wonder Woman, past uses of them typically had Wonder Woman discovering a mythical lost city – not traveling directly into the historical past. Marston's focus on this late in his career suggests a turn away from whimsical fantasy to more real-world concerns.

This is reflected elsewhere in Marston's later work. The *Sensation Comics* stories in 1946 and 1947 take a distinct turn towards materialism and away from fantasy. The twelve issues of *Sensation Comics* published in 1946 feature only one journey to a strange world – the aforementioned realm of the Bughumans. The other eleven issues include one time travel story (Boadicea) and ten stories concerned with contemporary 1946. These stories still have various fantastic inventions and the like, but they're mostly based around issues like family relations or romantic partnerships. This contrasts sharply with, say, 1944, where at least half of the stories employed fantastic settings of one sort or another.

This turn to materialism is wholly understandable in context. Remember, Marston firmly believed that the ascendance of women, and the concomitant male submission to female authority, was a historical inevitability. Not only did he make the claim in *Family Circle*, he made it in Wonder Woman, where American victory in World War II was positioned as a fundamental step in Aphrodite's eventual dominion over the world. Given this, the immediate aftermath of the end of World War II must have been a crushing disappointment for him. The waves of liberated women manning the factories went home, replaced by men. The women's sports leagues (a topic Marston repeatedly championed in Wonder Woman) vanished, and the Women's Army Corps nearly collapsed, falling to ten-thousand members whose long-term future in the army was in doubt: for two years, Congress delayed the bill that would make the WAC permanent, despite the Army's active support for it.

In short, almost none of Marston's beliefs regarding the post-war future actually materialized; instead, the causes he championed moved rapidly backwards. No wonder that his leaps into progressively more outlandish fantasies in the later days of the war, when victory was so close at hand, came crashing back to the ground. In many ways Marston's later work exemplifies not decline so much as despair. The stories in this era become anxious and pained – even Steve Trevor's continued pleas for Wonder Woman to marry him take on an increasingly desperate tone.

This also explains the increasingly nostalgic turn in the latter days of Marston's writing. The number of grotesque ethnic stereotypes markedly increased, and Marston brought back a number of old villains he'd ignored for several years. Not only does Doctor Psycho make a return, Marston also introduces Doctor Psycho's geologist brother (who is just as crazy and evil). But it's "Villainy Incorporated," Marston's much-vaunted final story in Wonder Woman #28, that's the ultimate in nostalgia.

"Villainy Incorporated" marks a return to the practice of devoting an entire issue of *Wonder Woman* to a single narrative. Through most of 1947, *Wonder Woman* ran three unrelated short stories, just like *Comic Cavalcade* and *Sensation Comics*. But "Villainy Incorporated" is overtly advertised as "novel-length" and features the return of no fewer than eight past villains, all of whom escape Reform Island to wreck havoc on the Amazons and Wonder Woman.

The result highlights one of the glaring weaknesses of Wonder Woman as a traditional superhero: her rogue's gallery. I've already noted that few villains developed in Marston's time proved to have any legs. Of those that did, one — Doctor Psycho — doesn't even appear in "Villainy Incorporated," which necessarily focuses on the female villains imprisoned on Reform Island. No, Wonder Woman's epic encounter with her past foes includes such lackluster enemies as the Blue Snow Man, Hypnota, and Zara, Priestess of the Crimson Flame.

The root problem here is that most superheroes have various inversions of themselves to serve as their villains. Batman fights curiously-themed outlaw criminals, Superman has brainy arch-enemies to contrast with his strength, Spider-Man faces other sorts of animal-based characters, and Iron Man battles other rich corporate types. But inverting Wonder Woman is difficult to do well. The entire basis of the character as Marston conceived her precludes a meaningful male threat, as Wonder Woman is defined primarily by her ability to overcome them. This leaves her with primarily female antagonists who are pretty much defined by pathological behaviors, which is unsurprising given Marston's background in psychology. Thus we get sadistic leaders (Queen Clea, Zara, Eviless), unfettered anger and dominance (Cheetah, Giganta), and characters with a rather garish and uncomfortable sense of gender dysphoria who favor presenting themselves as men (Blue Snow Man, Doctor Poison, Hypnota). This accounts for the entirety of Villainy Incorporated. But given that Marston's Wonder Woman is explicitly a moral parable, these clear-cut and pathological villains are woefully uninspiring. None present a serious conceptual threat to Wonder Woman. Most are left to tie her up and boss her around like every other villain she encounters, making them wholly interchangeable. The closest thing to a villain that works is Doctor Psycho, who serves as an equal and opposite threat to Wonder Woman – a man with powers of psychological persuasion who espouses a misogynistic viewpoint.

"Villainy Incorporated" does little more than reiterate the handful of decent ideas the original stories featuring these villains had. Taken as Marston's last word on the character it appears utterly cynical – as if he believed his tenure was best summed up by a greatest hits collection of its action-adventure moments. Yes, the usual discussion of loving authority and submission is there, but it's not the focus. There's no reasonable way to argue that Marston's last Wonder Woman story is first and foremost a restatement of the moral principles that underlie the character.

But if we're being honest, this is a fitting end for Marston's tenure. His agenda, at least in its pure form, failed. Women did not take over the world after World War II. Despite the regard we've held towards Marston's philosophical project, his idea of creating children-friendly female-supremacist bondage propaganda to help ensure world peace was never what you'd call a sound plan. On top of that, his vision of world peace was deeply problematic. He was unrepentantly racist and rarely showed any regard for non-American cultures, and as we'll discuss next chapter, his fetishization of strong, dominant women isn't without sexist implications.

So anyone looking for a thrilling capstone in which Marston definitively lays out his vision in a convincing way is going to be disappointed. His vision was always problematic and unconvincing. Ironically, he goes out on a crassly commercial and nostalgic note. In the end it's much easier to argue for the value of his commercial legacy than it is for his ideology. At least with "Villainy Incorporated" he went out on the note he's actually remembered for: raw populism.

But this strays dangerously close to DC's clear desire to sweep the subversive ideology of Marston's Wonder Woman under the table as an embarrassing historical footnote to the character. One of the basic premises of this book is that there's no such thing as an ideal feminism, and that all feminist progress is necessarily messy, morally compromised, and problematic. That Marston's vision was problematic and impossible to realize either artistically or socially does not mean it lacked value, especially given how utterly iconoclastic it was at the time. More bluntly, it's not as though DC was likely to improve the morality of Wonder Woman by replacing Marston with another writer. And indeed, Robert Kanigher turns out to be crushingly regressive, sending the character into a twenty-year tailspin.

So while Grant Morrison's embrace of Marston's "lush, pervy undercurrents" is misplaced, it's equally wrong to look at Marston as anything other than a weird and wonderful visionary. The problem is that his vision belonged to an era that was already receding into history by the time of his death. While it was undoubtedly the case that replacing Marston was going to lead to a downward turn in the subversive politics of Wonder Woman, the end of his tenure had already exposed a desperate need to find a new approach. As we said when we first defended Marston from the wealth of obvious ethical critiques his work raised, progress is mostly a matter of making new mistakes. By the time his last story was published, Marston had made all of his. Change, of one sort or another, was required.

Chapter 6: Harry G. Peter

One of the reasons Robert Kanigher's ascent as the writer of Wonder Woman doesn't mark an immediate and sharp transition point is the fact that Harry G. Peter remained the artist on the comic through 1958, working with Kanigher for many more years than he did with Marston (though on fewer issues, as both *Sensation Comics* and *Comic Cavalcade* ended shortly after Marston's death). To a reader of modern comics this may seem strange. As much as artists have major star power in today's comics, the comparatively slow work rate of modern artists (a factor of changing tastes, technology, and labor standards) makes it rare for an artist to outlast a writer on a book, let alone make it through a single year without at least one fill-in. In modern comics at least, a change of writer often heralds a new era, while a change of artist is practically routine.

Even in the Golden Age there was a sense that artists were somewhat interchangeable, though much of what we know about the writers and artists on Golden Age comics is reconstructed. For instance, by 1948 *Superman* stories didn't credit writers and artists at all, while *Batman* strips were credited to Bob Kane, even though he only drew the Batman and Robin figures while another uncredited artist handled the rest of the work, and someone else entirely, typically Bill Finger, wrote the stories. *Batman* is perhaps the most indicative example of the crediting practices of this era. To this day, when Batman appears in a comic, he's accompanied by a "created by Bob Kane" credit, despite the fact that by any reasonable definition he was co-created by Bill Finger, who died without ever having seen his name publicly attached to a Batman story or getting a penny of royalties for creating the character.

All of which makes it quite extraordinary that every single issue that Peter drew up through 1950 had his name clearly attached. It's not until *Wonder Woman* #45 in 1951 that a story finally went out anonymously. This level of respect for an artist who was not even credited as one of the creators of the character is almost unheard of in the 1940s, and indicates how much Peter's contributions to Wonder Woman's development went far beyond what was normal for an artist in that era.

We should look at Peter's artistic style in general. Upon a superficial examination, it could be taken as inferior to his contemporaries. His work is much more flat than what was required by the printing technology of the Golden Age comics. Peter has no particular love of shadow or depth, and hardly ever shows motion between the foreground and background of his panels. His action scenes favor static poses, like portraits, and he relies primarily on a perspective based on theatrical staging where the viewer looks straight at the action. Reading an issue of *Comic Cavalcade* in which his art is paired with the expressive angular action of Carmine Infantino's Flash, the frenetic action of Alex Toth's Green Lantern, it's easy to see him as by far the weakest of the three artists.

But it's not surprising that Peter's art is jarring in the context of the latter days of the Golden Age. In the late 1950's, Toth and Infantino were rising stars who would find a place among the greats of the following decades, while Peter was in the final years of his life and career. But even compared to contemporaries like Joe Shuster or Bob Kane, Peter's art is odd. Neither Shuster nor Kane are extraordinary artists from a technical perspective, but they're both phenomenally good at conveying a sense of tone. Shuster's clean lines and simple faces give the early Superman strips a vibrant and fast-moving energy perfectly in tune with the supposed mandate of the title; quite literally, he drew *Action Comics*. Likewise, Kane's drawings, while lacking the confident sense of Shuster's compositions, have a sharp angularity that drips with gothic menace wholly fitting for *Detective Comics*.

It's almost impossible to place Peter's art in this context. Certainly nothing about it screams *"Sensation Comics"* in the same way Kane and Shuster were able to exemplify their titles. Even in comparison to the other artists working at DC at the time of Wonder Woman's debut, there is something dated about Peter's work. His refusal to abandon the theatrical mode of treating the comics page as the equivalent to curtains around a stage, his over-reliance on awkward tableaus that turned as many characters as possible into positions where they faced the readers, and his tendency to use almost grotesque contortions of characters' mouths as the only means to depict emotion all exemplify a completely different tradition than evidenced by his counterparts on other titles. His linework is particularly notable, as its style suggests a hierarchy of characters. Good characters are expressed through relatively clean lines and simple faces, whereas villainous characters and horrific racial caricatures are defined by a comparative density of facial lines.

But if Peter seems out of place with his contemporaries, it's because calling Shuster and Kane his contemporaries is deeply misleading. Harry Peter was over thirty years older than either of them, and had a career stretching back into the early 20th century with illustration credits dating to at least 1908. He drew numerous cartoons for *Judge*, an early American humor magazine that influenced *The New Yorker*. In other words, Peter belonged to the Platinum Age, an era preceding the Golden Age, much as Thoth and Infantino belonged to the later Silver Age.

Figure 4: Harry G. Peter's early 20th century art for *Judge* (1908).

Peter's Platinum Age work is based on flowing, swirling strokes that display an even richer and more complex sense of linework than his Wonder Woman material. It's not merely a different style than his superhero work; despite the superficial difference in medium between the four-color printing of the Golden Age and the black-and-white drawings of *Judge*. Rather, it's that the basic nature of drawing Platinum Age cartoons and Golden Age superhero comics are starkly different. Sequential storytelling is not the same as illustration, and just as Marston frequently found himself in the space between two traditions, Peter's career does not bridge the two styles so much as it lurks between them.

Like Marston, Peter's first work for DC was on Wonder Woman. He'd done a smattering of stories for some minor companies, but it's not as though he was an established modern comic book artist. Given how odd his art compares to his contemporaries, his hiring is a bit unusual. Les Daniels quotes DC editor Sheldon Mayer as saying that Harry Peter was Marston's choice to draw Wonder Woman. Mayer wasn't initially fond of the selection, and suggests that Marston sought an artist who worked in an older style. But this raises a new question: why did Marston desire this old-fashioned style for Wonder Woman?

The most obvious answer comes from a particular detail of Peter's career in the early 20th century: his work drawing the Gibson Girls. The Gibson Girl was a particular style of female designed by Charles Dana Gibson in the late 19th century and popular into the early 20th century. She was among the first real pinup images, combining a tall and slender build with the ample hourglass figure characteristic of the Edwardian-style swan-bill corset.

This fact alone suggests Peter's appeal to Marston, who after all was trying to create a sex symbol of his own. But in 1941, when Wonder Woman began, the Gibson Girl's popularity had long since waned, replaced by the more overt sexuality of the Varga Girl and photographs of contemporary celebrities. Even in the context of looking for actively sexual

Figure 5: A characteristic example of Charles Dana Gibson's "Gibson Girl" style (1902)

artistry, the decision to reach back into the receding past of the Gibson Girl sticks out.

The Gibson Girl also had a clear feminist leaning that surely appealed to Marston. She was generally depicted as educated and independent. At worst they were equals to men, and at best they were teasing companions who visibly enjoyed the upper hand in the gender dynamic. In some ways Gibson's vision is even more progressive than Marston's, conceived as the product of America's melting pot of races, a sharp contrast to Marston's xenophobic tendencies.

Gibson acknowledged that his creation was not modeled on any real girls, but on a sort of ideal vision of American femininity – and a Darwinian vision at that, given that Gibson cited natural selection in a 1910 interview with the New York Times about the girls. He spoke movingly of how "in American pictures woman has been notable because the artist has approached and treated her with an innate respect – with gallantry, if you care to use the term; but with no more than she deserves. American men pay homage to their women – actual homage. That is true and to their credit, but sadly enough, makes them distinctive." The appeal of this sentiment to Marston goes a long way towards explaining why a former Gibson Girl artist would be his first choice to draw Wonder Woman, herself an extension of Gibson's views.

But there's a hint that Harry Peter sits at the end of an even older tradition. Thus far I've largely stressed his weaknesses when it comes to traditional American superhero art, but this is unfair to Peter, whose skills are clearly within the context Marston wanted. His relative weakness in facial expressions and in dynamic, kinetic action is counterbalanced by his elegant depictions of the human form, particularly the female form. In panel after panel, Wonder Woman is posed with curving, graceful lines; there's a sense of physicality to all of Peter's women. Their very lack of dynamic movement makes them distinctly corporeal, creating a material presence.

As I noted in the first chapter, his work resembles that of Victorian and Edwardian pornography, which for fairly straightforward reasons favored depictions of the body over the face. At least one nude drawing of Wonder Woman by Peter has surfaced, and it's difficult to believe it's the only one he ever drew. Peter, in other words, was an artist whose style was indebted to erotica and even pornography. But this still dances around the degree to which Peter's style was a *datedly* erotic one.

In this regard, there's one more influence that makes Peter's style a clear fit for Marston's intentions. Peter's work most resembles the pornography associated with the British Aestheticist movement of the late 19th century – the movement that, most famously, produced Oscar Wilde – and that movement's crowning popularity came during Peter's adolescence and young adulthood. It would have been quite familiar to him from the parodies in the British equivalents of magazines like *Judge*.

As one might guess from its name, aestheticism focuses on the value of experiencing art and the reactions art evokes; consideration of the aesthetic response is treated as the most basic and fundamental moral duty. In practical terms, this manifested in two main ways: the avid valuation of art and design, and the acceptance of alternative sexualities (primarily male homosexuality, at the time). But its key idea, for our purposes, is that it viewed ethics and philosophy as stemming from aesthetics – that aesthetics form a set of first principles from which the rest of one's thought extends. This is not a belief in aesthetics over morality, but a belief that it's impossible for any serious sense of morality to reject aesthetic pleasure. Thus, it embraced a sort of utopian hedonism.

To look at Marston's philosophy through the lens of aestheticism brings back the problem that haunts all of Marston's work: that for all of his moral justifications, the real point of Wonder Woman is just that he's turned on by sexually dominant women. However, Marston's insistence that the act of submission to powerful women necessarily

Figure 6: Harry Peter was heavily influenced by the often erotic work of Aestheticist artists like Aubrey Beardsley.

leads to an ethical good in fact echoes the aestheticist's claim that sound ethics will follow from a commitment to the aesthetic.

In this regard, Wonder Woman can first and foremost be seen as an attempt to make Marston's own impressions and experiences of female domination into a distinct and communicable object. The specific hiring of Harry Peter to actualize this idea into comic form, given Peter's own clear debt to the aesthetic movement and its styles, makes complete sense in this context. The aesthetic of Wonder Woman reflects the late 19th century artistic tradition that Peter grew up in and learned from.

There's a problem lurking underneath this, however. Marston and Peter aestheticize Wonder Woman, making her into a modern-day muse to be worshipped. In this regard she fits firmly into the tradition of the Gibson Girls, who were also muses to be admired and put, if not on a pedestal, at least on a wall. In all cases, however, it's heterosexual men who are determining the place of women. They are admired because men choose to admire them rather than disrespect them. Even Marston's women are given their power because of men who submit to them. Power, by default, flows from men to women.

Nothing in Marston's Wonder Woman is actually about women or their experience. This is the same problem that led Marston to be so crushingly wrong about what post-war America would look like. The "liberated" women who were working in factories weren't going out and taking jobs of their own, they were given the jobs of men who had to go to war. And when the men came back, they took the jobs back. Rosie the Riveter was, like Wonder Woman and the Gibson Girl, adored and idolized by men. But when her usefulness was at an end, she was as easy to knock off her pedestal as she was to put there in the first place.

Not to say that fetishizing women as strong and dominant figures to be adored and worshipped isn't an improvement over treating them as domestic slaves.

Marston's vision was fatally flawed, but it doesn't mean it wasn't progress. What it does mean is that we can see what the next step in Wonder Woman's ascent must be.

Chapter 7: Robert Kanigher (1948-1958)

The transition from Marston's Wonder Woman to Kanigher's is a gradual thing. One doesn't notice it happening so much as that it's already happened. The first moment of awareness comes when the comic seemingly loses its moral framework. Marston's stories stemmed from the complex weirdness of his philosophical and aesthetic system. Even his most banal stories – and Marston wrote many banal and subpar stories – have a compelling depth to them by virtue of being facets of a larger and more intricate object. Marston was genuinely unlike any other comic-book writer. He wasn't an industry professional who churned out a variety of stories and characters in different genres to fit a given freelance commission, only to later find success with a particular character. He wrote one type of story, and improbably found a home for it within the comics industry.

Robert Kanigher, on the other hand, was a consummate freelancer. He wrote dozens of different characters for DC, racking up more writing credits than any other writer in the company's history. His twenty-year run as writer-editor of Wonder Woman is his largest single contribution, yet it's a small fraction of his overall body of work. He has no identifiable style or interests, no ideology or beliefs; his most distinguishing characteristics lie in his adaptability and the sheer volume of his output. If he has a style, it's to hit his deadlines, which he did better than anyone else at DC. The contrast with Marston could not be sharper.

In many ways, this was exactly what the title needed. Kanigher's adaptability explains why his early work is indistinguishable from Marston's lesser stories. Within a year or two, however, a shift becomes apparent. Slowly, Kanigher dulls the edge of Marston's philosophical system. Reform Island and the Amazon principle of "submission to loving authority" are watered down to Transformation Island and the Amazon way of "living in loving kindness," and Marston's radical morals are steadily replaced by bland pablum, like, "When people everywhere in the solar system realize that love and kindness is the greatest 'atomic' force in the world, there need never be any unhappiness."

If this softening of tone were the only change to Wonder Woman, it would be possible to read it as little more than a response to arguments about the title's excessive bondage dating back to 1943, when Josette Frank penned a letter to M.C. Gaines expressing concern about these themes. Marston won those arguments while he was alive, but the concerns persisted, and after Marston's death such material was quietly taken out of the strip. More troubling, however, is how the comic veers away from the overt (if troubled) feminism of Marston's work towards outright sexism.

In *Sensation Comics* #94 the comic was completely redesigned to target a female audience. Every feature save for Wonder Woman was dropped, replaced with new backups like "Romance, Inc.," "Dr. Pat" (the cover helpfully clarifies she's a woman), and "Headline Heroines." The cover has Steve Trevor carrying a grinning Wonder Woman over a stream, drawn by Irwin Hansen instead of Harry Peter. Hansen's style – considerably more expressive and friendly than Peter's – would be featured on the covers of both *Sensation Comics* and *Wonder Woman* until Peter departed the strip entirely in 1958.

Internally, the changes were equally vivid. Wonder Woman's stories become much more concerned with the issue of her marriage (or lack thereof) to Steve Trevor; every issue of *Sensation Comics* from #94 through #99 looks at their engagement. The most ridiculous change to take place in this period appears in *Sensation Comics* #97, when Wonder Woman becomes the editor of the Daily Globe's "Hopeless Hearts" department, where she fixes people's love lives. Although this change only lasts a handful of issues, the resulting spectacle of Wonder Woman rushing between her Military Intelligence job as Diana Prince and her editor job as Wonder Woman is at once depressing and bizarre.

Even the basic ethos of the character gets a makeover. For instance, Wonder Woman's original reason for not marrying Steve Trevor was that she couldn't abide Trevor's failure to love her in her guise as Diana Prince. The implication was that Trevor was flawed because he only valued the traditionally beautiful Wonder Woman and not the plainer Diana. But in *Sensation Comics* #96, the reason becomes more pragmatic – if Wonder Woman gets married, she'll no longer be an Amazon and will revert to her Diana Prince identity forever, so Steve *has to* love her as Diana. In later issues the explanation becomes even less connected to any notion of female empowerment: Wonder Woman simply won't marry Trevor until she's rid the world of crime and injustice.

This is the pebble at the front of an avalanche. An obsession with marriage infects *Wonder Woman* as well: the "Wonder Women of History" segment devoted to positive female role models is scrapped in favor of trivia about wedding customs around the world. However, while the stories and backup features give every indication of being targeted at female readers, the advertisements are still for air rifles and Charles Atlas bodybuilding programs – stuff clearly intended for boys. This gives the books a decidedly schizoid quality.

While the stories may be targeted at female readers, the targeting is particularly crass, treating that readership without the slightest shred of respect. To be perfectly blunt, in the

1950s *Wonder Woman*'s attitudes towards women were depraved. Consider the story "Wonder Woman's Invincible Rival" from *Wonder Woman* #56, in which Steve Trevor becomes jealous of Wonder Woman for always saving him. In sharp contrast to how the strip worked under Marston, where this would be used to emphasize how female superiority is not a bad thing, Kanigher presents a lengthy sequence of trials and tribulations in which Wonder Woman secretly helps Trevor to realize he can do whatever she can, while remaining unseen so as to save his pride. This endorsement of the idea that women should stay out of the spotlight in order to assuage the male ego is completely contrary to everything that Marston designed the character to do.

Sadly, Trevor's wooing of Wonder Woman only gets worse. By the time we get to "Daily Danger" in *Wonder Woman* #96, his affections have become downright disturbing. Trevor gets Wonder Woman to agree to marry him if no one needs her help for an entire day. He then tricks her into situations where he might win such a bet – like trapping her in a diving bell with him, all alone under the sea. When she protests, he laughs at her. "All's fair in love and war, angel!" He doesn't win, of course, and yet at the end of the story he says, "My day will come! Just you wait, Wonder Woman – just you wait!" Wonder Woman grins lovingly at him, giving tacit approval for everything he's done.

Let's pause here and consider: Steve Trevor abducts Wonder Woman to force her to marry him. This is played for comedy, without ever considering the possibility that Trevor's actions are morally appalling – his bullying comes close to functional rape. He tries to cheat her using schemes that Marston (or any remotely sensible writer) would reserve for villains. Wonder Woman avoids forced marriage, but her escapes are not due to her own ingenuity or strength. They're just dumb luck, born of improbable situations where someone needs her help after all.

Kanigher's take on Wonder Woman is unquestionably sexist, in ways Marston's never was, and without any evidence of a larger moral system – indeed, Kanigher doesn't push any kind of a coherent philosophical position. His stories are just as likely to end with no moral whatsoever as they are to end with something that's horrifyingly sexist. His most bewildering ending comes in "Wonder Woman's Invisible Twin," from *Wonder Woman* #59. Wonder Woman is beset with a number of strange mishaps: she's suddenly tied up with invisible rope; she fails to successfully lasso gangsters; and so on. It turns out her double in another world is inadvertently affecting her, and they sort it all out. When we get to the final panel – the position normally reserved for a moral lesson – Wonder Woman says, "I've always been myself! It's just that what happened to my double in our co-existing world – affected me! Something that can happen to anyone!"

The story is superficially structured like a story with a moral. Wonder Woman looks out of the panel towards her readers, directly addressing us, and delivers a monologue that wraps up the story with the general claim that this can happen to anyone, just as in Marston's fables. But there's no moral here, only a reflection on how having your superpowers sapped by an alternate-dimension doppelgänger is just one of those things. It looks like Kanigher wrote a Wonder Woman-styled story with no thought whatsoever to its content.

Unfortunately, Kanigher's work at large supports this view. His plotting is lazy, and his stories often lack intelligible points. While this occasionally leads to the surreal brilliance of warning us about our counterparts in co-existing worlds, more often it leads to stories that have the singular goal of filling the six to ten pages assigned to them. This hollowness is most flagrant in the occasional features that describe the origins of Wonder Woman's equipment. The plots of these stories – and there are one or two a year in the first decade of Kanigher's writing – are practically identical. In flashback, Queen Hippolyta tells Wonder Woman that she needs one more object before she can go fight crime in man's world. Inevitably this entails a series of courageous feats to, say, recover a piece of her invisible plane from some dangerous circumstance. Over the course of roughly eight pages, Wonder Woman does what she needs to do and takes the item. The stories are nothing more than an excuse to cram several small action set pieces together in a loose frame.

This wouldn't be so bad if Kanigher had a sense of what makes an action set piece interesting, but he rarely does. In the nadir of this unfortunate subgenre, *Wonder Woman* #72's "The Secret of Wonder Woman's Sandals," Hippolyta presents her with a pair of miniature sandals that, in a staggeringly horrid pun, are said to "grow in proportion to your deeds! The mightier the feat – the larger they grow!" Moments after she says this, the sea around Paradise Island begins to boil (which is largely unexplained), resulting in Wonder Woman having to physically lift the island and move it. Quite reasonably, she now expects her sandals will fit, but only one of them has grown – she'll have to complete a second feat for the other one. "It may take years before anything momentous happens to need my help," Wonder Woman pouts, but then she hears a faint cry from the sea, dives in, and discovers a giant whale who's lifted a ship out of the water. She removes the ship from the whale, returns to Paradise Island, and lo and behold, her second scandal has grown. She declares victory.

If this sounds vapid and banal, it's not because of any distortion in the retelling. The story really does consist of Wonder Woman moving large objects around the ocean in order to grow her sandals. Hippolyta and Wonder Woman are the only characters, and none of the feats involve any dramatic tension beyond "Can she move this object?" Kanigher offers no interesting explanations to underscore her problems, he just strings together six pages of action. And though it's a particularly egregious example, for him it's hardly unusual.

It would be wrong to suggest that Kanigher was solely responsible for the decline in the comic, even though his dual role as writer and editor gave him almost complete freedom in determining its content. By the mid-1950s, Harry Peter's art weakened considerably, and near the end of the decade it was practically lifeless. There's no consistency to his character designs – their facial expressions rarely match their ostensible emotions – and his linework became scratchy and thin. Much of the blame deserves to be put at Kanigher's feet, but Peter was doing the title no favors, and there's an immediate spike in quality when he finally departs.

This may explain why Kanigher displayed little interest in the Wonder Woman comics of this period, but it's not like it was Peter who decided to have Wonder Woman meet Robin Hood twice in a two-year period, or who found the origins of Wonder Woman's tiara so compelling that he retold them multiple times. Even towards the end of his time on Wonder Woman, Peter was more likely to enliven a flat script with a clever splash page than he was to sandbag a promising story.

For example, *Wonder Woman* #90 features a relatively flat tale called "Wonder Woman, Amazon Baby Sitter!" In it, Wonder Woman has to care for a baby whale, a baby elephant, and a baby dinosaur, for completely specious reasons. She rescues them from improbable situations (like, the baby elephant parachutes from a plane and gets stuck on a rocky outcrop), but Peter interprets the plot with such joyful literalism – the opening splash page has Wonder Woman pushing around a pram with a dinosaur in it – that he almost succeeds in making the entire exercise worthwhile.

It's also worth noting that, generally speaking, most of the 1950s were a lousy decade for superhero comics. When Marston died in 1947, Wonder Woman was appearing regularly in four titles: *Wonder Woman*, *Sensation Comics*, *Comic Cavalcade*, and *All-Star Comics*. Five years later she was in just one (*Wonder Woman* itself) in large part because superhero comics had plummeted in popularity and were dropping like flies. *Comic Cavalcade* switched to being a funny animals book in 1948 before getting cancelled in 1954. *All-Star Comics* ended entirely in early 1951. *Sensation Comics* reinvented itself as a mystery comic at the start of 1952; it lasted three issues. As a result, Wonder Woman went from appearing in thirty separate issues in 1947 to just six in 1952. By that time, DC's publishing line consisted of thirty-nine comics, only seven of which were recognizably superhero titles. (A few were later reinvented as superhero comics once DC became an all-superhero company.)

This means the early years of Kanigher's writing coincided precisely with a massive downturn in the quality and popularity of the superhero comics industry. His Wonder Woman comics were lousy, but so the other superhero comics at the time. It wasn't until 1956 that the great revival of superhero comics began, in what is called the Silver Age, when Julius Schwartz revamped The Flash in *Showcase* #4, tapping Kanigher to write it. Barely a year later, Wonder Woman got her own high-profile relaunch, and with it a brand-new art team. So, at least in part, the low quality of Wonder Woman during Kanigher's first decade can be attributed to the fact that nobody cared enough to bother doing it well. The artist was literally dying (Peter passed away only a few months after Kanigher removed him) and the writer was phoning it in because the genre was apparently dying too.

That Kanigher was a disinterested writer with no conscious moral message to push doesn't mean that his comics lacked an underlying moral system. Kanigher claims in Les Daniels's history of Wonder Woman that he had no active set of concerns or plans; he simply worked on instinct. There is no reason to doubt this claim. But instinct, within the context of the superhero genre, has troubling implications.

By default, superhero comics are exceedingly pro-establishment. Even before the 1954 Comics Code mandated that "policemen, judges, government officials and respected institutions shall never be presented in such a way as to create disrespect for established authority," and that "divorce shall not be treated humorously nor represented as desirable," superhero comics were necessarily conservative in their leanings. Their entire premise is based on powerful individuals who can't be stopped by ordinary people, but who only want to protect those ordinary people in order to keep things the way they are. Superhero comics take place in a quasi-realist world, just like ours but with Batman, Superman, or Wonder Woman in it, which makes them hard-pressed to engage in any kind of contemporary activism. Contrary to Grant Morrison's ecstatically leftist reading of early Superman as a socialist hero, if a bulletproof man who can throw cars around wanted a socialist revolution that empowered the underclass, he would get it. But since the nature of superhero comics storytelling says he can't get it (as that would violate the quasi-realism) it's impossible to write a superhero comic where he wants it.

This isn't quite true. Marston, after all, managed to write a superhero who really did want to start a revolution. But he did this by sneaking content past his editors, playing up his insistence that America was a superior beacon of liberty and freedom to the world, while quietly remaking it into a feminist bondage utopia. It was, to say the least, a unique trick, but it depended on Marston's enormously complex and thorough moral system. In the absence of such a titanic effort to the contrary, superhero comics revert to the norm of reflexive support for existing structures of power. Under Kanigher, that's exactly what happened.

In the 1950s, Wonder Woman is repeatedly used to stress conformity and uncritical support for the status quo. Early in the decade Kanigher wrote several stories about the glory of menial jobs. In the lead story of *Wonder Woman* #39, "The Trail of Thrills," Wonder Woman reassures people with dull and unimportant jobs – light bulb replacer, for instance, or telephone time announcer – by showing them how their work actually matters. In the next issue, Wonder Woman similarly inspires a ferry operator to value his occupation. These stories are not actively sexist or objectionable, but there's something unsettling in the way Wonder Woman becomes a propaganda tool not to challenge the patriarchy, but to extol menial work. Even if one doesn't hold a quasi-Marxist position that says jobs of this sort are really about instilling conformity and unquestioning deference to authority, it's easy to see that a previously subversive comic calling for the rejection of the entire mainstream social order now glorifies its most banal aspects.

Even more troubling are stories like "The Earth Is a Time Bomb" from *Wonder Woman* #77. It ends with Wonder Woman hurling a planet-destroying bomb back at the planet that created it. This presumably results in the total destruction of that planet – a functional act of genocide completely ignored by the script. It's a particularly extreme example, but cases like Wonder Woman annihilating entire invasion fleets with nothing so much as a casual comment about how this is the fate for all who threaten America abound in Kanigher's work. Again, it's helpful to contrast with Marston, who goes out of his way to show how societies can be redeemed through submission to loving authority – a fundamentally optimistic moral about improving the world. Instead, Kanigher just blows them up and boasts about American supremacy. This shouldn't be taken as Kanigher being particularly genocidal or militaristic in his worldview; rather, in the absence of an active effort to do anything else, superhero comics will default to a moral about how powerful people can successfully use violence to maintain the status quo.

This introduces the other half of Wonder Woman. She's designed as a revolutionary progressive force for social transformation, but she's fundamentally enmeshed in a reactionary genre that celebrates the status quo. This restates the original problem that Wonder Woman faced. Her utopianism had already taken on a debased and material form, a pragmatic compromise that partially sold out its own ideals – that's what going to Man's World means. It's just that by

1958 the pendulum had swung against Wonder Woman in almost every regard. Her utopianism was gone, and nobody was making any effort with the comic. Man's World had won. From here, at least, things can only improve.

Chapter 8: The Silver Age (1958-68)

Wonder Woman was clearly near rock bottom in 1958. Given this, *Wonder Woman* #98, a soft relaunch with a new artist, is clearly a good thing. But any hopes of a swift restoration are dashed on the first page of The Million Dollar Penny," a story that shares its title and premise with a Kanigher story from *Wonder Woman* #59 earlier in the decade. In both iterations, Wonder Woman is challenged to turn a penny into a million dollars in just twenty-four hours. It's an irritatingly capitalist story, a rags-to-riches parable about the possibilities offered by industrial America. It's not the most frustrating example of Kanigher's predilections, but it's unmistakably an example.

The story isn't very good, but even if it were, it's in no way an intuitively sensible choice for the job Kanigher's trying to do. For the most part, *Wonder Woman* #98 retells Wonder Woman's origin – appropriate enough for a quasi-relaunch. But nothing about making a million dollars in twenty-four hours connects to Wonder Woman's origins, except as a vague initiation into Man's World.

It's a jarring concept in practice. Recast as a challenge from Hippolyta to build a summer camp in the name of Pallas Athena, this capitalist fantasy makes no sense in the context of an Amazon culture that's functionally withdrawn from society, secluded as they are on Paradise Island. The result is at once ludicrous and damaging, reducing the

Amazons to nothing more than a plot contrivance. The lack of effort on Kanigher's part is shocking. Not only does he lazily recycle old stories, he doesn't seem to be giving any serious thought to what stories he chooses.

Even though Kanigher remains as frustrating as ever, the improvements in the art are substantial. Ross Andru and Mike Esposito are not among the giants of the Silver Age, but their work is solid and stylish, with all of the dynamism that Peter's art lacked. Their grasp of faces is particularly strong, and under their pencils and pens Wonder Woman and Steve Trevor become characters with real emotional range, not the bland, programmatic ciphers that Peter drew, especially the last few years. This emotional range is more a feature of the art than a reflection of the stories themselves, but it *is* progress.

More broadly, Andru and Esposito fit well within the tradition of DC's Silver Age artists. Unlike at Marvel, where Jack Kirby's style applied to virtually all of their characters, DC had several artists of note, particularly Carmine Infantino, Gil Kane, and Curt Swan. This diverse pool of artists was united by an aesthetic that emphasized fluidity of motion and dynamic, exciting poses. Influenced by cinema, they paid attention to the camera angles of their storytelling.

For example, Andru and Esposito often foreground a character's face while other action happens in the background, creating a strong sense of motion in three dimensions. Although their skill at middle-range action shots pales in comparison to someone like Infantino, they're still deft at using the space of the page to create active, frenetic compositions, and their sense of when to move in and out of close-up is impeccable. They often use panels that are slightly too small for their subjects, such that parts of faces and bodies end up being cropped. This isn't done carelessly, but in a way that gives the impression of a photographer circling the action and grabbing snapshots of something moving too fast to capture perfectly. The compositions are always clear,

Figure 7: Ross Andru and Mike Esposito brought a kinetic and dynamic range of composition that had been lacking in Harry Peter's art, from *Wonder Woman* #101 (1958), copyright DC Comics, used under the principle of fair use.

even though the characters are on the verge of escaping the panels that depict them.

Kanigher's writing, however, was slow to modernize. Steve Trevor's behavior continued to border on the abusive, and Wonder Woman became increasingly jealous and petty. *Wonder Woman* #102 features a story with robot duplicates of Wonder Woman (a common Kanigher trope) and Steve Trevor has to figure out which of three is real. He ultimately kisses them all to make his decision, and at the end of the story Wonder Woman complains, "Did you have to kiss those – those robots first? Why couldn't you have started with me? How many other girls have you kissed?" It's disheartening.

Over time, though, Kanigher finds inspiration in his new art team. In *Wonder Woman* #105, he retells the origin story again, this time introducing Wonder Girl into the mix. Kanigher's usual storytelling foibles apply – plot holes abound, the Amazons are further marginalized, and the basic conceit isn't particularly original: young versions of existing superheroes have been around for years, at least as far back as 1946 with the debut of Superboy.

But Kanigher gets at least some credit for trying something new with the title. Wonder Girl is hardly a novel concept, but she's new within Wonder Woman, and she heralds a wave of similar inventions in the early 1960s: Wonder Tot and her playmate Mister Genie, Mer-boy and Bird-Boy as love interests for Wonder Girl, and adult versions of both to provide competition for Steve Trevor. Kanigher also develops a bevy of new villains. Most are, admittedly, as forgettable as Marston's, although Egg Fu – a Fu Manchu stereotype who happens to be a gigantic egg with a deadly mustache – is quite memorable.

Even Kanigher's non-recurring characters in this period have a spark to them that was lacking just a few years before. *Wonder Woman* #113 features reanimated Sphinx creatures in the Egyptian desert. It's not an award-winning idea, but compared to Wonder Woman's previous decade it's positively clever. The Sphinx Men are designed to work well as a visual spectacle, providing the comic with alluring and unusual images throughout the story, beyond the opening splash page. This characterizes Kanigher's writing more and more during the period. The next story has parade floats of giant animals coming to life and attacking things, another idea that provides visual fun for an entire issue. It's a sharp contrast to Kanigher's earlier plots, which were usually generic action set pieces strung together with no particular thought towards visuals or plotting (though occasionally Harry Peter got something fun to draw on the first page).

Coinciding with this period of improvement was the rise of a comic that would prove essential to Wonder Woman's future: *Justice League of America*. The premise of this comic was a straightforward reiteration of the Golden Age *All-Star Comics* (right down to using the same writer) with DC's current stable of superheroes. Unlike the previous Justice Society, however, full membership was granted to characters holding down their own books, including Wonder Woman.

This had the effect of integrating DC's line of heroes. While *All-Star Comics* purported to offer a team of superheroes, it was basically an anthology of individual adventures. In *Justice League of America* there's a much higher level of interaction among the characters; they teamed up regularly. Reading DC comics became an experience based on knowledge of and engagement with the line as a whole. Where *All-Star Comics* served essentially as a marketing tool, offering you an extra Doctor Fate story every few months in exchange for trying a few other characters, *Justice League of America* positioned itself as the flagship book of the entire line, the book that every DC comics buyer had to buy.

This was a significant change in the nature of comics. The Justice Society of the Golden Age played at being an overarching narrative, but in practice there was little real overlap among the titles. The tones of Batman, Superman, and Wonder Woman were all fundamentally different, and so too with the other heroes. While the Justice Society might claim that Wonder Woman and Batman were part of the same world, in practice it was impossible to imagine Marston's feminist bondage propaganda fitting in with the angular noir world of Bob Kane's imagination.

But *Justice League of America*, by putting its characters not just in one comic but in one coherent adventure, forced the reader to come up with a narrative frame that reconciled the disparate styles and storytelling of the various superheroes, and this extended to the nature of the characters themselves and their reasons for teaming up. In the 1960s, Superman had various superpowers including heightened senses and genius-like intelligence, in addition to being nearly invincible; in theory, he had no need to team up with Batman, who was just an ordinary human in a leather rodent costume. Any threat appropriate for Superman was by definition out of Batman's league, and any threat appropriate to Batman was pointlessly trivial for Superman.

Justice League of America ignored this disparity and treated both Batman and Superman as equal partners within a larger group of heroes with wildly varying levels of power. While this process was eased by the relative streamlining of DC's entire line into a distinctive Silver Age style, it still required an active, savvy readership who could switch between multiple codes of reference, and who intuitively grasped that characters appearing in *Justice League of America* were subtly but distinctly different from their respective solo books.

This reflected another trend in DC's Silver Age comics: gimmicky covers that suggested radical changes undermining the premise of the comic, or that were blatantly absurd. The auxiliary Superman titles *Superman's Girlfriend Lois Lane* and *Superman's Pal Jimmy Olsen* provided the best-known examples of this style: a cover where Superman holds Lois Lane's limp body and shouts, "Yes, Lana... it's true! I killed Lois Lane!" or, more humorously, one where Jimmy Olsen shivers in a leaking, rat-filled apartment with a broken window, begging for help, while Superman angrily declares, "That's what you get for being a wise guy, Jimmy! You'll just have to live in this rat-trap from now on!"

The stories themselves would invariably go to great lengths to make sense of the outlandish covers without actually undermining the characters. Again, these covers assume a readership well-versed and comfortable with the tropes of the series, who read not just for an entertaining story, but to see those tropes played with and subverted. Silver Age comics, in other words, assumed readers would engage with the comics on multiple levels.

Wonder Woman settles into this approach gradually over the course of Andru and Esposito's decade on the series. Only a few months into their tenure, Wonder Woman struggles to find an adventure worthy of her 100th issue, lampshading her status as a fictional character published by a comic-book company. A later story in *Wonder Woman* #112 has her soliciting reader comments for the letter column; when the letter column started up, letters were purportedly answered by Wonder Woman herself, and requests to meet her were patiently answered with reflexive explanations of her fictionality, often accompanied by musings on the nature of imaginary spaces and how reading a comic constituted a meeting in the imagination.

This kind of metafictional storytelling culminates in *Wonder Woman* #124, when Kanigher has Wonder Woman, Wonder Girl, and Wonder Tot team up in a single adventure, even though they each represent the same person at different points in her life. (This had previously been rejected in *Wonder Woman* #117, with Wonder Girl traveling through time in an attempt to meet Wonder Woman, only to be constantly frustrated in the attempt.) Kanigher's solution is to have Queen Hippolyta splice together film of Wonder Woman at various points in her life to create this "impossible story." It was popular enough that such stories became common in Wonder Woman for several years, with increasingly little effort given to explain how they work – eventually the "impossible" tag gets dropped entirely. It's utterly ridiculous, but the very existence of such a tongue-in-cheek presentation, turning the ostensibly impossible into something demonstrably feasible, shows a lively complexity that the comic lacked in the dying days of the Golden Age.

This increasing textual complexity pays clear dividends to the feminist themes of the title. Now that it's plainly designed to function on multiple levels, one can identify a feminist subtext that critiques the unfortunate tropes favored by Kanigher, though it's probably stretching things to suggest the 1960s gave him a wake-up call; for example, he still relies on domineering male characters who engage in flagrantly abusive behavior in their attempts to court Wonder Woman. But the fact that the comic actively solicits multiple levels of reading provides the opportunity for it to resist its own excesses.

This process begins in the Wonder Girl stories. Kanigher frequently writes scenes in which Wonder Girl angrily berates Mer-Boy for his efforts to woo her, presumably to give the character a sense of teenage outrage. So, for instance, in *Wonder Woman* #115 she spends the entire story infuriated with Mer-Boy, who has put up big signs stating that her refusal to go to the dance with him is unfair. She angrily proclaims that she never wants to see Mer-Boy again, engaging with him only to stop his public humiliation of her. It's not until he reforms his behavior and tries to save her from danger that she consents to going to the dance with him. While on one level this is seems to suggest that Mer-Boy was never actually that bad and that Wonder Girl was overreacting, it can equally be read as a parable about what is and isn't appropriate behavior towards women, as well as the importance of consent and boundaries. Because the title's been actively soliciting the reader to approach it on multiple narrative levels, this alternate reading allows Wonder Girl to give voice to the objections lurking around the default presentation of romance in Wonder Woman, and particularly how Steve Trevor's been a complete cad.

In a highlight of Kanigher's stories, and a highlight of Wonder Woman outright, "Wonder Girl vs. The Teenage Monster" (from *Wonder Woman* #151) pushes the Silver Age structure as far as it goes within the series. Wonder Girl wishes she had as many suitors as Wonder Woman, and dreams herself into Wonder Woman's place. In the dream she's pursued by a Steve Trevor who's been recast as a teenaged military pilot. (This is, of course, ridiculous. However, despite the fact that a teenager flying fighter jets for the military is preposterous, the story can be understood because it mimics a coherent structure from Wonder Woman's adult adventures.)

The antagonist of this story is an alien life form, an extraterrestrial made of orange glop. It quickly becomes apparent that the Glop is capable of digesting anything and then taking on its form and characteristics. Things turn bizarre when the Glop attacks a group of picnicking teenagers, who possess an amazing record player that can hold a hundred different records; at the time, they're listening to a pop song where the singer proclaims that Wonder Girl is his pearl. For reasons best left unexamined, one of the teenagers reacts to this attack by throwing the record player at the Glop, which then proceeds to digest the records and take on their characteristics. Accordingly, it spends the rest of the story serenading Wonder Girl with cheesy pop lyrics while trying to destroy anything that stands between them. The caption accompanying this rather unexpected plot development is one of the greats of the Silver Age: "What thunderous new development will now haunt the world because the Glop has found a voice from digesting a stack of 100 rock 'n roll records?" The answer consists of a massive blob of orange glop singing bewildering pop lyrics like "Glop... glop... glop... I've got an atom bomb! To blast the calm! 'Less my Wonder Girl herself comes off the shelf to me-me-me-me-GLOP!" Eventually Wonder Girl defeats the Glop by having a time machine tattooed onto her body so that she can send the Glop back to prehistoric Earth.

The manic inventiveness of this story is not its only strength. The central conceit also serves as an implicit critique of the very pop culture in which it exists. The Glop becomes a threat to Wonder Girl when it uncritically assimilates the ethos and aesthetics of contemporary pop music, mistaking its depiction of romance for an appropriate way to pursue her. Wonder Girl, in other words, is under attack from mass media's depiction of women, and deposits her slimy stalker back in the Stone Age where his objectifying attitudes belong. At the end of the story, Wonder Woman herself notes that sometimes dreams come true, while a supplemental caption asks readers to weigh in on whether the Glop should return in a future adventure. Such multiple levels of narrative coding – where imaginary stories within fictional stories are also treated as real – invite a multi-layered reading that can be reflexively extended to pop culture itself.

Unfortunately, this sudden wellspring of creativity within Wonder Woman was not to last. Ironically, the force that brought it down was the same one that allowed it several years of manic creativity: its fans. The first sign of trouble came just a few issues later, in *Wonder Woman* #156. On the surface, the comic was another inventive piece of trope subversion. In a story called "The Brain Pirate of the Inner World," Wonder Woman reads a newspaper article about the sudden popularity of her Golden Age comics. To see what all the fuss is about, she goes to a bookstore that has many of her old issues, where she's suddenly pulled into a Golden Age adventure. The rest of the comic pays homage to the Golden Age: Andru and Esposito mimic Harry Peter's art, and Kanigher brings back characters abandoned years before – most notably Etta Candy and the Holliday Girls.

But *Wonder Woman* #156 is not a straightforward reproduction of the Golden Age. Although its various tropes are invoked, such as the Holliday Girls, and how Wonder Woman loses her power when her bracelets are bound by men, the story is clearly not from the Golden Age. For one, it's a single twenty-four page story that doesn't break into separate adventures – a structure that simply didn't exist in the Golden Age. For another, the art is still clearly more sophisticated in its storytelling than anything Peter ever drew.

Most importantly, while the story may evoke the tropes of the Golden Age, they're not used as they were originally. One of the most notable things about Marston's Etta Candy was that her love of chocolate and her weight were never, ever used as sources of shame or embarrassment. Given Marston's larger philosophical beliefs, it's safe to assume that this was part of the point of the character: she was a strong, sympathetic woman who was not sexually attractive by mainstream standards. But in Kanigher's revival, Etta Candy's love of candy is no longer framed as empowering (remember her assertion under Marston that candy is superior to men) but as a personal weakness. Likewise, her weight is roundly mocked: the Holliday girls complain, "We'll never win this race – unless you stop stuffing yourself all the time!"

This gets at the real problem with Kanigher's return to the Golden Age – he pilfers its iconography while ignoring the actual content of the stories. This is due in part to the neutering of the entire industry by the Comics Code. It's difficult to imagine Marston's take on Wonder Woman surviving in the censorious climate of the 50s and 60s. But it's more telling that with all the tropes Kanigher revives in his "Golden Age" story, the phrase "submission to loving authority" is nowhere to be found. Kanigher doesn't really bring back the Golden Age with this story, just a pale reconstruction of it.

But what compelled Kanigher to bring back the Golden Age at all? The answer appears in the very next issue. Although *Wonder Woman* #157 doesn't feature any Golden Age styling, or an unusual plot beyond the fact that it unexpectedly ends in a cliffhanger leading to the next issue, there's still a major change in it: the letter column. Throughout the Silver Age, the letter column featured letters to Wonder Woman from readers, typically young and often female, and these in turn were ostensibly answered by

Wonder Woman herself. But in issue #157, the column was dominated by letters from adult male readers, answered by Robert Kanigher himself.

The implications of this change may not be obvious, but the first letter printed in the revamped column provides clarification. It's in regard to a throwaway line in *Wonder Woman* #151 that mentions fanzines, and is written by a self-professed comics fan from the fanzine scene. To most readers at the time this would have been baffling. Fanzines, for the uninitiated, are a portmanteau of "fan" and "magazines." They're self-published and generally not-for-profit works about a given subject – DC comics, in this case. Distributed informally through a network of fans who gathered at conventions, they provide some of the first material evidence of the growing existence of comics fandom as a coherent cultural force. Although this particular fan writes in praise of the issue, and argues that the comic shouldn't cater to fanzine culture, the very fact that this was being debated within the comic itself is a clear sign that something had changed.

But fanzine culture was an awkward fit with Wonder Woman. Comic-book fans were overwhelmingly male, and teenaged or older. *Wonder Woman*, on the other hand, still targeted female readers, with backing features about wedding customs and romance. Needless to say, the two groups did not get along. The implications of this become clear in *Wonder Woman* #158, which devoted the bulk of its letter column to the first part of a letter by a fan named Robert J. Allen, with the second half picked up an issue later.

Letter columns usually have five or six different letters; spending almost two whole columns on a single letter is almost unheard of. Allen's letter is a textbook example of the tone of fandom, with paragraphs and paragraphs of lengthy prescriptions for how to improve *Wonder Woman*. Although these had always been an element of the letter pages, they generally took the form of innocent "what if" suggestions – like having Wonder Woman team up with Supergirl, for instance. Allen's letter, on the other hand, is so micromanaging in its exhortations that it even details what size the cover logo should be. The second half of the letter consists of an eleven-part list, including instructions to be forwarded to the editor of *Justice League of America*, directions on what catchphrases Wonder Woman should and should not use, and a charge to bring back all of the Golden Age characters (coupled with an amusingly contradictory admonition not to use the Holliday Girls).

This description makes fanzine culture sound like a bunch of marginal loonies. To be fair, some of them were. But the letter columns over the next two years also included people who would go on to become major figures within comics: Michael Uslan, the eventual producer of the two Tim Burton Batman films; Marv Wolfman, who would go on to be a prolific comics writer in his own right; and Mark Evanier, who became a well-regarded historian of comics. Still, letter after letter for the remainder of Kanigher's tenure on the title offered detailed suggestions and comments on how to fix the title, often citing years of precedent and engaging in meticulous stylistic critiques. All of a sudden, *Wonder Woman* went from being a comic targeted at younger female readers to one that (poorly) courted the audience that preferred the rest of DC's offerings.

It's difficult to understand why this happened. Yes, *Wonder Woman* was the odd title out among those represented in *Justice League of America*, but her position in this regard was no different than it was with the Justice Society back in the 1940s. In neither case did she have the degree of autonomy from the rest of the line that Superman and Batman enjoyed, but she was still in a class of her own. Indeed, this liminal state didn't change after Kanigher's reorientation to court fandom, and it persists to this day: Wonder Woman is still part of DC's so-called "trinity" of major characters, even though she supports only one book, unlike Batman and Superman.

To say that her sales figures were falling (as Robert Allen suggests in his letter) isn't really accurate. According to the actual data, readership fell off a cliff *after* Kanigher began actively courting fandom. *Wonder Woman* sales were admittedly weak compared to the rest of DC's line throughout this period, but there's no obvious drop in the numbers to justify Kanigher's decision to change things. The problem, it seems, was that Kanigher mistook the vocal group of fans involved in fanzine culture as representative of his whole audience, and catered to the wrong tastes.

"The End... or the Beginning!" is the final story in the aforementioned *Wonder Woman* #158, and it suggests that Kanigher had begun to realize this. It's a metatextual story that announces a reboot of the series, retiring much of its supporting cast and promising a return to the Golden Age. It does this within the world of the comic. The various characters Kanigher created over the years are summoned to his office and let go personally. Wonder Woman frets, "You've really done it! You've killed them all!" Outside, a crowd protests the low quality of Wonder Woman comics. Kanigher depicts them savagely as comedic fools, and gives them dialogue ripped straight from nasty comments made about him within fandom. (My personal favorite is the near-perfect encapsulation of fan entitlement, "What could be more important than meeting our simple requests?") It appears that Kanigher was stung by the level of abuse and criticism he received over Wonder Woman, and felt motivated to respond. Certainly it explains why the revamp of the title coincided with Kanigher taking over the letter column.

But Kanigher was unable to get anywhere with fandom. He made his return to the Golden Age for six issues, done in the Harry Peter-esque style of #156, but fandom still wasn't happy. The remaining thirty months or so of his tenure are marked by an increasingly dispirited Kanigher trying to reassure angry fans in the letter column, while in the comic itself all the passion and creativity that had characterized the past five years inexorably drained away. Even the art grows flat and sloppy, as if Andru and Esposito have also given up on the idea of creating a comic book that will get people to stop insulting them. By the end of Kanigher's tenure, the pencils are being passed around several artists, and all of them treat the comic as a filler assignment between the jobs they want to do.

Wonder Woman was always going to be a tough sell to the male fandom of the Silver Age. Perhaps they could have been wooed by Marston's approach, lured into willing submission through Wonder Woman's charms, but it's impossible to imagine such an attempt under the Comics Code, or any modern media company for that matter. Besides, readers attracted to a genre dominated by muscular men punching things into submission are probably invested in the mainstream construction of masculinity. To many fans of such material, a female version of the genre is simply going to be seen as an inferior copy. This is a problem with those fans, of course, but it's still a real phenomenon.

Nowhere is this clearer than in the three team-ups Wonder Woman got in the late Kanigher era outside of *Justice League of America*. Two of these took place in *Brave and the Bold*, an anthology title that featured various superhero team-ups, at first between any two heroes, and exclusively with Batman from #67 on. Wonder Woman's two appearances are with Supergirl in #63 and then with Batgirl and Batman in #78. However, given that Batman was in every issue by #78, it's more accurate to say that Wonder Woman appears with Supergirl and Batgirl. Regardless, both stories are appalling.

In the first, Supergirl decides to quit being a superhero in favor of living a glamorous life in France. Superman asks Wonder Woman to intervene, but she too finds herself tempted. In one of the single worst scenes ever written for the character, she becomes distracted by clothes while she attempts to persuade Supergirl: "But your powers, they make you different – they ... ooh, that dress! It's adorable! Where'd you get it?" Eventually both characters realize that they can't settle down with hot men in France because they'd put those men in danger, so they return to their careers as superheroines. The Batgirl team-up is no better. In a ruse to fool a minor villain, Wonder Woman and Batgirl pretend to fall in love with Batman. Unfortunately, being women, they really do fall in love with him, which causes no end of headaches for the Caped Crusader. The third team-up, again with Supergirl in *Wonder Woman* #177, is a bit better, but not much – Supergirl and Wonder Woman are kidnapped by aliens who want a bride.

In the world of superhero team-ups, Wonder Woman's peers are knockoffs of Superman and Batman, not Superman and Batman themselves. But for Wonder Woman herself, as a *female* superhero, the adjective itself is all that's required to cut her down to size. Unfortunately, in the male-dominated realm of superhero comics after the Silver Age, with their fetishization of masculinity and their increasing sexualization and objectification of women, it's going to get worse for Wonder Woman. The misery heaped upon her in the last years of Kanigher's tenure becomes her status quo. And this status quo, in various forms, appears throughout the rest of her career.

It's difficult not to feel as though there could have been another way. Wonder Woman would have benefited greatly had she not spent twenty years saddled with a mediocre writer who had no interest in the original intentions underlying the character. But one suspects that the gravity of superheroes would have brought Wonder Woman into line eventually. After all, nothing outside of superhero comics has survived at Marvel or DC to the present day. Realistically, Wonder Woman's options were to conform or perish, like everything else that wasn't a straightforward superhero story. Even if someone else had written her in the 50s and 60s, kicking back against the push towards conformity, the outcome was the only realistic option besides outright cancellation.

For all of Kanigher's flaws, Wonder Woman could well have turned out worse. Kanigher kept the character alive through a major bust in superhero comics, and he ensured that she retained at least scraps of her distinctive identity into the Silver Age. If the Silver Age ensured that Wonder Woman would always be a second rate "female superhero" in the DC stable, it equally fostered a multi-layered mode of reading that allowed these scraps to continually subvert and scrape against the more inane content of the superhero industry. Yes, the fans that enabled those multi-layered readings were the same ones who eventually wrecked the character, but again, the alternative was worse.

We should also note that the alternative was only narrowly avoided. The tail end of Kanigher's tenure was a sales disaster. By 1968, Wonder Woman faced cancellation unless some clever new idea could be generated. The result was a desperate gamble. With Kanigher finally off the title, *Wonder Woman* entered one of its strangest phases ever.

Philip Sandifer

Chapter 9: The "I Ching" Era (1968-72)

The period from late 1968 to the end of 1972 in *Wonder Woman*, most often referred to as "the I Ching era," may be the most controversial period in the character's history. Famously, this period of the title so incensed Gloria Steinem that she successfully appealed to DC Comics to get everyone involved in it sacked. These events have overshadowed the comics themselves, which is a pity; Steinem's attacks on the comic are in practice utterly unfounded, based on a profound misreading, or, more likely, a not-actually-reading of it. To understand how and why Steinem was so wrong, we have to first understand what these comics actually were.

Let's start with the basic facts. The era covers *Wonder Woman* #178-203, a scant twenty-six issues, three of which primarily consist of reprinted material. In #178, after a filler issue featuring her team-up with Supergirl, a new writer and art team took over the title. The writer was Dennis O'Neil, while the lead artist was Mike Sekowsky. It took them just three issues to implement a number of drastic changes to the book.

The very first issue features a drastic makeover of her appearance as Diana Prince. Her sharply angled glasses and conservative business attire are dropped, and she's recast in a stylish mod fashion. A more drastic shift came in the following issue: Queen Hippolyta announces that the Amazons' magic has run out, forcing them a retreat to another dimension to recharge. Diana decides to stay on Earth, which entails the loss of all her powers, her costume, and her invisible plane. Instead she gets a blind Asian mentor named I Ching, who teaches her the martial arts. Finally, in *Wonder Woman* #180, Steve Trevor is shot and killed by the villainous Doctor Cyber. All of these changes remain in place through *Wonder Woman* #203, before they're swiftly recanted in the following issue.

To treat this twenty-six issue run as a single coherent era, however, is a bit of a stretch. Up to the end of the Kanigher era, for the first twenty-seven years of her existence, Wonder Woman had a total of two writers, two editors, and two regular art teams. Over the course of the I Ching era, it would have three different writers, four different editors, and two different art teams. (This rapid churn of writers and editors helps explain why the book required three reprint issues to cover the four-and-a-half years it ran.)

It's not as disorganized as it sounds. There's a consistent plot hook of a super-powerless Wonder Woman teaming up with a blind kung fu master, and while the creative team changed a lot, it was more a case of musical chairs than wholesale replacement. Sekowsky served at various times as penciler, writer, and editor of *Wonder Woman*; likewise, O'Neil both wrote and edited it. Every issue featured at least one of the two men in some role. Nevertheless, the comic was a team effort in a way it never had been before.

The most straightforward mistake made in characterizing the I Ching era is that it's a knockoff of *The Avengers*, a British television series. This is flatly ridiculous. All they have in common is that they're action-adventure stories with prominent female characters who dress in mod fashions. Wonder Woman is frequently compared to Emma Peel, the character played by Diana Rigg, but the basis for the comparison seems to be that both these mod women are teamed up with an older male character, and that the white pantsuit worn by Wonder Woman on one cover vaguely resembles one worn by Emma Peel. (Despite appearing in only a handful of issues, the white outfit is inexplicably treated as her "primary" costume for the era.)

This insistence on treating the I Ching era as an *Avengers* rip-off speaks to a much larger issue with the era's reception. Much of the controversy focuses on a very specific criticism that the decision to power down Wonder Woman was in some sense a betrayal of the character. This criticism takes two forms. The first and best known is a feminist critique of the decision to take away the powers of the most prominent female superhero. The second is a more fannish critique that suggests the character's lack of superpowers made her boring and generic.

This latter critique is more easily squared away, so let's begin with it. Implicit in the critique is the idea that being a superhero is inherently better than any alternatives. Within comics today, that makes sense – superhero comics and the American comics industry are largely treated as interchangeable. But in 1968 this simply wasn't the case. When the switch to the "New Wonder Woman" took place, DC was still publishing war comics, sci-fi comics, romance comics, horror comics, and humor comics, without any superheroes. Furthermore, in 1968 every DC title except *Superman* was outsold by *Archie*, and the majority of their line came behind things like *Tarzan*. Even the Catholic Guild's *Treasure Chest* outsold anything DC was putting out that didn't feature Batman or Superman. Abandoning the superhero genre in favor of something else amounted to a snub only in the eyes of the fanzine crowd that had already largely abandoned *Wonder Woman*. Unfortunately, over time that fanzine-reading crowd comes to represent nearly the entire readership of American comics. But in 1968, a rejection of the superhero genre was a move towards the mainstream, not away from it.

The "fannish critique" is deeply undermined by how good some of the people involved in this period actually are. O'Neil is a rock-solid comic-book writer with a number of classic runs to his name, and a reputation for dealing well with progressive issues. The final two issues of the era were written by Samuel Delany, one of the best-regarded science-fiction writers in the country, and who is particularly famed for his treatment of gender and sexuality.

Unsurprisingly, the storytelling techniques of the era take a dramatic step forward. Just at the level of basic craftsmanship, the tangible jump in quality for *Wonder Woman* #178 is shocking. Instead of beginning with a giant splash page previewing some iconic event in the story followed by a heavily narrated introduction, as was the case for every single issue Kanigher wrote, Sekowsky opens with two silent panels of Steve Trevor entering his apartment. This sounds like a small thing, but it's something that was virtually unseen in the previous era – a moment of storytelling that's allowed to work entirely through pictures. O'Neil strips away narrative captions except to clarify jumps of location and time, using curt phrases like "suddenly..." or "with the interruption ended, Wonder Woman returns as Diana Prince and..."; Kanigher relied on exceedingly descriptive captions, often several to a page, which said things like, "Around and around the ingenious Amazon whirls at eye-blurring speed until..." which goes to show how much O'Neil's writing quietly trusts the visuals to tell the story. In later issues, where Sekowsky illustrates his own scripts, there's an even greater inclination towards the visual – silent panels are a standard part of his repertoire.

More impressively, the storytelling and visual style change according to the needs of the story. Sekowsky favors silent or near-silent panels with stories set in the everyday world of New York City, in contrast to the action-adventure pieces. When he does a sword-and-sorcery story over issues 190-192, he dramatically increases the use of narration in order to provide a tone akin to the pulp magazines from which the style originates. The artwork, greatly assisted by the high quality of Sekowsky's inkers (most often Dick Giordano), shifts easily from bright uncluttered visuals to a grim, moody style characterized by large pools of black and shadow.

Rather than curtailing what the comic could do, the I Ching era offered more creative flexibility than what had been seen to date. For two decades, Robert Kanigher frantically reinvented the character every couple of years, and yet, save for the early stories where he passably imitated Marston, he never managed to write anything that didn't feel like a Robert Kanigher story. In contrast, the I Ching era's deft movement through different tones and genres while maintaining a sense of identity provides a massive breath of fresh air.

Its technical quality does not in and of itself constitute a defense of the era. After all, it's quite possible to tell bad stories well. The real question is, "In what sort of moral framework do these stories exist?" Coupling Robert Kanigher's unconscious support of existing structures of authority with a depowered Wonder Woman would have been every bit as miserable as Steinem accused the I Ching era of being. However, it's not impossible for a story with a female lead bereft of superpowers to be feminist. Indeed, Kanigher's tendency to emphasize the uniqueness of Wonder Woman by confronting her with an endless series of inadequate copies was a feminist problem in its own right, suggesting as it did that Wonder Woman's strength came entirely from the fact that she had magic powers. In this regard there's a real feminist possibility to be had: depowering Wonder Woman can show her strength coming from attainable character traits, not impossible magic.

The I Ching era was also engaged with the material world in a way not seen since Harry Peter drew it. Even into Kanigher's earliest days, *Wonder Woman* would look at people with supposedly dead-end jobs, or at equality in women's sports. But since the arrival of Andru and Esposito, these sorts of stories were almost completely absent; the book had zeroed-in on zany visual spectacle. The I Ching era, on the other hand, has three stories devoted to the mundane concerns of more-or-less ordinary people, and several more depicting of the lives of people far from the world of superheroes and the traditional adventure genre.

From a feminist perspective, this is very important. Feminist issues rarely involve fighting giant insects from outer space. The "protect Earth from alien invaders" approach doesn't immediately lend itself to social relevance. It took Marston's active subversion of the style into something resembling a Victorian fairy tale to make it consistently feminist. A story about a female small-business owner in New York City is fairly straightforward in this regard, all things considered.

While it's true this route was not taken consistently, it was at least taken frequently. Even in *Wonder Woman* #178, before she loses her powers, O'Neil puts Diana in trendy clubs to hang out with hippies. This contrasts sharply not just with the previous military milieu, but also with the mythical setting of Paradise Island; it harkens back to the days when the character regularly visited the campus of Holliday College. Significantly, O'Neil puts Wonder Woman in places where she might meet and interact with feminists. In 1968, feminism was a movement solidly aligned with the political left and with youth culture, and yet through the 1960s Wonder Woman rarely if ever encountered either.

There are some problems with the relationship between the I Ching era and youth counterculture. First of all, Diana's repeatedly identified as "mod" in the era. Mod style, however, is largely associated with the early 1960s. Not only had the mod style largely faded by the time of *Wonder Woman* #178, the psychedelic hippie culture of the later 60s had already peaked and begun to wane. But the I Ching era treats the two styles as essentially interchangeable, and like they're the height of edgy cool. In reality, it debuted the same month as the protests in Chicago at the 1968 Democratic National Convention, and Wonder Woman's depowering coincided with the election of Richard Nixon. Far from being exciting and revolutionary movements, the cultures depicted in *Wonder Woman* had been roundly defeated. Even though she was more current than she'd been in twenty years, she was still behind the times.

On top of that, the portrayal of these counter-cultures can hardly be called flattering. O'Neil's approximation of hippie dialect is hilariously bad. For instance, when Steve Trevor asks a hippie girl her name, she replies, "No names – we can have our own kind of happening, luv, without brand names to spoil our trip..." And though youth culture appears regularly in the comics, its portrayal is generally negative. *Wonder Woman* #185 features a small gang of hippies who recreationally enslave vulnerable women. Similarly, a story written by O'Neil in *World's Finest Comics* #204 depicts a student protest obviously modeled on Kent State, but has the student protesters throwing Molotov cocktails.

However, as with the heights of the Kanigher era, the multiple levels of reading that superhero comics encourage often works in their favor, and O'Neil in particular is a master at using them. The overall plot of the aforementioned "Kent State" story is that Superman and Wonder Woman are pulled into the future and discover that the Earth is a post-apocalyptic wasteland. Told that the future can be averted if someone's death at the riot is prevented, they rush back to 1971 and try to stop the riot. Between the bomb-throwing students and the violent cops who joyfully declare "I'm gonna pot me a long-haired freak!" before opening fire, they are unsuccessful. In the ensuing chaos they rescue a youth matching the description of the person they have to save, but there's also a police officer who fits, and he's killed in the firefight. The story ends ambiguously, without confirmation of whether or not they saved the right person. Obviously distressed, Superman says, "I don't know, Diana... we'll never know until it's too late!"

On the surface this is a bland piece of neutered liberalism that plays at raising real political issues, but only in their most caricatured and toothless forms, all the while suggesting equal culpability on both sides. Neither the student protesters vaguely demanding "equal rights" nor the brutal police are sympathetic. No actual political issues are raised or identified. The final message concludes that violence is dangerous, and

A Golden Thread: An Unofficial Critical History of Wonder Woman

the lives of protesters and authority figures are equally valuable. In the end, this sort of milquetoast moral – that "everybody's points of view are valid and everybody is equally to blame so we should all just calm down" – necessarily reinforces the existing structures of authority, who will presumably remain in power when everyone in fact calms down. It's a perfect example of the default authoritarianism that the increasingly corporate post-Comics Code industry favors, made all the more insidious by the fact that it actively pretends to be otherwise.

Aside from the surface text, the entire comic cuts against this reading. The typical reader is unlikely to believe the DC Universe is doomed to destruction by the year 2171. A savvy reader, of the sort who read team-up books like *World's Finest Comics*, is no doubt aware of the existence of the Legion of Superheroes, a futuristic team of heroes from the 31st century whose existence defies the idea that the world ends in the 22nd.

But even a reader taking the issue in isolation should have a hard time buying that the universe might be done for at the end. Superman and Wonder Woman are shown the man they have to save on a computer screen, but he's only shown from behind; his identity is unknown. However, he is unequivocally a protester – he's dressed in an orange shirt with a yellow collar, and carries a protest sign. This is what the man they save is wearing. The police officer, on the other hand, is in uniform. More to the point, he's obviously not a protester. There is simply no way to read the sequence in which the man they're told to save as pointing to the police officer. The comic itself betrays the supposed ambiguity of the ending.

Furthermore, the police officers are shown to be systematically corrupt – we see three of them, all of whom revel in the possibility of violently suppressing the protests. On the other hand, not only is a protester apparently integral to saving the planet, only one of them is shown to be at all violent, and his leftism is subtly undermined by his dialogue: he calls Wonder Woman "Miss," a term widely criticized by feminists in 1971. The resulting implication is that the cops are institutionally corrupt, whereas the protesters have only one or two bad apples in the bunch. Whatever the superficially ambivalent ending might suggest, the comic clearly and repeatedly indicates what side of the debate it's really on.

This is characteristic of the era. The counterculture is superficially treated as a visual style, a faintly ridiculous and rather seedy affair. This is certainly true in *Wonder Woman* #178, where hippies hang out in the bad parts of town, enmeshed in all manner of unsavory activities. But the changing narrative context of the superhero comic and the implicit assumption that Wonder Woman is the moral center of her own narrative both reveal a different message. Wonder Woman owns a mod boutique, which allies her with that culture, a culture in turn made interchangeable with the hippies. Even though these cultures are depicted as lurid and unseemly, they are fundamentally given a stamp of approval simply because the comic's heroine is one of them. Similarly, this is when Steve Trevor finally becomes attracted to Diana Prince, after twenty-seven years of spurning her. That this occurs after her mod makeover implies that the real barrier to his affections was not that Wonder Woman was better than an ordinary woman, but that Diana Prince was painfully dowdy and in need of a modern sensibility to surpass Wonder Woman and her star-spangled underwear.

In many ways, the single most significant advancement of the I Ching era comes in issue #180, in which Steve Trevor dies. Originally, he was a parody of Marvel's Captain America, designed to be repeatedly shown up by Wonder Woman. But over twenty-seven years of playing the role of her primary romantic interest, he steadily succumbed to the inexorable gravity of being Wonder Woman's "one true love." This was a disaster from a feminist perspective. It rendered Wonder Woman helpless and without a meaningful choice regarding her own romantic and sexual interests. Even when Kanigher introduced new characters as romantic rivals, it was clear that Steve Trevor was her only credible choice, and sure enough he was the only character to survive Kanigher's reboot in *Wonder Woman* #158. So over the long haul, Steve Trevor was the source of many of the Kanigher era's largest problems. The only way to fix it was to forcibly remove Trevor from the comic.

Wonder Woman suddenly became a much freer character. Almost immediately after Trevor's death, Mike Sekowsky took advantage of this with a story where a potential romantic interest betrays Wonder Woman. While it irritatingly makes her a victim to her own sexuality, this development was oddly empowering. For the first time since Marston had her decide she didn't like being dominated by Steve, *Wonder Woman* could depict romance with a healthy dose of skepticism.

Because Wonder Woman's personal life was no longer functionally owned by a square-jawed action hero, she could also enmesh herself into the world in ways she couldn't have before. Story lines where she owned her own business, boarded with ordinary families in New York City, and traveled extensively became possible. In effect, the removal of Trevor from the comic meant that Wonder Woman could stop being a domesticated housewife with a superhero sideline and start being an independent woman.

Removing Steve Trevor paid dividends in some Wonder Woman's other comic-book appearances during this period, most notably in *World's Finest Comics* #204 and *Superman's Girlfriend Lois Lane* #93, both of which rely on pairing Wonder Woman and Superman as potential romantic partners. While this prospective romance has its own problems (and will haunt Wonder Woman for the rest of her history), it shows how Trevor's removal improved Wonder Woman's status in the larger DC universe. Under Kanigher she was only allowed to team up with the characters like Supergirl and Batgirl – female clones of existing characters. Now, despite losing her powers, she's teaming up with

Superman and Batman as a peer, and outside of *Justice League of America*.

This is not to say that the I Ching era is perfect. It has several striking flaws, most obviously its name. The horribly named I Ching, Diana's blind martial arts mentor, is a paper-thin racial stereotype. O'Neil has been open in interviews about his regrets regarding the character. He admits that he picked the name because the eponymous system of Chinese divination had been popularly appropriated by Western culture in the 1960s, and that it was a patronizing, offensive choice. While it's a real flaw, I Ching is an ignorant stereotype, not a malicious one, and for which his creator has apologized.

More troubling is the way in which female characters are routinely put in sexualized peril throughout the period. Obviously, as defenders of the treatment of women in comics routinely point out, any comic about a female superhero is going to involve a fair amount of endangerment. But the fact that Diana and other female characters are imperiled throughout these comics isn't the disturbing part. What's disturbing is the way in which their peril is luridly eroticized, particularly on the covers in the latter part of the era, displaying an obsession with women in bondage not seen since Marston wrote the book. The covers of *Wonder Woman* #196, #199, and #200 all feature a chained-up Wonder Woman, with #196 having her clothes ripped to shreds and a gun pointed at her for good measure. Unlike with Marston, this does not come across as playful bondage. This is sadistic bondage that takes pleasure in Wonder Woman's terrified face and heaving bosom.

As much as we can romanticize Marston's "playful" bondage, we shouldn't pretend it wasn't problematic, even if the acknowledgment of Wonder Woman's sexuality is a bit of a relief in that we can be honest about the character again. The first and most troubling of the "bondage" covers, *Wonder Woman* #196, also provides the first-ever reprint of Marston and Peter's origin story from *All-Star Comics* #8. This is augmented by "The Stormy Menace of Goblin Head Rock," an unpublished Marston/Peter story featuring The Cheetah, and wholly consistent with Marston's long erased bondage-imbued utopianism. The return of Marston's ideology also informs two of the three bondage covers of the I Ching era: it's a female villain who's responsible for the bondage.

We're also only talking about the covers here. The stories inside are not the fetishistic bondage festivals their covers imply. One features Wonder Woman telling a thinly-veiled Hugh Hefner clone to his face, "I happen to agree with the people trying to kill you, Mister Dill! You are a symbol of sickness – you take feminine beauty and pervert it! You make your girls objects!" That the cover of the comic can be implicated in the exact same way as Mister Dill is unfortunate, but it doesn't completely undermine the story within, any more than the faux-ambivalent ending undermines *World's Finest Comics* #204. Indeed, Wonder Woman's criticism of Mister Dill ends up implicating any readers who might have bought the book because of the lurid cover.

This is the problem with the feminist objection. The I Ching era was called a betrayal of feminism, but such a critique implies that it's more in line with feminist ideals to have a less empowered woman fight generic space invaders in occasionally problematic stories than it is for an empowered woman to confront actual sexism and the material problems facing real women in stories that are no more problematic. This judgment hinges on the fact that the less empowered woman happens to have superpowers. This is ridiculous. The removal of Wonder Woman's powers didn't weaken the character; it refocused her on the concerns of real women, a strong turn from the endless treadmill of absurd action stories.

For proof of this, look at the final issue of the I Ching era, *Wonder Woman* #203. The creative team on this issue is one of the best creative teams ever to work on an American superhero comic. With Denny O'Neil editing, the phenomenally good Dick Giordano on art, and Samuel R.

Delany (one of the most acclaimed and respected writers to do a stint in comics) scripting it, one has every reason to expect good things. The issue doesn't disappoint; it's an overt and uncompromising work of feminism.

In the opening sequence, Diana gets harassed by men who say things like "Ain't that a pretty one?" and then get angry at her for being "a stuck-up dame" when she doesn't respond to their advances. Lest anyone think this is somehow uniquely bad behavior, the captions make it perfectly clear: "How many women get by without having to deal with this dilemma? ... But when a problem presents itself as often as this, what can you do but face it!" From the start, the comic acknowledges the realities of sexual harassment and assault in a way that's unprecedented in Wonder Woman comics, and not only before this issue, but frankly since.

The major antagonist is a corrupt department store owner who markets clothes to women but fails to pay his female employees the minimum wage, and makes them work in unsafe conditions. In what serves as a critique of the series' historical lack of engagement with materially real feminist issues, Wonder Woman fails to be adequately supportive of the feminist group she ends up meeting, and she's criticized for it by the other characters. Eventually a newfound friend explodes at her with the series' finest statement of a feminist argument to date: "I never asked to be denied what's denied me because I'm a woman! I'm told to be a whole person, but never fight, build, or envision – only to respond! Perhaps I'm incompetent and unsure, but I'm conscious of it and enraged at anyone who says I must stay that way! You're Wonder Woman! Skilled enough to overcome some of our problems, lucky enough to avoid others! But you know what all of them are! Now, walk away from my anger! Go on!"

Confronted with this, Wonder Woman admits that her friend is right, and that the corrupt department store owner is simply trapping his clients into a destructive cycle of cheap materialism. It's a tour de force, an uncompromising and unrelenting use of the comics medium to pick apart social

A Golden Thread: An Unofficial Critical History of Wonder Woman

issues and make a statement about them. Best of all, Wonder Woman helps put Grandee out of business, only to have an angry group of people burst in on the feminist group and accuse them of putting Grandee's employees out of work. It's a fantastic ending – one that fully embraces the moral and practical complexity of fighting for equality and the way in which gains in one area can lead to harm in others (which is, after all, the point her friend makes about Wonder Woman in general). That the cliffhanger of the comic is based more on the growing complexity of the issues at play, with a promise that they'll be more thoroughly explored next month, bespeaks a serious and mature approach to the question of what feminist comics should be.

Interviews with Delany about where he was going to go next with the story are even more heartening. He'd planned a six-issue arc about the sorts of villains who actually confront women – a supermarket mogul trying to stop a women's food co-op, or a sexist college advisor, culminating in a story in which Wonder Woman defends a female-run abortion clinic from male thugs. By all appearances, from Delany's plan and the single issue of the run that exists, it would have been one of the crown jewels of Wonder Woman's history.

Unfortunately, the run was never to be. In Delany's telling, Gloria Steinem, who was touring the DC offices while she was launching *Ms.*, heard about the depowered Wonder Woman and condemned it. The next day management sacked O'Neil, Giordano, and Delany, and Wonder Woman literally went back to the way she was, with Robert Kanigher taking over the book once more. To be clear, this didn't happen because of controversy over Delany's stories. It happened because of specific pressure from prominent feminist activists, Gloria Steinem in particular, to restore Wonder Woman to how she had been. Which raises an awkward question: how the heck did the feminist movement screw this one up so badly?

Chapter 10: Gloria Steinem, Wonder Woman, and Feminism

If understanding why Steinem's attacks on *Wonder Woman* were so wrong-headed required looking at the I Ching era, understanding how Steinem came to be so wrong requires looking at American feminism in 1972, and more particularly at Steinem's role in it. This doesn't mean a hit job on Steinem as a feminist – she is rightly praised as one of the most effective feminist activists in American history. But equally, her attack on Wonder Woman was not an isolated instance of her getting it wrong. There are systemic problems in Steinem's vision of feminism, which are rooted in the so-called "second wave" of feminism.

The standard history of feminism divides it into three "waves": the early 20th century women's suffrage movement being the first, the feminist activism of the 1960s and 70s (including Steinem) being the second, and a somewhat confusing mishmash of everything from the 1980s onward being labeled as the third. The names "first wave" and "second wave" were coined by the second wave to distinguish itself as a new women's equality movement. The term "third wave," on the other hand, was coined by Rebecca Walker in the wake of the Clarence Thomas/Anita Hill hearings to describe a new wave of feminism that she identified with. The characteristics of this "third wave" were primarily an expansion beyond the concerns of the second wave, and specifically into the intersections of gender with other forms of discrimination, beginning with race (Rebecca Walker is the daughter of Alice Walker, author of *The Color Purple*).

The largest problem with the "waves" model becomes apparent when one looks at its origins: every wave is defined in terms of the second wave. The second wave named the first wave as their precursors, whereas the third wave self-identified as breaking with the second. That the second wave is, at this point, some forty years old means that the third wave, allowed only to exist in its shadow, has to shoehorn several decades of feminism under one umbrella. This is, of course, ludicrous: the feminism of the 2010s is as distinct from the feminism of the 1990s as the feminism of the 1990s was from the 1970s. But more to the point, only the second wave gets to define itself on its own terms. Even today, forty years after Steinem founded *Ms.*, she remains the default image of feminists that everyone else has to react to – the one wheeled onto TV talk shows and invited to pen editorials whenever feminist issues enter mainstream American discourse. And this has real negative consequences: it is Steinem's brand of feminism that's generally reacted against when women declare themselves not to be feminists, and her approach that is caricatured with the patently offensive slur "feminazi."

This is not to say that the second wave was unsuccessful. They were enormously effective at attaining political goals that materially improved millions of lives. The political right describes this success as being "strident," a word that would be laughable if it didn't actually succeed in making effectiveness a bad thing in a political movement. But even on the left, one senses a continual anxiety about the basic fact of the second wave's success, that feminists have something to apologize for. This is flatly ridiculous. The question of how well second wave feminism performed at its desired tasks is straightforward: they nearly ran the table, with the failed

Equal Rights Amendment their only significant legislative defeat.

Nor is it reasonable to complain excessively about the causes they championed. The legacy of second wave feminism is not only a rousing string of victories, it's a rousing string of victories that mattered: the passage of no-fault divorce laws, the ruling that pay equality applies to the substance of a job instead of the title, the election of people like Bella Abzug and Shirley Chisholm to public office, the opening of battered women's shelters, Roe v. Wade, banning discrimination based on gender when extending credit, banning discrimination against pregnant women in employment, massive progress in the quality of rape laws, and massive progress on the subject of sexual harassment. All of them were genuinely important advances for women, and this isn't even a complete record of their successes.

That said, for all its glories, second wave feminism came to a deserved and necessary end. The reason for that is the same reason anything had to come to an end, including Marston's tenure on Wonder Woman: it was insufficient. There needed to be more. The first major blow came when a wave of black feminists – Rebecca Walker among them – argued persuasively that they were excluded both from the civil rights movement, which focused overwhelmingly on black men, and from the feminist movement, which focused primarily on white women. Despite the quality of their arguments, the second wave largely (though not completely) ignored them.

Other fault lines appeared around queer theory, transgender politics, and the need to look at the situation of women as a global phenomenon instead of an American one. All of these were issues the second wave not only failed to respond to, but for which its approaches were fundamentally inadequate. Beyond that, and relevant to Wonder Woman, changing attitudes towards sex and sexuality made the second wave's largely straightforward anti-pornography stance increasingly limited, as it became evident that many women found liberation through performing in pornography (Steinem's piercing account of the degradations of Playboy bunnies aside), and many more enjoyed pornography on its own merits.

It's important to look at why second wave feminism was ill-equipped to tackle these issues. For instance, the sense of exclusion on the part of black women was clearly not due to any racism as such on the part of second wave feminists. Steinem and others shared podiums with black women repeatedly and were outspoken advocates of the civil rights movement. The problems that arose were subtler than that, stemming from the movement's approach. Second wave feminism was small at first, as any social movement is. More to the point, the people who got involved in feminism prior to its broader successes were necessarily going to be more affluent, better educated, and, in America at least, mostly white. And so the concerns of second wave feminism, for wholly understandable reasons, reflected the concerns of its early leaders: middle class white women. But as the movement succeeded, it brought in a more diverse set of women who chafed at the way in which feminism seemed to disproportionately focus on the needs of just a fraction of women. Yes, feminists in the second wave (and Steinem in particular) focused on the concerns of poor women, but it's still the case that the leaders of the second wave were not a massively diverse bunch.

A telling example of this homogeny comes in the "Personal Report" that leads off the first issue of *Ms.*, Steinem's high-profile feminist magazine. The piece attempts to establish the diversity of the magazine's staff by listing their places of education: "Malcolm X College, Darien High School, Vassar, Smith, the University of Delhi, Millsaps College, Columbia, Radcliffe, Willamette University, the Sorbonne, the University of Wisconsin, and VISTA." It's true, there is a real gulf of experience between the Sorbonne and Malcolm X College, but it's also worth noting that the list consists entirely of universities, with the exception of Darien

High School, which is located in a Connecticut town with a median family income of nearly $200,000 a year. Only VISTA, a federal volunteer program based on fighting poverty, offers anything resembling a break from overwhelming economic privilege.

The other problem that second wave feminism faced was a failure to adequately think about the ways in which the concerns of women were inextricable from the concerns of other groups. Second wave feminism focused largely on the patriarchy: the way in which men dominate society. The so-called third wave, along with other social justice movements, has shifted that focus to what is called the kyriarchy: the way in which those in power use a linked system of dominance and repression based on race, sex, class, religion, and other systems to maintain their power. So in modern social justice the problems of racism are not an alternative set of concerns to the problems of sexism, but a different manifestation of the same problem. This is a crucial shift, and the failure of second wave feminism to grasp it is a fundamental part of its eventual obsolescence.

Steinem, however, never got this. To this end, let's look at two pieces of Steinem's writing, one from the prime of her career – an essay entitled "Transsexualism" first published in 1977 – and a recent editorial on the Democratic primary race between Barack Obama and Hillary Clinton in 2008.

"Transsexualism" is an essay that gets at the frustrating tendency of Steinem and other second wave feminists to ignore or erase the experience of people outside the relatively narrow band of people that generated the movement. What's most striking about the essay is the sheer dismissiveness with which it writes off transgender people. Her main example is the story of Renée Richards, who successfully sued the United States Tennis Association so that she could play in the US Open as a woman. In the course of the essay, Steinem waffles back and forth on pronouns, at times using the male pronoun to describe Richards, most blatantly while criticizing the New York Times for using the female pronoun and the name "Renée" while comparing this issue, apparently without any sense of irony, to their policy at the time of not using the title "Ms." for women who requested it. The use of a diminutive like "Miss" (offensive as it may be) is in no way equivalent to the outright denial of someone's identity, and Steinem's suggestion that it is demonstrates the at times pernicious narrowness of her interests.

It would be one thing if this were an anomalous detail in the essay, but it's not. Steinem goes on to complain that Richards caused "the hard-won seriousness of women's tennis [to] be turned into a sensational circus by one transsexual," seemingly upset that someone with different issues of marginalization, discrimination, and oppression than hers dared to get in the way of her cause. She refers to sex reassignment surgery as "self-mutilation," bemoans the focus of the medical profession on hormone therapy and surgical intervention instead of more important concerns, and suggests that it's a pity that transgendered people don't just stay as they are and undermine gender dualism.

This last point is worthy of special condemnation. Steinem, in all sincerity, proposes that people suffering from gender dysphoria – an agonizing mental health condition that leads to a tragically high suicide rate among the transgender population – should suck it up and forego surgery and hormone treatment because it would be more convenient to her political cause. This is, in many ways, the most straightforward example of the problems with Steinem's work: the way in which the entire identities of people outside her narrow circle of interests are erased and subsumed into her single-minded agenda. And in her 1995 collection *Outrageous Acts and Everyday Rebellions*, in which she had "Transsexualism" reprinted, she doubled down on this assertion celebrating how "gender rebels like those described in 'Transsexualism' can live and be themselves – with or without surgery," a statement that not only spectacularly fails to retract any of the horrifying positions in her essay but that reiterates that trans men and women are "gender rebels" as opposed to actually men and women.

Given the complete lack of repentance for the errors in her earlier work, it's unsurprising that she is similarly single-minded and offensive in her more recent work. In January of 2008 she published an op-ed in the New York Times on the subject of the race between Barack Obama and Hillary Clinton for the Democratic nomination for President. That she supported Clinton is neither surprising nor problematic; it's the amount of tone-deafness her piece displays regarding race in America that's truly distressing.

To be fair, Steinem does at one point in the column offer a strong characterization of the problem, saying that she is "not advocating a competition for who has it toughest. The caste systems of sex and race are interdependent and can only be uprooted together." This wouldn't ring so falsely if she hadn't spent the preceding six paragraphs of the column talking about how "gender is probably the most restricting force in American life," and making the somewhat jaw-dropping claim that "black men were given the vote a half-century before women of any race were allowed to mark a ballot," a statement that capriciously ignores the fact that for forty-five years after the passage of the Nineteenth Amendment blacks were routinely denied voting rights via poll taxes and literacy tests, "grandfather clauses" that allowed whites to avoid disenfranchisement.

Similarly, her piece opens with a lengthy meditation on the idea that Barack Obama wouldn't have been a serious candidate if he were a woman, taking this as evidence that gender discrimination is clearly more prevalent than racial discrimination, without ever bothering to entertain the idea that perhaps Hillary Clinton would have had a much tougher road if she were black. This sort of claim is typical of Steinem – in the preface to the second edition of *Outrageous Acts and Everyday Rebellions* she (rightly) complains about the term "feminazi" before attempting to compare it to the hypothetical term "nazijew," declaring it "equally cruel and ahistorical," seemingly unaware that there's something tangibly different about the hypothetical appending of the Nazi label to the very people they systematically exterminated. So while she pays lip service to the ideas that racism and sexism are interconnected and that social justice involves advancing both, the overwhelming point of her editorial cuts against this. They may be interconnected, but it's clear that Steinem believes women's rights should take precedence, with the rights of racial minorities following dutifully in the background.

With these positions and their attendant flaws in mind, we turn our attention to Steinem's attack on Wonder Woman's I Ching era, an attack which is by and large wrong in the same ways as the rest of her work.

To start, let's look at the exact particulars of what happened. Samuel Delany has given an account of his sacking in which he says that Steinem was being shown through the DC offices (presumably in the lead-up to *Ms.* being published by Warner) and was shown an issue of *Wonder Woman*. In Delany's account, she didn't read the issue. Instead, she asked what happened to the costume, and implored DC to consider the importance of Wonder Woman as an image. The next day, apparently, the edict came back to restore Wonder Woman's powers and pull the plug on Delany's arc. While this is obviously a self-serving account, and it's unlikely that Delany would have been in the office to witness it first-hand, parts of it seem altogether compelling. It's not difficult to believe that Steinem didn't read the comics in question. For evidence of that, one doesn't need to look further than the existent writings on Wonder Woman written or published by Steinem.

Two key texts present themselves in this regard, both from 1972. The first is the debut issue of *Ms.*, which famously featured Wonder Woman on the cover, and a four-page feature by Joanne Edgar. The second is a collection Steinem edited for DC, a reprinting of several Golden Age Wonder Woman stories alongside essays by Steinem and Phyllis

Chesler. Both documents go to some length to obscure and distort the history of Wonder Woman.

For instance, Joanne Edgar's feature includes an account of reading Wonder Woman during her childhood, and lists the supporting characters she loved, including Mer-Boy and Etta Candy – with the latter described as "fat and frustrated" and as someone who "stuffed her problems with chocolate," which is utterly at odds with Marston's actual portrayal of her.

But Joanne Edgar was born in 1943, two years after Wonder Woman's debut. Etta Candy stopped appearing regularly in Wonder Woman in the early 1950s, and Mer-boy made his debut in 1959, by which point Edgar was sixteen. Edgar singles out Marston for praise, despite the fact that he'd departed the title when she was four. While it's not impossible that she read some old issues, the comics she describes were not the contemporary comics of her childhood. There is essentially no way that she was reading those comics when they came out. Other details – particularly the claim that one of the popular comics among her friends was Donald Duck – suggest the mid-1950s, which would have put Edgar at the right age to be reading Wonder Woman. The caption at the head of the article comments that "Wonder Woman had feminist beginnings, but like many of us, she went into a decline in the fifties." So Edgar's childhood reading Wonder Woman comics was, in point of fact, the very period her article ostensibly criticizes, and would have included neither Etta nor Mer-boy.

Equally revisionist is Edgar's account of Marston's feminism, which she snidely calls a "self-styled version of feminist philosophy" before dismissing it entirely, as though it was soundly refuted by the existence of female villains. This is followed by a predictably distorted account of the I Ching era, which avers that Wonder Woman's "vulnerability to men" was worse than when she fawned pathetically over Steve Trevor, that giving her "conventional emotions" was somehow bad, and that I Ching's gender was more offensive than his racial stereotyping. "In other words, she became a female James Bond," Edgar concludes, apparently unaware that James Bond is not normally associated with sword and sorcery epics.

Steinem's introduction to her 1972 collection of Marston-penned Wonder Woman stories, while more on target, is shot through with similar revisionism. Steinem makes Marston's belief in female superiority sound like an incidental implication of his views, but as we've seen, female superiority is central to what Marston believes. Her claim that "as for men, we do get the idea that they have some hope – even if vague – of collective redemption" is a transparent whitewash. The hope of men in Marston's stories is in no way vague. Their redemption is explicitly and repeatedly said to lie in submission to female authority. While Steinem doesn't like that – she's opposed to any sort of biologically essentialist arguments – it remains the case that it is unequivocally Marston's viewpoint. As our earlier look at his underlying beliefs revealed, Marston's biological essentialism is integral to his entire belief system. Similarly, Steinem cites Wonder Woman's deliberations in a story in which Steve Trevor briefly acquires Wonder Woman-like powers (a story discussed back in Chapter Three) only to pointedly ignore the fact that the story unequivocally answers her question about whether Wonder Woman likes being dominated by men with "no, she does not."

This revision extends to a selection of stories that over-represents those in which Marston deals with mundane social issues and avoids those that more explicitly spell out his philosophy. The piece from *Sensation Comics* #48 in which Wonder Woman asserts that she can't love a man who is dominant is a marked exception. But even there, Steinem claims that the story's moral is that "she could only love an equal," a claim that is possible only if one excises every discussion of submission to loving authority in the course of Marston's work – which Steinem does. She also strips away the eroticism of his era. Given her categorical dismissal of bondage in her essay "Erotica vs. Pornography" this is hardly surprising, but it leaves her troublingly unmoored from actual facts. Steinem's introduction appears to have been cribbed directly from Edgar's *Ms.* magazine article. Both essays select the same quotes from Marston, and make similarly worded (and nonsensical) "female James Bond" claims. (Significantly, Steinem, who is ten years older than Edgar, actually did grow up when Marston's comics were coming out.)

Furthermore, they both discuss recent anthropological discoveries in Brazil, obviously drawn from the same source material, and towards nearly the same conclusions – that there was some early stage of human development in which human society was matriarchal, and that this is the origin of myths about dangerous and powerful "Amazonian" women. To call the underlying science "shoddy" is to be overly charitable. Worse, however, there's a problematic sense of absolutism; a master narrative of female identity that reaches back into the primordial past of humanity is too appealing for Steinem to pass up, facts be damned. (One of the more staggeringly laughable moments of Steinem's introduction is the assertion that the invention of society predated the idea that having sex led to childbirth, an idea that ended a prior matriarchal state of being.) This longing for a matriarchal past and its destabilizing of patriarchy cuts against Steinem's earlier dismay at Marston's biological essentialism. Situating matriarchy in a long-distant primordial past implies that it's the natural order of things, with patriarchy being a later corruption that should be rolled back. This implication fits awkwardly with her rejection of biological essentialism and smacks of trying to have her cake and eat it too.

This is all the same mistake. Steinem's marginalization of the transgender community, her marginalization of race in America, her misrepresentations of human history, and her misrepresentations of Marston are all symptomatic of the exact same problem: a single-minded obsession with her vision of feminism. What's ironic is that this vision is practically indistinguishable from Marston's. They're both flagrantly matriarchal, only Marston eroticizes female dominance and makes it central to his vision, whereas Steinem and her followers try to pretend it's not what they're calling for. So it's hardly a surprise that Steinem misread the I Ching era if she read it at all, and thus failed to realize that it was engaged in a genuinely feminist message of the sort she claimed to want.

What's most galling about all this is how Steinem ended up playing the stooge for a larger corporate decision. Both Edgar's *Ms.* piece and Steinem's introduction to the Marston collection tout the upcoming 1973 relaunch of Wonder Woman, which makes them marketing tools for other products within the Warner Communications stable. Even the cover of *Ms.* #1 is revealing in this regard – its image of Wonder Woman features a version of her costume that she'd never worn in the comics before, but that she'd come to wear in 1973.

Far from leading the pack on the revamp of Wonder Woman, one gets the sense that *Ms.* and Steinem were just being used to cross-promote a Warner product. There was never any real intention of restoring a more feminist Wonder Woman. After all, the person they replaced Delany with was not Dorothy Woolfolk, as Edgar said it would be, but Robert Kanigher, the very person responsible for the 1950s decline in Wonder Woman that Steinem and Edgar make so much of. And as we'll see in the next chapter, any suggestion that Kanigher's scripts were progressive is absurd; they're among the worst scripts Kanigher ever produced, marked by appalling racism.

I don't mean to imply any sort of conspiracy theory whereby Warner Communications wanted to bring an end to the subversive nature of the I Ching era, and used Steinem as a pretext to do it. If nothing else, Steinem was wholly unnecessary. Had Warner wanted to kill the I Ching era they could simply have sent a memo. Perhaps, once Delany's arc hit the hot-button issue of abortion, they would have anyway. But I suspect Delany's account is more or less accurate: Steinem by chance found out about the I Ching era and condemned it without really looking at it. Warner Communications saw an opportunity to use their new feminist magazine to promote the relaunch of a once-popular comic-book title. And so it was done with next to no thought, because that sort of synergy is simply instinctive to a major corporation.

What I find more troubling is how utterly naive Steinem was in being complicit with the move, and how blind she remains to it. To this day she talks about the I Ching era as if it were an anti-feminist disgrace, and that bringing it to an end was a positive move that "saved" the character. But this naïveté is implicit in the very notion of *Ms.* as a magazine. Did Steinem and the rest of the *Ms.* editorial collective really believe that Warner Communications, a company with an all-male board, was going to bankroll subversive feminism looking to bring down the patriarchy? Did they really think that their audience was of interest to Warner as anything other than a momentarily trendy and reasonably wealthy demographic worth catering to? How could a company without any women on its own board look like it was on her side? By all appearances, Steinem seriously believed that Warner Communications as a corporate entity was going to listen to her and follow her lead on purely moral grounds, out of the goodness of their corporate heart. Phrased that way, it's no surprise she botched it.

In a larger career that includes failures like her lack of engagement with the trans community, it's not as though her failure with regards to a comic book is a particularly severe offense. But the nature of this failure with Wonder Woman serves as a perfect image for second wave feminism's larger failures. It favors a narrative that, while not necessarily illegitimate, is restrictive and erases an unfortunate number of real people.

More important, I think, is the way in which the I Ching era, particularly the direction implied by the final Samuel Delany issue, does a better job with these issues than Steinem does. This, in turn, gets at the most lasting problems of second wave feminism. It's not that it proved inadequate (all movements do in time) but that it continues to steal oxygen from the feminist movement in its wake. The "third wave" is all too often rejected by the remaining adherents of the second wave; the attempts to pull in a larger diversity of viewpoints, and any softening of previous rigid positions, are viewed as a selling out of feminism. At times this becomes deeply abhorrent: Steinem's flawed position on transsexuality echoes that of the Michigan Womyn's Music Festival, which engages in some of the most appallingly transphobic behavior imaginable in the name of "feminism" (banning trans women from attending, and campaigning to publicly out them), and of Julie Burchill, whose appalling column in *The Observer,* "Transsexuals Should Cut it Out," goes so far as to refer to trans women as "dicks in chick's clothing."

Other times it's more subtle and insidious. There's a tendency to treat the feminists of today as somehow lesser than those of the second wave, as though third wave feminism isn't "real" feminism. Steinem herself is guilty of this. In her essay "Why Young Women Are More Conservative," she essentially argues that younger women tend to be lousy feminists while older women are better ones. It was penned in 1979, but she reiterates its conclusions throughout the 1995 second edition of *Outrageous Acts and Everyday Rebellions,* applying them unequivocally to the younger women of the third wave.

If we were to ask where Gloria Steinem could have gotten a primer in 1972 that showed how gender discrimination intersects complexly with racial and economic discrimination, and of how corporate and commercial interests are intertwined with feminist concerns, there would be an obvious answer. She could almost certainly have found such an explanation in *Wonder Woman* #204, by Samuel Delany. That issue, after all, was a story about how the need to protect women from a predatory business can cause harm for other people, including women who relied on that business for their jobs. It was about what feminism should do when social justice concerns intersect and overlap. But instead of reading it, Gloria Steinem got it cancelled.

Chapter 11: Julius Schwartz (1973-76)

It seems almost unnecessary to criticize the first year's worth of post-I Ching *Wonder Woman*. It is deplorable, yes. But if we're being honest, what else would we expect from the setup? To some extent, all we need to say is that Robert Kanigher returned as both editor and writer.

Astonishingly, this fact doesn't quite capture how bad the comics are. The plotting is both incoherent and mean-spirited. Ignoring Delany's cliffhanger entirely, Kanigher opens with a sniper who murders "Dottie Cottonman, Woman's Magazine, Editor." This isn't even a *thinly*-veiled reference to Dorothy Woolfolk, the female editor who Steinem claimed would be taking over *Wonder Woman*. I Ching is dead four pages into the issue, as is the sniper. Diana, amnesiac from the experience, flees instinctively to Paradise Island (which has quietly returned to this plane of existence without telling anybody), where her memory and powers are restored. And with that, every idea from the I Ching era is unceremoniously dumped so that we can move on to Kanigher's new ideas.

As it happens, these ideas are absolutely awful. The next issue features the most infamously tasteless *Wonder Woman* cover of all time, with a spread-eagled Wonder Woman tied to an extravagantly phallic missile. Inside we see her crying at being described as a "Plain Jane." After that issue it's revealed that a secondary character who's been in the background of all three issues is Wonder Woman's previously unknown twin, who was stolen and raised by Mars to attack Paradise Island. This evil Wonder Woman is helpfully distinguished from the real one by being black. Her name is Nubia. At this point, mercifully, Kanigher's well of new ideas for the character dries up. He turns to rehashing old Golden Age plots with new artwork, and doesn't even bother to explain why Steve Trevor, previously dead, is now alive again.

After eight issues of this, it was clear even to DC that the character was in trouble, so they put Julius Schwartz in charge of editing the book. Schwartz was a literary agent (representing Ray Bradbury and HP Lovecraft, among others) who had a reputation as someone capable of reinventing concepts. It was under his editorship that the Silver Age revamps of superheroes like Flash and Green Lantern began, and by 1973 he'd also done similar work for Superman and Batman. Wonder Woman, by this point, was just about the only major character he hadn't edited, so calling him in when the series was in obvious distress after a cataclysmically botched relaunch was common sense.

Schwartz took a relatively restrained approach that didn't reinvent the character, but he nonetheless made a decisive break with the past. Penned by Len Wein, his first issue as editor mocks what came before. Wonder Woman encounters Superman for the first time since her powers returned, and he expresses bewilderment that she hasn't mentioned this to anybody. Wonder Woman realizes that there are gaps in her memory, and it's revealed that the Steve Trevor who inexplicably appeared in the last five issues was a hallucination engineered by Hippolyta for Wonder Woman's psychological well-being. Aghast at the holes in her memory, Wonder Woman initially declines Superman's invitation to rejoin the Justice League, but is ultimately convinced to undergo a dozen trials monitored by League members as proof of her readiness to rejoin.

As Schwartz admitted in interviews, this was a pragmatic plot setup. Its sole purpose was to provide an excuse for two years' worth of stories with high-profile guest stars. Each of the next ten issues dutifully features at least one member of the Justice League lurking around and watching Wonder Woman in action, giving the book a needed sense of direction. The ensuing stories are by no means world-beaters, at least at first, though they hold together better than Kanigher's recycled Golden Age yarns. But around the fifth trial, monitored by the Justice League's new token female, Black Canary, things start to turn around.

The plot of the Black Canary issue, *Wonder Woman* #216, is not in and of itself anything special. An extravagantly rich man named Mr. Diamandopoulos has only one uncompleted life goal left: to learn why men can't set foot on Paradise Island. Ergo, he sets out to invade Paradise Island, while Wonder Woman and the Amazons defend it. This isn't the first time the question's been asked, and as is always the case, the answer is inconsistent with every previous answer. This time it's that if a man sets foot on Paradise Island, every Amazon will instantly fall in love with him, to the point where they will attack each other and cause the collapse of Amazon civilization. (The script, somewhat archly, refers to this as Aphrodite's "idea of a great cosmic joke.")

This highlights an issue that's been implicit in the last few chapters, but is worth stating explicitly. With feminist critique, what often matters most is not the overall description of what happens but the details, context, and tone. Gloria Steinem, for instance, was in no way unreasonable to be concerned about the broad description of a depowered Wonder Woman. It's very easy to imagine a number of ways that could be done in a sexist and offensive manner. The problem was that not only was the I Ching era not telling the story in any of those ways, it was going about it in a compelling and feminist manner. I say this because on the face of it, the "no men on Paradise Island" rule sounds appalling. In its practical execution, however, it's altogether more compelling.

The key scene comes after the revelation of why men can't set foot on Paradise Island. The story cuts to Diamandopoulos as he makes his way onto the island. Upon reaching it, he's surprised to see that nothing happens. Wonder Woman comes up behind him and explains that the Amazons have tricked him. He's not on Paradise Island. Diamandopoulos breaks down and confesses – he was motivated by his love for the Amazons, and says that Wonder Woman is "the only woman impressive enough... beautiful enough... formidable enough for Diamandopoulos." He only wanted to impress her. In response, Wonder Woman condemns him for having "threatened to destroy that civilization to impress one you claim to love," and that all he's really doing is flaunting his "petty male ego." Black Canary's subsequent narration continues the critique.

This is a compelling sequence for several reasons. First, Diamandopoulos's stated motivation should sound familiar – it's not all that far from Marston's original conception of Wonder Woman. Diamandopoulos's supposed love for Wonder Woman is based on exactly the same logic that Marston used to suggest that men would gladly submit to such a character, but here it's a submission that inverts Marston's utopian aims. This inversion allows Elliot Maggin, the writer of the story, to finally raise one of the major critiques of Marston's work within the context of the comic itself, namely that his idealization of women is still a form of objectification. Under Maggin's pen, male desire for women becomes dangerous in the general case, providing a new context for the revelation of why men can't set foot on Paradise Island. It's not the desire to submit to men that is dangerous, but rather the desire to be wanted by them in the first place.

The issue ends with Black Canary removing the description of what happens if a man sets foot on Paradise Island from her report to the Justice League, because "there are some things that must be known to no man – not even the men of the Justice League of America." This is something we've not seen in Wonder Woman before: an affirmation of the idea that there must be some spaces that are reserved for women, from which men must be excluded. This is not a rejection or slight against men. After all, Black Canary is on her way to an otherwise all-male meeting of the Justice League; clearly she's not becoming a lesbian separatist. Rather, it goes hand-in-hand with Maggin's implicit critique of Marston. It's an acknowledgment that feminism is not primarily about repairing the relationship between men and women, it's about allowing women the opportunity to define their own lives, existences, and narratives outside of male desire. And for all his valorizing of women, Marston doesn't really allow for this.

This willingness to examine and critique the central premises of Wonder Woman ramps up two issues later, when Martin Pasko takes over as the regular writer of the comic. In turn, this marks a transition in the nature of the "Twelve Labors" plotline. The idea of Wonder Woman having to complete twelve labors to return to the Justice League is an adaptation of Hercules, acknowledged when Wonder Woman first takes on the tasks in issue #212. Pasko transmutes the idea from being a mere lift of the Hercules story into a modern-day feminist reworking of mythology.

To some extent this is a bland interpretation of the comics. The "superheroes as modern mythology" approach doesn't just border on the cliché, it falls right in the middle of a major metropolitan area. But one doesn't reach cliché without at least some underlying truth, and if there's one comic where we have to accept the relevance of mythology, it's Wonder Woman. She's overtly grounded in it.

There's an odd interplay between the Twelve Labors of Hercules and Wonder Woman, given that one of the classical labors involves Hercules's theft of Hippolyta's girdle, an item woven into the origin of Paradise Island. By reenacting the twelve labors, Wonder Woman is playing around with some very fundamental symbolism for her. Under Pasko, the implications of this come to the fore – of the six labors he scripted, five serve as commentary on Wonder Woman's nature.

Pasko's first two stories appear together in issue #218. In the first, Wonder Woman is challenged by a villain who uses hypnotic powers to turn her various weapons and accoutrements against her. This is a literal story of her reclaiming her identity: the hypnotic powers directly parallel her own investment in control and submission, and the fact that she has to reclaim the iconic elements of her character from someone else's control is symbolically rich.

In the second story she takes on Felix Faust, a recurring foe of the Justice League who has determined that the Statue of Liberty was, unbeknownst to everybody, constructed at a moment when "the magical forces in the universe were in alignment" such that "it embodies the spirit of liberty actually as well as symbolically." Accordingly, Faust animates the Statue of Liberty and has it fly to his side so he can shrink it down to an amulet and use it to destroy freedom forever. Even though this is certainly a bit of inspired and over-the-top zaniness, the Statue of Liberty is nonetheless a specifically feminine representation of freedom; Faust's description of it as an actual embodiment of the spirit of liberty applies equally well to Wonder Woman, who naturally liberates liberty from Faust's schemes.

Pasko's next story, "World of Enslaved Women," is easy to be conflicted about, and not just from the title. It takes place on a standard-issue alternate world named Xro, where dictatorial men oppress women, but after two women from that world discover feminism in ours, they start a revolt back home. However, it turns out that emotions and beliefs get turned backwards when crossing over, so the male overlords decide to kidnap feminists from Earth, who will then undermine the female revolution on Xro by speaking out in favor of the patriarchy.

It's easy to object to this story. The two women who cross from Xro to Earth are named Frdn and Stnm, a fairly obvious reference Betty Freidan and Gloria Steinem. The way in which it's discovered that people's natures flip when they cross between worlds is that Stnm is crushed by a falling rock and Frdn laughs over her dead body. Let me be clear that you did, in fact, read that right – the comic not only kills Gloria Steinem, it has Betty Friedan laughing over her corpse.

Equally troubling is the explanation why Diana's observer in this story, the Elongated Man, isn't affected when he travels to Xro: men are immune to the effect. ("Imagine that," the Elongated Man contemplates, "a dimension where nature is sexist!") Furthermore, the feminist icons are kidnapped by luring them to a beauty salon, as if that were the secret weak spot of all women.

But as with the I Ching era, this critique misses the forest for the trees. Taken as a whole, the story is unequivocally feminist. The very first page carries a dedication to renowned science-fiction writer Janet Kagan, making it clear that this is a story serious-minded people have given real thought to. Looking at the premise in more detail, the nature of Xro as a reversed Earth means that on Xro women are physically superior and mentally inferior, suggesting that women are mentally superior in our world. But given this, the fact that Xro is ruled cruelly by men is one of the bleakest jokes in Wonder Woman – it grimly reframes one of Steinem's best and funniest essays, "If Men Could Menstruate," in which she suggests that they would brag about how long and how much. Implicit in the story is that there's nothing about the nature of women that makes them unworthy of leadership; that their oppression takes place even when everything else is reversed highlights how arbitrary their oppression is.

The story also fingers the real culprit through its naming conventions – the dictatorial megalomaniac is named Mchsm, i.e., machismo. Even the bleak joke of crushing of Stnm makes sense in the context of Steinem's attacks on Wonder Woman. It's not a stretch to think Pasko would sympathize with his colleague Dennis O'Neil, or that Schwartz (with a background in literary science fiction) would have been aghast at Delany's unceremonious sacking. It's certainly easier to explain than Kanigher's seemingly unmotivated killing of Dorothy Woolfolk.

Finally, there's the handling of the beauty salon. Both Wonder Woman and the Elongated Man express their concerns, calling it a sexist establishment. Elongated Man says, "I thought duding yourself up for a man was supposed to be sexist – so there's no such thing as a beauty parlor for liberated women!" But his wife Sue Dibny explains: "This place doesn't give a hang about what men think is beautiful, dear – it teaches women to make up to please themselves!" And it's true, at first, that this is what the salon appears to be. This foreshadows notions of third-wave and sex-positive feminism; it's remarkable that the argument is being expressed in 1975. Admittedly it's a mixed bag, as the beauty salon is actually a trap designed to enslave women and overthrow feminism, but it's significant that the argument gets advanced in the first place.

The result of all of this is a story that once again tests Wonder Woman not according to arbitrary fictional criteria like "Is she able to stop these missiles?" but according to criteria relevant to her larger role as a fictional character. What's at stake is not simply the fate of some imaginary people, but a larger philosophical question about the nature of feminism – one that animates the larger debate about what Wonder Woman should be. Pasko stakes out a subtler feminist position than the totalizing one advanced by second wave feminism, while simultaneously telling a story in which feminism is unquestionably endorsed and patriarchy is unequivocally opposed, with the latter shown to be destructive and pervasive in complex ways. For the first time since the I Ching era, Wonder Woman is living up to the challenge laid down by that era. In this story, more than any other, Wonder Woman's twelve labors become, in a literal sense, the tasks needed to reestablish her as a viable superhero after the twin trials of Steinem and Kanigher.

Schwartz stuck around on the title for five issues following the twelve labors arc, with Pasko writing. The first of these features Steve Trevor's proper return to life. This fact isn't particularly interesting in of itself – superhero comics are notorious for the cyclical death and return of major characters – but for the way in which it's done. Most of the story appears to be about men landing on Paradise Island, and the resulting destruction of the Amazons (who are, apparently, back to "aging to death" when men are on their soil). It turns out to be a test devised by Hippolyta, who declares her disgust at the idea that the overwhelmingly male Justice League would dare to test the worthiness of an Amazon.

As a reward for passing this murky extra trial, Aphrodite decides to bring Steve Trevor back to life. This is treated as a source of ambiguity. The issue ends with Diana and Steve embracing, but instead of exchanging tender words, they express considerable anxiety. Diana says, "You've been gone so long – I – we hardly know each other." Hippolyta, who's watching, wonders if she's made a terrible mistake.

This apprehensive tone regarding the relationship between Steve and Diana continues over the next four issues. Trevor chafes against his role, frustrated at his new "man out of time" aspect (a plotline that returns to the original conception of Steve Trevor as a knock-off Captain America, the "man out of time" plot having been added to Captain America during his 1960s revival). Trevor's disquiet is juxtaposed with lightly political stories that grapple meaningfully with questions of feminism and the depiction of women. The final storyline of Schwartz's editorial tenure features a troubled singer à la Judy Garland trying to turn her life around, where it's made clear her issues result from being objectified and used for her talent.

It's all terribly promising. At this point, much of what was good about the I Ching era has been restored. Though not flawless by any measure – Wonder Woman never has been perfect – the comic does what it's meant to do, telling action-adventure stories that are genuinely about women and women's issues, and treating those issues with dignity and respect. By the end of 1976, *Wonder Woman* was in good hands. Clearly, then, it was time to reinvent the wheel. And this time, at least, there were more fortuitous reasons for a change.

Chapter 12: Lynda Carter

In talking about a character like Wonder Woman who's featured in multiple different media, it's easy to lose sight of the fact that these media are in no way equivalent in terms of their popularity and impact. Comics are a much smaller medium than television; indeed, most media are. A given episode of a reasonably popular television show will be seen by more people than any novel, comic book, or most movies. So while Wonder Woman may be a comic book character first and foremost, the fact that she had a popular television show makes that the medium through which people have most likely encountered her.

Although she's had several television appearances, by far the most successful is the one starring Lynda Carter, called *The New, Original Wonder Woman* and later *The New Adventures of Wonder Woman*. While the sales figures from Wonder Woman's heyday in the 1940s don't exist, DC marketed the launch of her newspaper strip by claiming her comics had over ten million readers. In contrast, the Lynda Carter series routinely pulled ratings in excess of fifteen million. Compared to the nearest year (1969) for which we do have sales figures, the Lynda Carter series reached about a hundred times as many people as the comics.

The Lynda Carter series was not the first attempt to bring Wonder Woman to television, but the third. The first was in 1967, headed up by the producer of Adam West's *Batman* series, with a script titled "Who's Afraid of Diana Prince?" by comedy writers Stan Hart and Larry Siegel. Five minutes of the show were filmed as a test sequence, which is about five minutes too many. The central joke is that when in costume, Wonder Woman imagines herself as being extremely beautiful, seeing herself in the mirror as a buxom model played by Linda Harrison (Nova in *Planet of the Apes*), whereas in reality she's unattractive and delusional. The entire premise of the show is body shaming.

Mercifully, that concept was never pursued. Instead the property lay dormant for seven years, until ABC attempted a TV movie in 1974 starring Cathy Lee Crosby. This version is widely reviled, which isn't entirely fair. It's not particularly good, true, but there's nothing offensively bad about it. Unlike the I Ching era, the ABC movie really is a blatant rip-off of *The Avengers*, only with Wonder Woman's origin story awkwardly tacked onto the beginning and a renegade Amazon shoved in towards the end. It's a harmlessly forgettable mid-70s TV movie, a footnote at best for Wonder Woman.

The breakthrough came in 1975 with another TV movie, a pilot for a new take on the character that moved the action back to World War II, mirroring the period when Wonder Woman was at her peak success in the comics. It was a smash hit. The spring of 1976 saw two more specials, followed by a full-season order, and then it jumped to CBS for another two seasons. These seasons featured a pair of reboots, the first moving it to the present day, and the second to a West Coast setting in preparation for the aborted fourth season.

Many things were good about the Lynda Carter series. For one thing, it was actually a Wonder Woman series, not some random script with the trappings of Wonder Woman grafted on. And then there's the casting of the two leads. Lynda Carter gets the most attention, and we'll get to her, but the casting of Lyle Waggoner as Steve Trevor was just as inspired and went miles towards addressing the first and most obvious problem in trying to make a Wonder Woman series.

Steve Trevor has always been a bit of a problem for Wonder Woman. Even though Marston always intended Trevor to be undermined, the nature of the stereotypical masculine lead will tend to dominate the narrative without an active effort to undercut him. This dynamic is magnified by the norms of the Hollywood celebrity culture. In American film and television, male stars are generally bigger names than the female ones. Given that Lynda Carter was a relative unknown prior to being cast, there was a real danger that she'd be upstaged by her male co-star, whoever he turned out to be. She could easily have been the star in name only as the male action-hero rescued her from peril over and over again.

In this respect, the casting of Lyle Waggoner was a stroke of genius. He was an established television star, but his prior roles, most notably on The Carol Burnett show, were comedic. On top of that, he did a semi-nude spread as the first *Playgirl* centerfold. So his casting in Wonder Woman helped to undermine the Steve Trevor character automatically. Lyle Waggoner was still close enough to a square-jawed action man to play the role straight, but his very presence serves to send up the traditional male lead. It's never quite possible to take Waggoner seriously as an action hero, and that keeps him from upstaging Lynda Carter. This isn't a criticism of Waggoner, who's a fine actor; what he accomplishes – being a male action lead who doesn't hog the narrative – is a harder task than just being a square-jawed leading man.

All that would have been for naught if Lynda Carter hadn't been a revelation. Her largest claim to fame was winning Miss World USA and reaching the semifinals in the Miss World competition. In the world of television she was relatively unknown, but she proved to be a skillful actress. Whether her skill was sufficient to excel in other roles is difficult to judge, as we'll see later, but in *Wonder Woman* she was phenomenal. She was graceful and poised even while wearing a flatly ridiculous costume. On top of that, she managed an expression of bemused detachment that continually sold the otherness of Wonder Woman and the fact that she wasn't from the culture in which she existed.

It's possible to frame both of these things as artifacts of her limited experience. Her otherness can just as easily be treated as a form of woodenness, while her grace and poise can be attributed to the fact that as a model she had plenty of experience looking dignified in silly outfits. But whether or not Carter was a talented actress in general, she was perfect for Wonder Woman, and her pairing with Waggoner allowed the series to function with an almost meticulous sense of irony.

The pilot illustrates this sense of irony well. Wonder Woman gets to make several entertaining and wry commentaries on the silly people in man's world – most satisfyingly when she observes that the robbers she caught "steal money, and I have to fill out forms." This is not the broad comedy of Adam West's *Batman*. Rather, *Wonder Woman* uses light comic touches, allowing the show to deliver a standard set of action-adventure thrills while also having room to reflect on the frailties of its typically male-dominated genre. This cuts both ways, for the show also creates distance between Wonder Woman and society. For instance, people openly remark about how strange Wonder Woman's costume looks, and stare incredulously at her on the street. Other lines are oddly orthogonal to any logic – one gangster's comment, "I never shot a woman before, except in self defense," raises no end of delightful questions.

In many ways this process resembles the space opened in the late Kanigher era, where the more complex forms of fan engagement allowed his Wonder Girl and Wonder Tot stories to raise themselves above his otherwise mundane work. By casting actors who had a bit of ironic detachment from their characters, the show opened itself to multiple layers of interpretation. That, in turn, allowed the series to continually comment on and critique itself. The show simultaneously enabled its viewers to enjoy its action plots and to recognize the absurdity of them.

The comparison with the late Kanigher era is apt in other ways. Although the multi-layered readings and irony of that period were compelling, they were also by and large cover for the fact that the comic had long since abandoned all notion of a serious engagement with any feminist philosophy, or, indeed, anything at all. Similarly, as irony-laden as the TV series is, it's difficult to ignore the fact that it has next to no taste for actual moral positions. The decision to backdate the series to World War II conveniently allows it to use Nazis as villains, thus freeing it from any obligation to talk about anything remotely relevant to the lives of women in the mid-1970s.

And then there's its terribly mealy-mouthed sense of feminism. Take, for instance, Wonder Woman's declaration in the pilot that the Nazis would let women fend for themselves, a claim that exists to describe why they're bad. Strange, but fair enough. Even stranger, she goes on to clarify that women are the wave of the future, which leads to the question of what, exactly, they're going to be doing if not making their own decisions and expressing some degree of autonomy – i.e. fending for themselves.

This unnerving hesitance over the role of women is an unfortunate and consistent feature of the series. In "The Feminum Mystique," a two-part story, they trot out the old standard of men invading Paradise Island, this time to steal the supply of "feminum," the material that Wonder Woman's bracelets are made out of. As with much of the series, it's easy to like – notably for Deborah Winger's delightful portrayal of Wonder Girl. But there's a chilling aspect to it as well: the second part hinges on the Amazons' failure to adequately appreciate the Nazi threat – skeptical of the Nazis' danger, they giggle about how attractive they are, only to get blindsided by an attack. This is a general theme of the story – Wonder Woman has to convince Hippolyta that the Nazis are so dangerous she can't leave man's world.

The peace-loving, feminine Amazons are explicitly tied to the Neville Chamberlain viewpoint that the Nazis could be stopped via appeasement and negotiation: Hippolyta asks Wonder Woman, "Why don't you just reason with your Nazis?" With the Amazons standing in for a 1960s style of pacifism, the series makes one of the most clichéd attacks on that viewpoint ("But what about the Nazis?") while equating that viewpoint with feminism. This isn't good.

The second series transitions to the present day, but little changes. To some extent this is deliberate and conscious – the show even retains Lyle Waggoner as Steve Trevor's son, helpfully named "Steve Trevor," which allows him to play essentially the same character some thirty-five years later. The Nazis are replaced by hazily defined "international terrorists" as the standard threats, and business continues more or less as usual. These episodes are more frustrating than the World War II ones, because while the show is free to comment on contemporary culture, it only leads to an uptick in cringeworthy moments – like the former executioner who becomes an assassin because the state has abolished capital punishment, and all he knows is how to kill.

Worse is the third episode of the second season, "The Man Who Could Move the World," in which a Japanese-American becomes a terrorist in rage over the death of his brother in an internment camp during World War II. The episode is outright horrifying. It equates objecting to the appalling treatment of the Japanese-American population with outright villainy, and throws in a side-order of gratuitous Yellow Peril in which Asians have menacing psychic powers and a propensity for setting up elaborate death traps; the Japanese in particular are apparently all samurais. The story pays lip service to the fact that the camps were horrible, only to turn around and proclaim, "War is cruel and unjust," and it suggests that it's wrong to hold on to anger over the camps after some weak attempts at reparations have been made. ("That's why pencils have erasers," Wonder Woman remarks, a line that sounds ominously like the suggestion that the mistreatment of Japanese Americans should just be erased from history.) Worse, it's made explicit that Wonder Woman knew about the camps during World War II and didn't object, rendering her tacitly supportive of them as a necessary evil. The story ends with the misguided Japanese man accepting how nice all the white people are and agreeing to use his psychic powers only for good.

Given that the series is prone to such virulent reactionary tendencies – let's stress that "The Man Who Could Move the World" was made in 1977 – it's little surprise that feminism itself is at times held in contempt. For instance, in one episode the audience is invited to laugh at a former assassin whose partner has decided she should retire and become a secretary, much to her chagrin (because it's funny to parody women who want to be more than secretaries). In most cases this would merely be generic sexism, but to have it take place in *Wonder Woman* is considerably more troubling because it undermines the show's ostensible premise about female strength.

The series' mistrust of the idea of powerful women also manifests in opting for female villains who pose a sexual threat. This is made even more grating by the frequency with which these villains are contrasted with the "plain" Diana Prince. These villains typically seduce Steve Trevor as part of their plans, thus affirming the sexist message that beautiful women will betray you and only a plain woman like Diana Prince can be trusted – as she can't get a man, she isn't threatening. These women get their comeuppances, whereas the litany of sexist men who moon over, harass, and assault Diana or Wonder Woman rarely if ever get more than a light scolding, as Lynda Carter is left to uncomfortably squirm away from their pawing hands. This tendency reaches its upsetting culmination in the episode "Death in Disguise," which has as its central gimmick an assassin who dresses in drag. It manages to combine homophobia, transphobia, and misogyny in its suggestion that the most dangerous thing about a woman is the possibility she could be a man. It's difficult to find anything good to say about it.

It is apropos that *Wonder Woman* was launched the same year as the publication of Laura Mulvey's "Visual Pleasure and Narrative Cinema," a landmark of feminist film theory. Mulvey's article is grounded in complex points of psychoanalysis that are beyond the scope of this book, but the main thrust of her argument centers on the way in which the portrayal of women in film reinforces systems of patriarchy. At the heart of her argument is the Freudian idea that women represent anxiety over castration because of their lack of a phallus. Accordingly, this anxiety has to be contained through any number of systems. In film this is exemplified by the way in which looking at women is treated as an act of pleasure – a concept Mulvey calls "scopophilia." Mulvey distinguishes between two types of scopophilia – one that is voyeuristic and sadistic, based on devaluing the woman, the other based on fetishizing the woman, which turns her beauty into something that is reassuring and safe.

It is tempting, given the degree to which the psychoanalytic concepts Mulvey employs have little currency in contemporary psychology, to dismiss her argument. But faced with something like "Death in Disguise," in which the idea of a woman who secretly possesses a phallus is treated as an enormous threat, her explanation becomes rather telling. Wonder Woman herself is an almost textbook example of fetishistic scopophilia: the attractive woman rendered as a safe and benevolent protective presence who passively desires the male object. There's no denying that one of the basic pleasures of *Wonder Woman* is that Lynda Carter is an extremely attractive woman who spends much of each episode wearing what's essentially a bathing suit.

Similarly, the camerawork in *Wonder Woman* is a straightforward execution of the approach Mulvey describes. Shots in which the camera tracks the eye movements of male characters looking at Lynda Carter (whether as Wonder Woman or Diana Prince) are exceedingly common. Scenes where Diana and Steve talk in his office are routinely shot with the cameras positioned behind Steve's desk. The audience's point-of-view is thus aligned with Steve Trevor's, and both follow Diana around the room. The camera is typically positioned at desk height, conveniently centered on Carter's posterior and chest.

The progression of the opening credits makes for an interesting commentary on the development of the show. In the first season, they're comprised almost entirely of comic-book-style images of Wonder Woman running around heroically. In the midst of it is a clip that becomes the first clip of the title sequence in the second season. In it, an animated version of Wonder Woman is tied to a post, breaks free of her bonds, then cross-fades into an image of Lynda Carter, who looks at the camera and beams. In other words, Wonder Woman escapes her peril by turning into a flesh-and-blood object of desire – swapping bondage fetishism for good old-fashioned scopophilia.

In a surprisingly apt description, Mulvey says, "Man can live out his phantasies and obsessions through linguistic command by imposing them on the silent image of woman still tied to her place as bearer of meaning, not maker of meaning." While the use of bondage imagery may draw on Wonder Woman's original depiction, Mulvey's description doubles as an almost literal account of the second season's opening credits.

The arc of the series turns away from comic book elements and towards real life. The comic book style of the opening sequence is reflected in the episode captions that identify locations and settings, but halfway through the second season this is all jettisoned in favor of an entirely live-action opening, and the abandonment of other comic book touches. (The third season keeps this sequence, but swaps the theme music for an astonishingly bad disco version.)

This transition captures the heart of the problem inherent in a television adaptation of Wonder Woman. In television, the scopophilic pleasures described by Laura Mulvey are in full effect. The very nature of casting a model in a role that involves her gallivanting about in a bathing suit is based around the idea that male viewers are going to enjoy ogling her. Even with Lyle Waggoner softly subverting the male role, it's impossible to get around the fact that the show is targeting male audiences with little more than the promise of titillation.

Of course, Wonder Woman has always been overtly sexualized. Marston's conception of her as a figure to which men would willingly submit is still based on the external idolization of women by men. But there's an intrinsic difference between the sexualization of an ink drawing and the sexualization of an actual human being. Carnal desires projected on a page of ink necessarily exist entirely within the realm of imagination. The sexualization of Lynda Carter has an actual person as the object of desire.

Carter found this process disturbing. After the show was done, she expressed horror at her objectification, noting in a 1980 interview, "I hate men looking at me and thinking what they think. And I know what they think. They write and tell me." The interview as a whole is a chilling discussion of her anxiety over all this. It's easy to see why. Carter played Wonder Woman in her late 20s, after which she was consigned to occasional guest appearances on mediocre TV shows; her only other starring roles – in 1984's *Partners in Crime* and 1994's *Hawkeye* – didn't last for more than a single season. She was the acting equivalent of a one-hit wonder. Once her time in that role was done, she was used up and spit out, a sexual commodity.

In comics, this problem can be partially alleviated: regardless of how hyper-sexualized and visibly modeled on pornography such portrayals may be, they don't involve the crass exploitation of a real human being. But this is, in some ways, a subset of a larger issue. Something profound is lost when Wonder Woman is turned into a role played by an actual person. Whether in Marston's original conception or in the many later (functional) versions, Wonder Woman represents a utopian view of femininity and its role in the world. Yes, there has always been and will always be a sexualized component to her, but she is firmly a sex symbol, not a sex object. Creating an equivalence between her and a real person destroys this; saying that "Lynda Carter is Wonder Woman" (as stated by the poster that prompted Carter's horrified comments regarding her own objectification) renders her a mere sex object and drains much of her symbolic function.

Even still, there was much social good that came out of the television series. As has been reiterated throughout this book, feminism isn't just an abstract ideal, but the messy process of historical progress. One can't compare *Wonder Woman* to a theoretical vision of feminism. One has to compare it to what else was on American television at the time.

Action-adventure dramas fronted by women were in short supply in the late 1970s. *Wonder Woman*'s only equivalents were *The Bionic Woman, Charlie's Angels, Police Woman,* and *The Hardy Boys/Nancy Drew Mysteries,* which stopped featuring Nancy Drew regularly after its first season. The bulk of the genre featured no major female stars, or had women relegated to supporting roles. *Police Woman* and *Charlie's Angels* were little more than excuses to put female characters "undercover" in ludicrously provocative positions, with *Police Woman* having a particularly infamous episode about an evil trio of lesbians. In contrast, the networks were clogged with male-led action shows. So the handful of female-centered action dramas that did exist genuinely mattered – *Police Woman,* for all its flaws, has been directly linked with a rise in female applicants to police forces.

Whatever its problems, *Wonder Woman* remained a rare opportunity for women to see themselves in roles typically reserved for boys. This has always been one of the basic benefits of the character: she serves as one of perilously few alternatives to male heroes. Having a massively successful television series for three years gave her unprecedented exposure in this regard, something that did real good. For all that's made of the fact that Wonder Woman is one of three superheroes to be published continually by DC since her debut, the truth is that her inclusion in DC's "Trinity" of characters (as opposed to the Flash or Green Lantern, who went on hiatus in the 40s before their rebooting in the 50s) comes from the fact that she, along with Superman and Batman, had hugely popular television series. Regardless of its faults, the Linda Carter series is why Wonder Woman is a cultural icon as opposed to a fairly well-known comic book character.

Chapter 13: Return to World War II (1977-78)

The television version of Wonder Woman was, culturally speaking, far larger than the comics. Given that, it's just sound business to adjust the comics to match the television show, more or less, and thus presumably appeal to fans of the television show who might cross over into reading the comics.

The previous times the comics reverted to Golden Age styles, no explanations were really offered. Given this, the sheer length to which Martin Pasko goes in *Wonder Woman* #228 to explain things is remarkable. Instead of simply rolling back the continuity or changing the setting by fiat, Pasko has Wonder Woman pass through a "space warp" that brings her not only to the 1940s, but to a world in a parallel universe called Earth-2. Here, superheroes arose during World War II instead of in the 60s or 70s, and they continue to exist in the present where the majority of Earth-2 stories are set. Wonder Woman meets her parallel universe equivalent and returns to Earth-1, but instead of following her, the narrative remains focused on Earth-2 and on that version of Wonder Woman.

The idea of Earth-2 has been a part of DC comics for some time. The short form is that after superheroes became popular again in the Silver Age, DC contrived to bring back the original versions of characters like the Flash and the Green Lantern, and so declared that the Golden Age comics took place in a parallel universe called Earth-2. (The long form, on the other hand, has become shorthand within comics fandom for the sort of astonishingly over-complicated things that happen in superhero comics.)

In 1977, when faced with a need to migrate Wonder Woman to a World War II setting, the obvious route was to use Earth-2. But the nostalgia implicit in Earth-2 necessarily has an odd relationship with Wonder Woman. It's worth noting that Earth-2 is not a universe that houses the old Golden Age characters, but the universe in which the old Golden Age comics took place. When *All-Star Comics* was revived, it was not revived with a new first issue but with issue #58, despite the fact that issue #57 had come out a quarter century earlier, an affectation that existed purely to stress that this was a continuation of the Golden Age.

In practice, however, things were more complicated. For the most part, the point of Earth-2 was to justify bringing back the original versions of characters revamped for the Silver Age. The 1950s relaunch of the Flash, for instance, was a whole new character with a different origin, with a several-year gap in the publication of his comics. It's straightforward to determine that his pre-hiatus comics were Earth-2, and his later ones were Earth-1. But for Wonder Woman, along with Batman and Superman, no such break in publication exists. So there's no actual transition point where their comics leave Earth-2 and enter Earth-1.

Nevertheless, there are Earth-1 and Earth-2 versions of all three characters, with Superman and Wonder Woman continuing to be active in the present of Earth-2 (Batman has retired). The result of this is that the nostalgia of Earth-2 erases the actual past of the comics. For the three most recognizable characters in DC's stable, the "multiverse" (a large collection of worlds of which Earth-1 and Earth-2 are merely the best known) serves not to legitimize their past, as it does for those characters reconceptualized from older premises, but to replace it with a false structure that cuts the comics off from their actual histories.

This relationship with the past is made even more complex with *Wonder Woman*, where the title reverts back to the Earth-2 continuity for a couple years. In most comics featuring Earth-2, stories are set in the present day – that is, several decades after World War II. However, Pasko sets *Wonder Woman* #228 in World War II, so not only does the title position itself in the same universe as the original Marston comics, it actually co-exists alongside them, ostensibly serving as "untold tales" of Marston's Wonder Woman.

This doesn't mean the stories strictly adhere to Golden Age continuity. A rather testy letter in *Wonder Woman* #233 points out that Steve Trevor has unexpectedly gotten into the hair dye – he's become brown-haired, to match Lyle Waggoner. Likewise, Etta Candy has been moved from Holliday College to the WAC, as she is in the TV series. The editorial reply points out more changes: General Darnell has been renamed General Blankenship in order to match the TV series, and Diana Prince is now a Yeomen rather than a Lieutenant.

But contrary to the letter writer's claim that *Wonder Woman* is now a TV comic, as opposed to one set on Earth-2, there are numerous traits that clearly hail from the comics and not the TV show. Wonder Woman is back to being powerless when men bind her bracelets, and uncontrollably angry when her bracelets are removed. Etta Candy, while now in the WAC, has resumed her chocolate-munching ways. The stories feature the return of tropes like Transformation Island (the Kanigher-era name is used) and Marston-era villains like The Cheetah and Psycho Pirate, neither of whom had appeared since Kanigher's 1960 Golden Age revival.

These tropes are clearly brought back in service to nostalgia. The nature of Wonder Woman's bracelets, and what happens if they're removed or bound by men, are details that only ever made sense in the context of Marston's larger theories of dominance and submission. It should go without saying that those theories haven't returned. Instead, we just get candy for readers with sufficiently obsessive knowledge of Wonder Woman.

But the Earth-2 exploits of Wonder Woman in her solo book are not the whole story of this era. In 1977, Wonder Woman was extremely popular again. The numbers alone are compelling. In 1973, immediately after the I Ching era, Wonder Woman appeared in seven issues, six of them *Wonder Woman* itself. This number slowly increased over the next few years: ten in 1974, eleven in 1975, and eighteen in 1976. Then, in 1977, she suddenly found herself in thirty-two comics, followed by thirty-six in 1978, and a peak of thirty-nine in 1979. The increase coincides exactly with the Lynda Carter series, and come 1980 the numbers go back down. But in 1977, her own comic was back to a monthly schedule after years of coming out bi-monthly, and she was making regular appearances as one of five features in *World's Finest* and as part of an ensemble in both *Justice League of America* and *The Super Friends*.

The last time she appeared in multiple series, in the 1940s, all of her stories were written by Marston and drawn by Peter. While at times there seemed to be some logic to what sorts of stories would go where, by and large the titles were interchangeable. But in 1977 it's substantively different. *World's Finest* and *Wonder Woman* both offered Earth-2 stories, but *World's Finest* had a take that was much more straightforward and action-filled. *Justice League of America*, on the other hand, featured the Earth-1 Wonder Woman as part of the current team, as did *The Super Friends*, but filtered through the lens of the popular Saturday morning cartoon.

There's a fundamental difference in what a popular Wonder Woman means between the 1940s and the present. Back in the 1940s, there was only one definition of Wonder Woman: the character as written by William Moulton Marston and drawn by Harry Peter. What was popular was not a general cultural concept, but a specific series by specific creators. Three decades later, the matter is more complex. There are at least four separate versions of Wonder Woman in the comics market in 1977, plus a TV story. What's popular is not a specific type of story or a particular take on the character, but the very idea of Wonder Woman herself.

This results in a different sort of storytelling. The partial reversion of Wonder Woman to her Golden Age roots makes it clear that while any change or reconceptualization of Wonder Woman can be undone, this process of departure and return to the "original" concept will cause a certain amount of drift in that concept over time. For instance, from this point on Etta Candy is, in all of her appearances, associated primarily with the military instead of Holliday College. More strikingly, this period marks the last time Wonder Woman is primarily associated with World War II – future versions of the character simply drop her into the modern world (as the television series did in its second season).

It becomes impossible, over the long term, to simply stick with a singular vision of Wonder Woman and tell stories about her in a straightforward manner. Once you have a multiplicity of versions, none of which are singularly authoritative, they all exert an influence on the character. Wonder Woman always reverts to a kind of "average" form in which the more popular versions carry more weight and the less popular ones are comparatively marginalized. Any given Wonder Woman story ends ups playing three roles, simultaneously telling its own story, commenting on past ones, and exerting some amount of gravity (whether large or small) on the larger idea of Wonder Woman.

The most interesting example of this in the Earth-2 period comes from *Wonder Woman* #240, in "Wanted: One Amazon – Dead or Alive!" In this story, the Duke of Deception tricks Wonder Woman into attacking American forces, which gets her arrested as a traitor. Even though the Americans have some relatively unimpeachable reasoning to think she's turned traitor, an angry Wonder Woman compares her arrest to slavery, and says that she feels betrayed. Meanwhile, a vociferous mob gathers; they are shown to be paranoid and cruel. Wonder Woman's solution is to have the Flash impersonate a Nazi and attack the courtroom where she's being tried. The mob realizes that if the Nazis hate her so much, she must in fact be good.

Wonder Woman and America are shown to be in potential conflict, with America's tendency towards paranoia and suspicion at odds with Wonder Woman's mission. This is very different from Marston's jingoistic worldview. Wonder Woman no longer represents of a specific philosophy, but rather symbolizes in a very general sense both feminism and peace – she is, in other words, an almost straightforwardly leftist character. In this regard, the idea of putting Wonder Woman in conflict with the broader culture makes sense.

But this need to pit her against enemies that are defined in a broader cultural context also underlies why the World War II setting wasn't going to work. It's inherently problematic to combine nostalgia with a character who is fundamentally affiliated with progressive values. The comic that looks at this most clearly is the 1978 one-shot *Superman vs. Wonder Woman*, a 72-page story published in a deluxe format with larger than usual pages. The story follows a fairly standard plot for comics like this. Set in World War II, Superman and Wonder Woman individually investigate a situation from different angles. Eventually they meet, and for relatively contrived reasons they come to blows. The fight ends inconclusively, and the heroes team up.

What's interesting is the cause of their conflict: Superman and Wonder Woman separately discover threats to the Manhattan Project. Upon discovering the nature of the project, Wonder Woman reacts in horror, and declares that using the atomic bomb would make America as bad as its enemies. Supported in this opinion by Hippolyta, Wonder Woman attacks Enrico Fermi's trial reactor in Chicago, and Superman rushes to stop her.

This dispute is inextricably tied to the two characters' concepts. Wonder Woman, as an inherently progressive character, would naturally be opposed to atomic weapons.

And Superman, defined at this point as fighting for "Truth, Justice, and the American Way," is equally certain to back the official judgment that the bomb has to be developed. The conflict between them is exactly the sort of story that both characters increasingly require.

There's a fundamental problem here, which is that in a story about the Manhattan Project, Superman's victory is historically inevitable, which entails unfortunate implications for the ideology he represents. To its credit, the comic struggles mightily against this, as writer Gerry Conway explores any angle he can think of to get out of the fact that history will 'side with Superman. Only Wonder Woman's viewpoint is given substantial voice, with Superman's support for the Manhattan Project being largely tacit. The story bends over backwards to shift the blame for the first atomic explosion: German and Japanese supervillains fight over a prototype bomb and accidentally setting it off.

This is narrated portentously: "According to history, the first atomic explosion occurred at 5:30 A.M. on July 16, 1945, at the Almogordo, New Mexico, Air Base. Such is history. The truth, however, is this: On June 12, 1942, at 9:32 P.M. of a summer's eve, Prometheus returned to Earth, and for one hellish moment, the sun seemed to kiss the sea --! From that moment on, the world would never be the same." In the end, Wonder Woman and Superman meet with President Roosevelt, who assures them, "As long as I am President, America will never use the bomb to kill. Never." It's a move that shifts the historical inevitability from the issue Wonder Woman and Superman fought over – the Manhattan Project – to the fact that Roosevelt dies prior to the end of the War, such that Truman is the President who actually uses the bomb. The comic concludes with Wonder Woman's reflection on the inevitability of the bomb and the fact that it's a danger that can never be undone.

But none of this helps. The weight of material history is too heavy for the comic to be about anything other than why Wonder Woman's hippie idealism has to fail – highlighted by her eventual acceptance that the bomb was inevitable. We saw back in the Kanigher era how comics, by pursuing apolitical writing, ended up writing alarmingly reactionary stories that were at times diametrically opposed to feminism. That superhero comics at this point in their history are actively concerned with nostalgia only exacerbates this. In a genre where the status quo can never change, a progressive figure like Wonder Woman has a difficult road. To set her comics in the past, where any fight for a progressive cause is often doomed from the start, is a bridge too far.

The problem of nostalgia is more severe for a progressive character like Wonder Woman than it is for more conservative ones like Superman or Batman. Nonetheless, it's a problem for all superhero comics, to some extent. The existence of a large and entrenched fandom means the comics are constantly pulled towards what they used to be, and away from engagement with the world outside themselves. This is particularly maddening in *Wonder Woman* #242, which shows the end of World War II prior to issue #243's reversion to Earth-1. Its purpose is to explain the status quo for people addicted to comics trivia, and to get in some choice details about Etta Candy and Holliday College to reward the knowledgeable. But nowhere in the issue are there any interesting questions raised about Wonder Woman's role in post-War America. The main plot involves a race of aliens who try to forcibly evolve humanity to their final state so that their aggressive instincts won't prove a problem when they become a space-faring civilization. Instead of any serious moral debate over the hive-mind consciousness these aliens offer, Wonder Woman squares the issue away with a bit about time-travel paradoxes and convinces the aliens to go home.

In reality, the aftermath of World War II was an occasion for serious thought about the nature of society, with the technocratic ideal implied by "the hive mind" getting real consideration. This was, in fact, a debate that Marston was eager to have, hence his publication of his thoughts in

American Scholar. More to the point, the post-war era was where Marston's system ran aground, as his "historically inevitable" developments failed to materialize. But *Wonder Woman* #242 has no interest in that, because its only use for history is the nostalgia of its readership. The rise of nostalgia, in other words, puts Wonder Woman into a strange position, locking her in as a sexually transgressive figure of progressive politics, but giving her an audience that is actively disinterested in them. And even when the yoke of historical inevitability is lifted from her stories in *Wonder Woman* #243 (which inverts the earlier story that moved the series to World War II, only this time it's the Earth-1 Wonder Woman who shows up on Earth-2 for the narrative to follow back), her necessarily chilly relationship with comics fandom remains a problem.

Chapter 14: Repeated Turmoil (1978-85)

In 1985 DC Comics decided that their aggregated approach to handling their fifty-year history had become incoherent. With an excess of universes and the perception that the "alternate world" idea had become a crutch to storytelling, as well as what was viewed as an overly convoluted history, DC launched a twelve-issue limited series entitled *Crisis on Infinite Earths*. This served to reboot every title's historical continuity (or lack thereof) into a singular, streamlined, and hopefully more easily understood DC Universe.

For the most part this forms the topic of the next chapter, but the existence of *Crisis on Infinite Earths* provides a dividing line for the whole of DC Comics, and to some extent for the whole of the American comics industry. For Wonder Woman it's a particularly stark line – the *Wonder Woman* series that had been running since 1942 came to an end at the beginning of 1986, and returned in 1987 with a heavily retooled origin story and a brand new direction. It's now impossible to read the final years of pre-Crisis *Wonder Woman* without that context looming over it.

The fact that *Crisis on Infinite Earths* canonically excised pre-Crisis stories, declaring them to have "never happened," relegates the latter days of *Wonder Woman*'s first volume to a sort of twilight state, tagging them as a dead end. It's not the first such dead end in the series' history, but the other dead ends have left us with some odd remnants. For example, the Wonder Family days of the 1960s are reflected in the continued existence of a Wonder Girl within the Teen Titans franchise. Even the I Ching era is reflected, if not in the comics, then in its famous status as a controversy that spread outside the insular world of comic-book fandom. But the dying embers of the pre-Crisis era are by their nature unheralded failures rejected in favor of the transformative event. the only feature of this era to carry over is the introduction of a new costume, replacing the eagle on Wonder Woman's breastplate with a more easily trademarked double-W symbol, a change explained in-story as a request by the Wonder Woman Foundation (itself a comic analogue to a real organization) to stand for women.

The other major problem for Wonder Woman in this period is one I've alluded to several times already, which is the continual revamping of the underlying concept of the comic. For maddeningly long stretches of the character's history she was unable to go more than about 18 months without a change in writer and, accordingly, a change of direction. The roughly four-year stretch from 1978 to 1982 had five major changes to the creative staff with either the writer or editor being swapped. The result was an inordinately choppy period of sustained awkwardness.

This can't be laid at the feet of the talent – the people working on *Wonder Woman* weren't always exceptional, but they were consistently solid. Rather, the character and the book were never given room to breathe. With every new editor or writer came an overhaul to Wonder Woman's supporting cast, civilian job, living situation, or the nature of her mission from the Amazons. The process of experimentation and reversion described last chapter happens too fast, such that little gets added to the concept, while more and more gets eroded away by the constant resets.

Despite the chaotic nature of this four-year period, the comic is written as a continual narrative with no overt "relaunch" issues anywhere in it. And yet, when such an overt relaunch comes along in 1982, the comic undergoes considerably less change than many of the upheavals in the previous four years. These two facts make for odd bedfellows.

Over these four years, the comic almost completely abandons single-issue storytelling in favor of long plot arcs, many of which are foreshadowed for several issues before they actually move into the spotlight (a style of plotting imported from Marvel Comics). But despite such long-form coherence, the comic is more fragmented and unsure of itself than ever. The problem is that this style of plotting – a style shared by soap operas – works in part because of big, iconic, and consistent characters in the stories. Soap operas tend to be anchored by characters that have been around for years, even decades, and despite repeatedly outlandish plots they remain doggedly consistent as characters. Similar characters exist in the Marvel titles *Wonder Woman* tries to emulate. Spider-Man not only has a memorable rogue's gallery (and one that intersects with Peter Parker's social world) but iconic and recognizable characters like Aunt May, Mary Jane Watson, and Gwen Stacy. The X-Men have several high-profile characters like Storm, Wolverine, and Colossus, all of whom anchor the team's shifting roster (in addition, once again, to a fantastic collection of villains).

Wonder Woman doesn't have this. Her rogue's gallery is lackluster, as previously discussed; when one of your four recurring villains is Angle Man you are pretty clearly in trouble. Her supporting cast is weak, too. The only supporting characters to make regular appearances outside of the era they were created in are Hippolyta, Steve Trevor, and Etta Candy, and when they're not getting randomly reinvented they're getting randomly killed and resurrected. By 1978 the character was too old and too iconic to acquire a new supporting cast. The churn of continual reversion was already too much a part of comic-book storytelling, and Wonder Woman didn't have a very strong foundation to revert to.

A Golden Thread: An Unofficial Critical History of Wonder Woman

No one person can be easily blamed for this (though Kanigher is perhaps the largest problem). No, this is a systemic failure, not an individual one. A series of small poor decisions added up for the character – a failure to adopt the innovations of the Silver Age in a timely manner, Steinem's ill-considered attack on the comic, the hasty response to it, and the need to move the comic to World War II to match the more popular television series, all conspired to weaken the character. Lacking a strong core, new writers and editors were tempted to "leave their mark," and so Wonder Woman was set largely adrift.

But it's not as though all of the individual changes to take place in this era are difficult to understand or justify. For all that I praised Pasko's handling of Steve Trevor's resurrection, the subsequent two-year pause in that plot left the story of Wonder Woman's conflicted emotions moribund, making the decision to kill him again a sound one. Others, however, are quite puzzling. For instance, it's never quite clear why Diana Prince quits the UN job she'd been working since the end of the I Ching era in order to become an astronaut.

However, as bizarre as the astronaut plot is, at least it created an opportunity to give Wonder Woman a supporting cast, which she didn't have at the UN. And sure enough, in the first NASA-based issue of the comic, *Wonder Woman* #252, writer Jack C. Harris introduces several new supporting cast members. Unfortunately, just three issues later, Harris was off the title, replaced by Paul Levitz. And in Levitz's second issue he reveals that the character Harris had been treating as Diana's love interest is in fact a member of the villainous Royal Flush Gang, leading Diana to quit NASA and return to the UN by issue #257. (Levitz, it seems, thought it was silly that someone who had been to space repeatedly with the Justice League would become an astronaut.)

Levitz was only on the title for a handful of issues, and in #259 Gerry Conway took over. Conway goes a comparatively long time without feeling the need to revamp the title, instead picking up on one of Harris's plot threads involving a villain called the Bushman, which he expands to a grand conspiracy in which it's ultimately revealed that Morgan Tracy, Wonder Woman's former boss, is an international criminal mastermind.

But then Len Wein replaces Ross Andru as Conway's editor, and it all changes again: Steve Trevor is brought back from the dead once more, only Wonder Woman's memory of him has been erased. And so in issue #272, Wonder Woman has yet another new status quo: this time she's working for the Air Force with Steve Trevor, Etta Candy, and General Darnell. At least some effort has been made to enliven the supporting cast, which had been abandoned with Levitz's abandonment of NASA. Diana Prince shares an apartment with Etta Candy, who has reacquired some of her personality and charm. Instead of a straightforward Steve/Diana/Wonder Woman love triangle, there's the added wrinkle of General Darnell falling for Diana, with the laudable move of his affections being pointedly unrequited.

This jumping around between concepts makes the storytelling seem sloppy and facile at best, and openly offensive at worst. Conway's run is most guilty of this. To pick the most troubling example, Conway pens a story where Wonder Woman, after deciding that she just can't handle the pressures of man's world without Steve Trevor, retreats to Paradise Island. To be clear, these pressures are not based on Trevor, but on world events. The key scene in Wonder Woman's breakdown comes as she watches the news on television, becoming more and more horrified as the headlines roll past.

Crucially, these headlines are clearly based on real events. References to the Ford Pinto, the Iran hostage crisis, discussions of deadly fires due to slashed municipal budgets, pollution, and other issues all push Wonder Woman to the edge. On one level this is interesting and gratifying. The truth is that 1980 was a time of political upheaval, and a comic like Wonder Woman should have a lot to say about it. On the other, one would be forgiven for hoping that Wonder

Woman has the emotional strength to carry on in a world where the Ford Pinto is hazardously designed.

The real problem, though, is that what Conway ends up saying through the comic is deeply depressing. One of the snippets of news – "President refuses to respond" – is a line that, in the context of Wonder Woman's breakdown, comes perilously close to an endorsement of Ronald Reagan in the upcoming election. More damning is the next issue, #271, when Hippolyta sends Wonder Woman back into man's world with a new mission: "As you can see, it shows war in distant lands... madmen holding the reins of government... hatred everywhere... violence against the innocent... mass insanity... perhaps the coming of a new dark age! I looked, and I knew that evil was incarnate in the world. All of this, daughter, cannot be mere happenstance. So much evil, so much madness, must have a cause... and a creator."

Let us pause here and consider the sheer conspiracy-minded paranoia involved in this. It implies that all of the world's ills are the product of a single bad actor – that there must be, in 1980, a Hitler-like figure upon whom everything can be blamed. The image supporting Hippolyta's monologue gets at the real point: a picture of the Ayatollah Khomeini is clearly displayed alongside the declaration of evil being incarnate in the world. As it turns out in later issues, all of the world's ills are actually the responsibility of a shadowy terrorist organization called Kobra. On the eve of Reagan's election and the appallingly successful backlash against the gains of feminism, Conway sees Wonder Woman's mission as nothing more than "smash the bad guy." It's a complete rejection of the idea of underlying social causes in the world.

To be fair, there's an explanation available besides the idea that Gerry Conway is a reactionary opposed to many of the basic ideas of Wonder Woman: he's just being lazy. Certainly the plotting of his run on *Wonder Woman* suggests that. When he takes a two-issue break from the main story to tell an "untold tale" from Wonder Woman's NASA days (in reality unused scripts from the period where Wonder Woman was appearing in *Adventure Comics*) he references events that happened after Diana left NASA. While complete accuracy in comic book continuity is an unrealistic expectation, flubbing an eight-month-old plot point speaks to editorial sloppiness, especially since the continuity reference (an off-handed remark in dialogue) is unimportant to the overall story, making it a completely avoidable error.

This gets at the real issue with this period; much like the worst moments of the Kanigher era, and indeed like the worst moments of every other era, it's all too clear that nobody particularly wanted to be writing Wonder Woman, having no ideas for the character other than disliking whatever the last guy (and it was still always a guy) did.

Thankfully, things started to turn around a bit in 1982. Much of this comes down to one person: DC Comics' publisher and president, Jenette Kahn – by far the most successful woman in the comics industry – who insisted Wonder Woman remain in print. Kahn created the Wonder Woman Foundation, a charitable organization, to celebrate the character's 40th anniversary, and shortly thereafter oversaw another relaunch. This one, however, actually had a few things to recommend it.

First, it had Roy Thomas writing the stories and Gene Colan doing the art. On the one hand, this is an example of what had been not working terribly well for several runs previously: taking popular Marvel creators who had recently migrated to DC and throwing them at the book. But in this case, both creators had distinctive styles to bring to Wonder Woman.

Colan's art was moody and expressive, honed on a lengthy run of Marvel's *Tomb of Dracula* series. The cover to his first issue, #288, is adorned with a large caption around the title that proclaims, "Look out, world! Wonder Woman is bustin' loose!" The text takes up a third of the cover's space. Underneath it, Wonder Woman fights her way through a

Figure 8: Gene Colan's striking cover to *Wonder Woman* #288 (1982), copyright DC Comics, used under the principle of fair use.

group of generic gangsters, one of whom turns towards the reader, raising a hand to his face to shout out, "An' this time, nothing will stop her!" Wonder Woman, meanwhile, has a confident strut as she marches diagonally across the page, straight towards the shouting gangster in the lower right-hand corner. With one hand she throws a foe behind her towards a pile of already defeated gangsters; with the other she deflects the bullets the remaining gangsters are firing at her. Her face is contemptuous.

Her pose, however, is awkward. Unrealistic and awkward poses for superheroines are nothing new – sadly, they're routinely contorted into bizarre positions, usually to play up their physical assets. But Wonder Woman's pose has a striking asexuality to it. Her legs are emphasized, but not in the normal elongated and eroticized sense – they're strong and muscular. Her arms are at odd angles, but the one blocking bullets serves to obscure part of her chest. The image, though unnatural, doesn't sexualize her. It highlights her strength and power in a way that contrasts sharply with the jocular tone of the gangster's words and the caption. The resulting cover is not so much appealing as intriguing, restoring some of the alien glamour that had been systematically drained from Wonder Woman over the preceding decades.

As the new writer, Thomas brought a grand scale to the comic. Instead of undoing the status quo from the previous run, he added to it: he introduced a new villain, the Silver Swan, reintroduced Doctor Psycho, and quickly put Steve Trevor in serious danger. After his first arc, which aggressively piled on the concepts, Thomas moved on to a second arc, boldly proclaimed as "a 3-issue epic guest-starring just about everybody!" Arguably, he may have taken this a bit too far, as Wonder Woman is barely included in the second issue. The story involves an alien called the Adjudicator who comes to Earth to judge and destroy it, and the efforts of Wonder Woman and other heroes (mostly heroines, actually) to stop its horsemen of the apocalypse. The story leaps between an epic tone –

"Nor needs he any spoken word from the spanner of space/time continuums that birthed him to know his mission. It is to sow death, in his own grotesque image, upon the world designated by his creator. Without end is the circle of Earths which lie strung before him now, like soap bubbles from the pipe of a playful deity."

– and a sharp, materialist edge. In one sequence, a starving Hindu man whose food has been reduced to dust by Famine spies a passing cow, and is nearly tempted to slaughter it before stopping himself and dropping the knife. The narration through this section maintains Thomas's strong sense of cadence and flow, allowing him to transition seamlessly from this small moment of nobility of an ordinary human back to the cosmic scale of things in the very next panel, leaping from a close-up of the man dropping the knife to the Adjudicator looming over events and judging them.

Unfortunately, Thomas's run on the title was short. He grew frustrated that he wasn't given the full book to work with, as the comic was running with a substantial backup feature starring The Huntress. After only eight issues, he turned the title over to Dan Mishkin. Mishkin wasn't equal to Thomas as a writer, but he largely kept the ship upright. Like Thomas, he displayed little interest in undoing what came before him, making his mark by adding more to the character. He quickly introduced another supporting character for Diana Prince's military life, Major Griggs, as well as Sofia Constantinas, a sort of latter-day Paula von Gunter who goes from being an antagonist to an Amazon-in-training.

Mishkin is also keen to explore the comedic aspects of the series. This culminates in issue #323, in which Etta Candy has to adopt the role of Wonder Woman to resolve a series of misunderstandings and miscommunications that have led to a fight breaking out between Angle Man, Doctor Psycho, the Silver Swan, and the Cheetah. After forty years of being a comedy-relief sidekick, this amounts to Etta's finest hour, and it's long overdue.

Mishkin also interrogates the nature of some of the series' premises, resisting the notions that Hippolyta and the Amazons are consistently in the moral right and that Steve and Diana are intrinsically meant for each other. On this last point he's aided by Thomas, who came back for *Wonder Woman* #300 along with his wife, Danette Thomas, making her the first woman to get a writing credit on a Wonder Woman comic. The resulting 75-page issue contained work by a plethora of artists, including the return of Ross Andru and Dick Giordano, and focused almost entirely on Wonder Woman's relationship with Steve Trevor.

Over the course of the issue she finds herself in various dreamscapes and alternate worlds: in one, she meets her daughter, Lyta Trevor from Earth-2 (where Diana apparently married Steve); in another, she marries Superman; she also marries a villainous inversion of Steve Trevor named Trevor Stevens. Meanwhile, in the non-dream portions of the comic, a story plays out in which Wonder Woman finally agrees to marry Steve Trevor shortly before an accident that appears to kill Diana Prince takes place. The issue ends with Trevor jilting Wonder Woman at the altar because he can't get Diana Prince off of his mind now that she's dead. The overall implication is that there's something fundamentally impossible about their romance, and Diana decides that she's going to reveal her secret identity to Steve.

Here the limitations of Mishkin's writing are exposed. As a change to Wonder Woman's status quo it's a sensible one, opening up more doors than it closes. You lose the ability to do the increasingly tired "maintaining a double identity in front of Steve" plots, but as long as Diana's identity is kept secret from other people there's still plenty of opportunities to go there with other characters. In turn, you gain the ability to do plots with Steve as an equal partner to Diana, instead of a dim-witted subordinate who can't see the obvious. Unfortunately, Mishkin teases this out over far too many issues, milking the "Is she going to tell him?" conceit far beyond what it can sustain, only to cop out in the end: Steve doesn't want Wonder Woman to share her secret. All the buildup was for nothing, and a genuinely interesting idea ends up being rejected.

More to the point, there weren't nearly enough issues of Mishkin's run, or of the series in general, to deal with the consequences of this turn of events. Mishkin's run ended with issue #325, Mindy Newell came on for an aborted three-issue run, and then Gerry Conway wrapped things up with a final issue. But even if Mishkin had been able to continue on the book, the sad fact is that it probably wouldn't have mattered. By 1984 the series had been cut back to bimonthly production due to low sales. For all that the quality improved when people didn't try to redo the premise every eighteen months, the team of Dan Mishkin and Don Heck was, apparently, not enough of a draw to sell books. But even past that, the ways in which Mishkin makes the series work are to fight against its underlying premises. We should know by now that narrative gravity would eventually nullify any gains won in this fashion, with Diana going back to dote pathetically on Steve, and Etta Candy marginalized or written out.

In this regard, *Crisis on Infinite Earths* is almost welcome, simply because it opens up the possibility of a talented creative team establishing a new status quo for Wonder Woman that can actually stick. The character certainly needs it after the preceding eight years. As it happens, the book will get exactly that with George Pérez, who worked on *Crisis on Infinite Earths* and was one of the hottest artists in comics. Though Pérez's run breaks from the past, almost everything he deemphasizes was something Mishkin had already been pushing against. As much as this era winds down with the same sort of failure and reinvention that led to the I Ching era, and as much as its specific concepts and ideas were abandoned, the seeds of Wonder Woman's eventual rebirth are visible in this strange twilight period.

Chapter 15: Crisis on Infinite Earths (1985-86)

As discussed last chapter, the *Crisis on Infinite Earths* by Marv Wolfman and George Pérez is a stark dividing line in the history of DC Comics. It revamped DC's entire fictional universe, but it's also a substantial division in the history of comics at large, and the transition it signaled is worth explaining on its own merits. Superhero comics changed over the 60s and 70s from being stories about characters as such to being stories about the state of well-recognized franchises. (Wonder Woman, a character who routinely suffers from commercial failure and reboot, demonstrates this particularly well.) But with *Crisis on Infinite Earths*, the focus changed from the individual states of character-based properties to the overall universe. So DC Comics stopped being as much about the state of Wonder Woman, Batman, and Superman, and became more about the state of DC Comics in general.

Much of this was due to a fundamental shift in how comic books were sold. Even before *Crisis on Infinite Earths*, comics were no longer being sold to a general audience through newsstands, but to a devoted audience through specialist comic book shops. This profoundly changed the nature of the comics themselves. Longer-running storylines became more and more acceptable (as a dedicated fan is likely to buy every issue) as did stories that assumed extensive knowledge of other comics. And then there was the creation of "event" comics, often featuring particularly hot writers and artists. These were comics that anyone reading any of DC's or Marvel's titles would be expected to buy, not just because they featured all their favorite characters à la *Justice League of America*, but because they set the tone and established major events for the entire line.

Crisis on Infinite Earths was the original event comic, and took this "setting the tone" mandate as far as it could possibly go. It rewrote DC's entire continuity in such a way that every book had to reboot itself afterwards. Multiple books, *Wonder Woman* included, ran "final stories" for the old continuity, and more launched in new directions following the Crisis miniseries, although several of these were delayed by a year or more, resulting in a continuity that was even thornier than the old one.

The main villain of *Crisis on Infinite Earths*, the Anti-Monitor, can destroy entire universes within the DC Multiverse: he wipes out Earth-3 (a world featuring villainous versions of the Justice League, with Lex Luthor as the world's only superhero) within the first few pages of the crossover. This establishes him as dangerous not only in the practical sense of killing people, but in an overall sense – he can damage entire lines of comic books. The crossover itself, then, focuses primarily on establishing what about the DC lines enable them to stand up to this threat. The answer, typically speaking, comes down to why the characters are so important in the first place.

To understand how this sort of storytelling works, we should look first to another character: Superman. *Crisis on Infinite Earths* features both the "modern" Earth-1 and the "Golden Age" Earth-2 versions of Superman. After the Multiverse collapses into a single Earth, the two Supermen explore it (alongside the Flash – the first character to pass between the two worlds) so as to explain the new status quo. In the final issue, it's the Earth-2 Superman who deals the final blow to the Anti-Monitor, not because he's more powerful than anyone else – in fact, he's less powerful than the Earth-1 version – but because his status as the first superhero, canonically defined through his appearance in *Action Comics* #1, can countermand the threat to DC Comics as a whole.

Within *Crisis on Infinite Earths*, Wonder Woman fares rather poorly. She hardly appears before joining the final assault against the Anti-Monitor, where she's abruptly vaporized. In the epilogue, however, it's established that the Anti-Monitor's blast has sent Wonder Woman back in time, devolving her into the clay from which she was formed as part of Paradise Island itself, thus providing a cyclic nature to her story. The Earth-2 version of Wonder Woman, like the Earth-2 Superman, is spared outright destruction by the merging of universes, becoming a part of the Greek pantheon itself. Of the four pages following the resolution of the main plot, a whole page is devoted to Wonder Woman, but this extensive focus at the end of the comic is the only real attention she gets for the entire series.

Ironically, then, *Crisis on Infinite Earths* managed to show the role Wonder Woman plays in the DC Universe with more accuracy than its writers intended. She's at both the center of what DC Comics is (being one of only three characters published throughout the 40s and 50s) and the margins (due to her relatively low popularity). So when it comes to the bit of the comic that actually defines the DC Universe she's central; in the actual story she's basically ignored. This surely isn't something that Wolfman and Pérez intended to say about the character, but it's cuttingly accurate nevertheless.

The impact of *Crisis on Infinite Earths* was not restricted to the miniseries itself. Ongoing comic series, including *Wonder Woman*, published issues tying into *Crisis*, and throughout the period comics came out focusing on the legacy and legend of their characters, reflections on the past that ran alongside the launches of the future.

There are two such series for Wonder Woman, the first being the final three issues of *Wonder Woman*. The crossover issues with *Crisis on Infinite Earths* are in general a bit infamous for their lack of actual engagement with the events of the miniseries, and at first *Wonder Woman* is no exception. On top of that, this marks the brief tenure of Mindy Newell as writer. By her own account, Newell was badly sandbagged by her editor, who was mildly obsessed with Aztec mythology; he insisted she bring back some concepts from an earlier story which he had edited. So the new writer had to simultaneously juggle a storyline she didn't want, tie into a crossover, and deal with the fact that her book was ending. That the results are lackluster is hardly a surprise.

Newell brings the Amazons into the conflict and puts Paradise Island under a major attack. This is resolved in issue #329, the final issue of *Wonder Woman*'s original run, in which Gerry Conway comes back to finish things off for the character. Unfortunately, Conway's conclusion is in line with the rest of his work on Wonder Woman. He has an alliance of Aries and Hades lead armies of the undead against Paradise Island on behalf of the Anti-Monitor, for more or less specious reasons, giving Wonder Woman the opportunity to inspire the Amazons to fight back; he then has her marry Steve Trevor, to whom she revealed her secret identity without much fanfare in the previous issue.

So Conway's definitive ending of Wonder Woman (with no direct foreshadowing of her imminent involvement in *Crisis on Infinite Earths* #12) is that she defeats the gods and marries her man. It isn't just painfully uninspired, but a complete rejection of what the character was. Even though the god she defeats is the God of War, her purpose and value are still rooted in fighting things and getting married. And actually, it's even worse, as Steve Trevor deals the final blow to Aries – which makes it Wonder Woman's final legacy to be saved by a man before she's married off.

The second series to tie into the Crisis was *The Legend of Wonder Woman*, by Kurt Busiek and Trina Robbins, and it's a much more complex animal. Trina Robbins was a well-regarded writer and artist from the San Francisco underground comix scene of the 1960s and 70s. *The Legend of Wonder Woman* marked one the first times a major figure from the underground was allowed anywhere near a mainstream superhero property, and in that regard it's something of a landmark. Furthermore, Robbins has, over the years, positioned herself as a comic book historian who's written and spoken extensively on Wonder Woman, making *The Legend of Wonder Woman* a sort of definitive take on the character from a high-profile commentator.

Unfortunately, much of what Robbins says about Wonder Woman needs to be taken with a grain of salt. She largely aligns herself with Gloria Steinem's position on the character, a position we've already seen the problems with. In addition, Robbins insists that Wonder Woman has always had a primarily female audience, which is a problematic claim at best. Her evidence for this primarily consists of the claims by Steinem and Edgar, which are suspicious (as noted), and the fact that in the 1960s the majority of letters in the letter column were from female readers. This latter claim ignores the fact that in a single issue the letter column switched from featuring young readers whose letters were supposedly answered by Wonder Woman herself to letters from dedicated comics fans, of whom the overwhelming majority were male. This fact alone demonstrates that the contents of the letter columns cannot be taken as an accurate representation of the readership.

Furthermore, Wonder Woman's adventures regularly appeared alongside other male superhero characters, and she debuted in a male-targeted book. One of Marston's explicit intentions was to provide propaganda to change the views of young men. The idea that the Wonder Woman of the Golden Age was a uniquely female-focused character that differed from the Golden Age superheroes at large is an ahistorical invention.

The Legend of Wonder Woman exerts a similarly troubling revisionism. It pays homage to the Golden Age: Robbins draws in a Harry Peter-esque style, while Busiek brings back the obscure villain Queen Atomia from the very end of the Marston era, and dusts off the Land of Mirrors from the

Kanigher/Peter era. But it's yet another in a long line of Golden Age recreations to excise Marston's sexual politics. Along with her demonstrably false claims about Wonder Woman's early readership, Robbins is quick to assert that the bondage elements of Wonder Woman are extraneous to the character, projected upon her by men. Though technically true, it does rather ignore the fact that the men most responsible for projecting them onto her are her creators. The secondary issue – that Robbins's angle seems to assume that women are categorically uninterested in bondage – is also problematic, though a subject for a later chapter.

The resulting four-issue "Golden Age" miniseries is miles away from what the Golden Age Wonder Woman was actually about; only some relatively whimsical plotting remains from Marston's actual comics. The story focuses on Suzie (described by Robbins as an authorial stand-in to fulfill her childhood fantasy of meeting Wonder Woman), a young girl who lies her way into Wonder Woman's care, threatens blackmail over her secret identity, and teams up with the villains, before she finally repents and decides to be a good girl because Queen Atomia was mean to her. For the most part it's a bland morality play about Suzie's selfishness. One gets the sense that Busiek and Robbins see Wonder Woman's value as little more than generic children's literature about fantastic worlds, only with a female protagonist – essentially as Alice in Wonderland, but with lots of punching.

It's the most frenzied erasure of the original conception of Wonder Woman to date, a desperate attempt to define the character in any terms other than her progressive and feminist ones. It's fitting that 1986 was a bad year for Wonder Woman's feminism – being at the height of the Reagan era, it was a bad year for most people's – but going into her relaunch, she finds herself in arguably the worst shape she's ever been. Even in the dying days of the Kanigher era, previously her lowest ebb, there was at least a concrete connection to the Marston era. Now, however, the character has been repeatedly defined in ways that ignore, distort, or openly erase her roots. It seems she's only important to DC because she's been around for 45 years, and that her original source material is a source of embarrassment to the company. With that now completely excised by the Crisis, the character can be rebooted from scratch in an atmosphere that actively denies and rejects the relevance of Marston's concept of the character. That *Wonder Woman* #329 is dedicated to the memory of "Charles Moulton" is all too fitting – he is, after all, a man who never existed, and all that's allowed to remain of him is a pseudonym instead of an actual presence.

Chapter 16: George Pérez (1987-92)

By this point in the book, the general arc of these things is surely predictable. Things go terribly wrong for Wonder Woman as a title; a big change comes through and saves it by the skin of its teeth; someone else screws it up again. It's difficult to romanticize this process. Occasionally it lines up well with the broader culture: the complete abandonment of Marston's entire concept of Wonder Woman during *Crisis on Infinite Earths* loosely coincides with the major backlash against the second wave feminists who'd appropriated her. But equally, Wonder Woman spent most of the 1960s in dreadful shape given her progressive credentials, and the peak of second wave feminism proved a disaster for her. It's also difficult to treat this process as a narrative of progress, even of the two-steps-forward, one-step-back variety – Wonder Woman often backslides into an even worse state than she'd been in previously, and in many ways her worst days are yet to come.

My argument, of course, is that this messy and rudderless process is the true shape of progress. The world does not move in a clean line whereby it solves one problem and moves on to the next. History is chaotic. Nowhere is this more salient than in the progress of the oppressed, who all too often find their victories in strange places and their defeats in moments that, to the victorious history-writers, look like triumphs. Wonder Woman doesn't just embody the idea of feminism: she demonstrates this odd process of progress and history.

Even by these standards, the 1987 relaunch of *Wonder Woman* is odd. The entire existence of her relaunch is in part predicated on the egregious and willful damage to the concept done over the preceding two years. Expecting DC to come up with a better version of the concept, shortly after they casually dismembered it, was by any definition a long shot. The early returns were discouraging. Post-Crisis, Superman was relaunched with John Byrne, a superstar artist and writer poached from Marvel. Batman was relaunched with a four-issue story written and drawn by Frank Miller, another superstar whose *Batman: The Dark Knight Returns* is one of the most acclaimed superhero comics ever, typically mentioned in the same breath as *Watchmen*. Wonder Woman, on the other hand, was slated to get Greg Potter, whose only extended work in superheroes had been on writing *Jemm, Son of Saturn* for DC. Clearly, it was never DC's intent to match every major property with A-list creators.

But as industry legend has it, there came a stroke of luck. George Pérez, the artist responsible for *Crisis on Infinite Earths* itself, spontaneously volunteered to take on the art chores for Wonder Woman, to give it a high-profile launch. As the new take on the character was developed, his role slowly grew, and eventually he was plotting and drawing it, while Potter was reduced to nothing more than filling in the dialogue; after two issues, he was replaced with Len Wein. This, in and of itself, is not promising. Artists who take up writing can be quite good – Frank Miller, at least in the 1980s, is a prime example. Pérez had minimal writing experience beyond some co-plotting credits for his work with Marv Wolfman on *Teen Titans*. In this regard he was a creative gamble, even though he did offer more-or-less guaranteed sales.

Every once in a while, however, a gamble pays off. And in this case the result was a sixty-two issue, five-year run of Wonder Woman that redefined the character and is rightly considered one of the best periods in the character's history.

Part of this quality is simply due to stability: Pérez's tenure on *Wonder Woman* was the longest since 1968. Given the problems caused by incessant churn since the I Ching era, this is no small thing.

But it's not as though *Wonder Woman* benefitted from the intense stability offered by twenty straight years of Robert Kanigher. Thankfully, Pérez turned out to be a revelation as a writer. It's an unsurprising truism that artists-turned-writers tend to write things that are fun for them to draw and play to their strengths. Pérez's strengths, then, work strongly in his favor. He's good at drawing extremely detailed panels with lots of characters in them, all of whom are visually distinctive and recognizable. Accordingly, he writes *Wonder Woman* with a huge cast of characters, rendered in gloriously complex and detailed page layouts. There's a lot going on in any given issue, and this new version of Wonder Woman starts with exactly what her predecessor so visibly lacked: a substantive supporting cast. Pérez also proved capable of juggling them – his skill at drawing a distinct cast of characters applied equally well to writing them.

The relaunched *Wonder Woman* had advantages behind the scenes as well. It was edited by Karen Berger, a rising star who'd overseen the bulk of Alan Moore's work on *Swamp Thing* and who brought Neil Gaiman and Grant Morrison into US comics. Berger's influence was considerable, and in many ways Pérez's *Wonder Woman* reads like a toned-down all-ages version of the fantasy-horror genre that defined many of the other books Berger edited. It's not difficult to imagine a world in which the relaunched *Wonder Woman* tied in slightly less with the surrounding DC Universe, with Pérez and Berger staying on a year or so longer than they did, leading it to be spun off into the Vertigo line that Berger created to house the more adult books.

Berger's influence on Wonder Woman also manifested in more material terms: she got more women to work on it, bringing back the actually quite good Mindy Newell and getting in female artists like Colleen Doran and Jill

Thompson while Pérez just served as writer. The combination resulted in a twenty-issue stretch of the comic in which every single issue has a woman either writing or drawing it – by far the longest run of female creators to date, and a record that maddeningly took until 2008 to beat.

The usual starting point in describing Pérez's tenure on *Wonder Woman* is to talk about how he brings the Greek gods to the foreground. This is certainly the biggest change, but in many ways it's more useful to look at how he handles the two major supporting characters retained from the pre-Crisis version of the character: Steve Trevor and Etta Candy. Under Pérez, Steve Trevor is no longer the traditional square-jawed action hero, but is introduced as someone who dislikes guns, and who got relegated to a desk job for testifying in front of a Congressional committee against several of his bloodthirsty military superiors. His crash on Paradise Island becomes an attempt by one of those superiors to kill him for revenge. On top of this, Pérez draws him as a considerably older character (he now has a receding hairline) and this distances him even more from the straightforward masculine hero.

Etta fares more ambiguously – almost all of her original charm is gone, and those who appreciated the character in part because of her visible lack of body image issues would be dismayed to find her constantly talking about her weight loss (a topic Pérez's successor, William Messner-Loebs, will tackle explicitly). But it's Etta who now becomes Steve's love interest. Among the changes Pérez makes to Wonder Woman, this is in many ways the most significant. In almost every problematic era of Wonder Woman prior to Pérez, the biggest problem is the handling of Steve Trevor. By conceiving of Steve as someone who was not romantically attached to Wonder Woman, Pérez kills the problem off for once and for all – Trevor is never again such a problematic facet of Wonder Woman.

Indeed, Pérez goes one step further to ensure that future writers would have a hard time pairing Wonder Woman with Steve Trevor. This comes with the explanation for Wonder

Woman's outfit, which is flagrantly American even though she's no longer explicitly sent to defend the United States in particular. Pérez changes the origin story so that it's Steve Trevor's *mother*, a soldier in World War II, who crashes onto Paradise Island. Diana Trevor raises Wonder Woman as a surrogate daughter (passing down the name Diana as well as the costume design) and tells her to take care of her son, thus establishing a sibling relationship between Wonder Woman and Steve Trevor. Sure enough, this revision spelled the much-needed end to the tiresome Diana/Steve romance that dogged the comic for its first forty-five years. (It's worth noting that Diana Trevor mirrors the Earth-2 Wonder Woman. Her appearance in a version of the iconic costume is used as a cliffhanger, and her parting words to Wonder Woman proclaim, "The future should always resonate with the echoes of the past." It's difficult to read this as anything other than a reference to the pre-Crisis history of Wonder Woman, with Diana Trevor serving as a literal echo of that past.)

This focus on the human aspects of Wonder Woman's world extends beyond Steve and Etta through a sizable cast of new supporting characters. The two biggest are Julia and Vanessa Kapatelis, who serve as Wonder Woman's surrogate family in the mortal world. Julia is a middle-aged history professor, while Vanessa is her teenage daughter. Vanessa's a surprisingly well-written teenager with a substantial supporting cast of her own, including a friendship with another teenager, the troubled Lucy Spears. In one of the best issues of Pérez's run, the characters grapple with Lucy's suicide. This is the second time he confronts real-world issues; previously, he introduced Mindi Mayer, a careerist publicist whose subsequent death prompted an issue on drug addiction that's another highlight of his run (and we should note how rare it is that a comic about drugs is actually good).

Pérez's run is not focused primarily on the mythic aspects of Wonder Woman, inasmuch as primacy implies a lack of focus on other aspects of the character. Nevertheless, it's clear that mythology is important to Pérez's work on Wonder Woman in a way it wasn't in any previous era. Not only are there substantially more Amazonian characters than ever before, Pérez makes use of the Greek pantheon, with Zeus, Aphrodite, Athena, Hermes, Aries, Hera, Hephaestus, Poseidon, Hades, and Eris all making appearances and getting non-trivial character development. (Hermes is particularly vibrant, and he progressively steals more and more of the book out from under the other characters. A plotline that has him rooming with Steve Trevor is one of the biggest delights of this generally delightful era.)

But Pérez's use of the gods goes beyond merely developing them. For all the focus he gives to human characters, none of them are introduced until the second issue. The first twenty-four pages of the thirty-two page first issue don't even feature Diana, and her initial appearance in the Wonder Woman costume is saved for a last-page reveal. Considering that the standard length of a comic book is twenty-two pages, were it not for its extended page count Wonder Woman wouldn't even have appeared in the first issue of her own book. Instead, the first three-quarters of it are given over entirely to the origin story of the Amazons and their relationship with the gods.

Pérez's stories are rarely about the gods as such, but rather about the relationship between people and their gods. Diana is repeatedly shown to be a character with a deep and profound faith in her gods, and this faith is established as her greatest character strength – not just in terms of the moral sense it gives her in the human world, but in the sense that her faith sets her apart from other Amazons. Equally, hers is not a blind or unproblematic faith.

It's significant that Pérez gives her faith in the Greek pantheon and not a monotheistic system. The difference is that the Greek pantheon is a set of deities representing specific concepts, as opposed to a general and diffuse authority. Accordingly, interrogating the relationship between people and the Greek pantheon has a different set of connotations than does a general exploration of the relationship between people and the divine.

More specifically, the use of the Greek pantheon makes the relationship not just about people and religion but between people and larger social orders. This is something stressed from the very first story arc of Pérez's run, which concerns the prospect that Ares's influence over the world has grown too strong, a problem that manifests itself materially through the near-onset of nuclear war between the United States and the USSR. The gods correspond not only to broad concepts but to social relations and material social phenomena. By positing a pantheon of deities who double as social relations, Pérez implies the existence of an absolute social order. The nature of his pantheon suggests that human social relations – the material concerns that Wonder Woman has always been invested in – are fundamental forces of the universe. In a sense, this is similar to Marston's treating of dominance and submission as fundamental human characteristics, albeit on a larger and less philosophically detailed scale.

Pérez establishes the Amazons as intermediaries between the gods and humans, and Wonder Woman as the ambassador between the Amazons and humanity. This is a significant shift in Wonder Woman's role – she's no longer a warrior fighting for America. Instead, her role within the comic is much more akin to what Marston envisioned, an inspirational figure who modeled a particular set of values in an attempt to promote them.

This is an improvement over Marston's original model. Pérez has Wonder Woman go out of her way to declare she doesn't want to be a crime-fighting superhero, or a member of the Justice League, because that would imply support for institutionalized violence. Unlike his alterations to Steve Trevor, this was not a change Pérez could make stick. It is, however, good while it lasts, in that it opens the door for Wonder Woman to have plot lines that aren't simply about protecting the world from a variety of threats. Such stories still exist, obviously – they are, after all, the bread and butter of superhero comics – but the fact that the character isn't defined primarily in terms of her engagement with them means that the stories have to be about their moral concerns in a more complex way.

The storyline that runs from issue #36 through #41 serves as a prime example. In this story, a group of human emissaries journey to Themyscira (the renamed Paradise Island) as part of a traditional ceremony. The ceremony, however, is cast into chaos by the goddess Eris, who contrives to turn the delegates against each other. The story contains a suitable amount of punching and explosions to fit smoothly into the superhero genre, but its major focus is on the nature of heroism and inspiration. Considerable time is spent in the characterization of the individual delegates: an anti-apartheid activist, an American feminist, a Russian neurosurgeon, a Scottish veteran who helped build the bridge over the River Kwai, a Unitarian minister, a Rabbi, a blind humanitarian worker, an architect who focuses on the needs of the physically disabled, a Haitian zoologist, and a young survivor of Tiananmen Square.

This list is overtly political in a way the comic had too often shied away from in previous eras. More to the point, once the characters turn against each other (thanks to the manipulations of Eris) the story becomes about much more than punching things. It's really about two groups of good, heroic people – the twelve delegates and the Amazons – and how the intervention of Eris inevitably draws them towards conflict even as they try to make peace. Pérez makes this explicit through Lois Lane, another of the twelve delegates. She provides continual narration in the form of her eventual news story, which reflects constantly on the larger social implications of the events.

Given this frame, Wonder Woman's role is telling. Eris's machinations become truly destructive when she captures and corrupts Wonder Woman, and it's only when Wonder Woman breaks free of the goddess's control that order is restored. Furthermore, Wonder Woman is only able to break free thanks to the intervention of both Hermes, who is stuck on Earth, and Rovo Quashi, the blind humanitarian delegate from Ethiopia. Wonder Woman's role, then, is to demonstrate how to overcome Eris so that peace can be brokered between the Amazons and humans. This is possible because of her ability to move between the worlds of gods and mortals.

This captures the basic way in which the new model of Wonder Woman works under Pérez. Because she embodies both an absolute concept and humanity itself, she serves as an example for how to interact productively with broader social forces. It's possible to oversimplify this to an observation that Wonder Woman's a role model, but this isn't quite true. Wonder Woman's actions can't be directly emulated by her readership. Furthermore, Pérez constantly stresses the fact that she isn't human, keeping her at a remove from the mortal cast (it isn't until the seventh issue before Diana even learns English so that she can speak to them). Rather, she provides an interface between the concrete world of humanity and the more abstract realm of gods and social forces, inspiring the humans within the story to then serve as role models for the audience.

Pérez reinforces all this by offering a relatively radical and compelling view of the world, even though it's not as philosophically systemic as Marston's. Wonder Woman's primary patron and the goddess to whom she is most devoted, Gaea, never actually appears in the comic. That is not to say that she's unimportant – she's explicitly one of the most important gods that Diana worships. Rather, she occupies a space akin to what most people's gods are: figures that aren't present in their lives in any material sense.

To some extent this is another facet of Wonder Woman's carefully constructed status as a liminal figure between the divine and the material, but there's more to it. Mythologically speaking, Gaea is a primordial mother deity with little evident role in any surviving texts. But in the popular culture of the

1980s, the name was most obviously linked with the Gaia hypothesis of James Lovelock, which posited that the Earth self-regulates itself to sustain life. Although Lovelock's theory isn't considered credible these days, it was in vogue in the mid-80s. Accordingly, Wonder Woman's devotion to Gaea ought to be read as devotion towards the concept of the world having an underlying order and purpose – one based specifically on a sort of bland hippie view of nature as a source of peace and harmony.

Within the context of Pérez's Wonder Woman, this is an underlying principle of the world, so it would be inappropriate to give it a physical avatar like the rest of the gods, as that would suggest she's just another Greek god. But equally, though she doesn't appear, she is not quite absent. I mentioned earlier that the first issue of the reboot barely focuses on Wonder Woman herself at all, but on the Amazons. Its first two pages describe a prehistoric man who is humiliated in combat with a sabertooth tiger and ostracized from his tribe. He lashes out and kills his partner, because he views her attempts to comfort him as emasculating. Her soul is then elevated from her body towards a mysterious higher order – a "voice as if from the Earth itself – whispering, calling, beckoning – making something happen that you cannot understand." This section, crucially, is narrated in the second person – the unnamed caveman is referred to as "you," implicating the (likely male) reader in this violence.

This is later suggested to be the origin story of Gaea herself. She in turn creates the Amazons by gathering in her womb the souls of women whose "lives [were] cut short by man's fear and ignorance." In other words, Gaea's influence manifests most directly through survivors of abuse. This abuse is clearly meant to stand in for the larger phenomenon of misogyny and sexism, hence the tying in of a prehistorical act of sexual violence. The implication is that the sustainability and harmony of the world is based on the ability of the feminine to survive masculine oppression. This reflects the pragmatic vision of feminism that we've seen throughout this book – rather than being a well-defined ideology, it's a continually evolving approach to interacting with the larger culture.

Pérez explicitly posits his version of the Amazons as evolving from Marston's. The key moment comes in issue #50, when the Amazons make their return to Man's World. As they do, they climactically cast off their bracelets, which are described as "symbols of their bondage" and "dark tokens of isolation and ambivalence." The fact that bondage is explicitly mentioned here and that the bracelets were such an important symbol in Marston's comics (recall that if they were removed from an Amazon she would go berserk) makes this an overt commentary on Marston's conception of the character. It is unequivocally a rejection of that take, but we should be careful in how we characterize this. Pérez is not criticizing Marston as such, but refining him. Marston's singular vision of how feminism can save the world is not so much wrong as inadequate – an outmoded version that the Amazons can now move beyond in favor of a more diverse and complex vision based not on dominance and submission but on the existence of a higher principle that can unify diverse groups – peace, as Pérez would have it.

The history of Wonder Woman is littered with writers who fail to live up to the challenge of Marston's iconoclastic vision – only a handful of periods in her history, like the I Ching era, have reached new heights. Most struggle and fail to make her as good as she used to be. Pérez is one of the few exceptions – a new high-water mark that other writers have to aspire to.

Chapter 17: William Messner-Loebs (1992-95)

The William Messner-Loebs era of Wonder Woman is a strange beast. On the one hand, its ending is an unmitigated disaster and one of the nadirs of the comic. On the other, its beginning manages the impressive feat of actually improving upon George Pérez, albeit because the end of Pérez's tenure is the weakest part of it, bogging down in a sloppily handled crossover.

For all that Pérez attended to his non-mythic supporting cast, his tenure was rather focused on mythology. In contrast, Messner-Loebs focuses almost entirely on the non-mythic world. This doesn't exclusively mean the real world – Messner-Loebs's first extended story arc is a six-issue piece set in outer space – so much as what's tangible, material.

This is not a significant departure from the ethos of Pérez's approach so much as an extension of it; Messner-Loebs very much follows Pérez, playing gleefully with the "fish out of water" aspects of Diana. It's less a change of course than it is an exploration of the other side of the coin – Pérez focused on the gods as a metaphor for human behavior, while Messner-Loebs looks at what the experience of the material world would be for someone who comes from the gods.

In this regard, the outer-space arc was well-advised. First, it created an easy opportunity to break from Pérez. By putting Wonder Woman in space for several months, Messner-Loebs could change anything about her earthly status quo without fuss. In particular, this lets him take Themyscira (Paradise Island) off the table without having (initially) to do a story to justify it – when Diana returns she simply discovers that it's vanished.

But the off-world start also lets Messner-Loebs make a broad statement of intent that goes beyond what he would otherwise be able to do with an Earth-centered story. The plot of his space story is standard pulp sci-fi fare: Wonder Woman leads a slave rebellion on another planet. But underneath the cliché is an interesting alternate take on the story. Instead of making rousing speeches about dignity and freedom, Wonder Woman leads her revolt quietly, hiding the extent of her powers for months as she steps in to help the other enslaved women. As a result, when she's eventually attacked by a sadistic guard the rest of the slaves all rebel in her defense, at which point she reveals her powers and leads them to freedom. It's not subtle in the least, especially given that the slavers are explicitly misogynistic, but it's an effective subversion of a genre cliché that gives a sense of Messner-Loebs's focus in his run: what a female alternative to the standard male action hero paradigm might actually look like. As good as it is, however, the real sparks start to fly once Messner-Loebs returns to Earth.

Other than the disastrous storyline that consumed his final year on the title, the thing Messner-Loebs's run is most known for is a delightfully bizarre storyline in which Wonder Woman has to take a job at Taco Whiz, a fast food joint, in order to pay for a place to live. The plot is memorably captured by a Brian Bolland cover that features Wonder Woman, in costume, wearing a "Taco Whiz" baseball cap and holding a serving tray of Mexican food and coffee. The hat obscures one eye, but her other one looks out at the reader as she grins cheekily and proclaims, "Hey... it's a living!"

This approach is almost a direct copy of the I Ching era. The setups are nearly identical: Paradise Island has vanished from the world, and Wonder Woman is forced to make a living with a real job. Although this storyline didn't attract the level of controversy that the I Ching era did (which is to say that Gloria Steinem stayed out of it), it still garnered some criticism. There are two reasons for this. The first is a complaint of realism – Wonder Woman shouldn't need to work to make money because of her membership in the Justice League. Messner-Loebs deals with this by establishing that the Justice League computer has a glitch and won't release her paychecks – a piece of cynical bureaucracy that fits perfectly with the lowly materialism he's going for. But this is exactly the sort of "let's not explore the consequences of these ideas too much" that happens constantly in superhero narratives. It's no different from the "Why doesn't Wonder Woman just violently overthrow misogynistic regimes that oppress women?" question that the comic has to ignore in order to have a plot, or, for that matter, "Why doesn't Wonder Woman use her powers to become a billionaire and start tons of charitable foundations?"

The second objection is the more interesting and troubling one, which is that it's somehow degrading to have Wonder Woman working a lousy fast-food job. There is something very unpleasant about this accusation, namely the intense classism inherent in declaring that Wonder Woman is somehow degraded by taking a lousy job of the sort that millions of people take to make ends meet. The objection tacitly argues that there's something wrong with having Wonder Woman face problems that resemble those of ordinary people, as though an engagement with the reality of the material world lessens the character. This argument is, of course, desperately anti-feminist, reducing Wonder Woman to a theoretical abstraction instead of something that exists in the real world and has material consequences.

In practice, what Messner-Loebs does here is good for the same reasons the I Ching era was good: Wonder Woman engages with real issues and thus fulfills the designed purpose of using comic books and superheroes for material progress. Unless one is committed to separating Wonder Woman from the political – and I cannot conceive of any good reason to want that – there's no way to write the character without connecting with the everyday world. Messner-Loebs gives voice to the idea that the Taco Whiz job is beneath Wonder Woman through numerous characters who express surprise and shock at her continual insistence on going to work. Wonder Woman, for her part, says that she finds work relaxing and that she enjoys having a job, a moment that would cut the "demeaning" argument off at the knees for anyone who actually read the comic, and that provides an interesting improvement on Kanigher's 1950s praise for menial jobs, which was based on their supposed value to society instead of on any sort of personal value. (So that's another parallel to the I Ching era.) This attitude even extends beyond Wonder Woman herself – in a particularly charming touch, Taco Whiz becomes a de facto gathering place for the superhero community on the grounds that nobody there bugs you for autographs or looks at you strange for wearing a superhero costume.

Messner-Loebs also continues Pérez's tradition of occasionally tackling real-world issues directly, again with a contrast in focus. Where Pérez dealt with drug addiction and teen suicide – both noble issues, but ones that are easy to romanticize as tragedies – Messner-Loebs's two "big issue" plots are eating disorders and deadbeat dads. The eating disorders plot is particularly refreshing, subverting one of the more troubling aspects of Pérez's run by having Etta Candy, who Pérez had made extremely body-conscious, be revealed as anorexic, a move that serves as a tacit critique of the endless tendency to slim the character down and make her more conventionally "sexy."

The other big "issue" story comes in *Wonder Woman* #81, in which Wonder Woman attempts to get the father of her boss's daughter to pay child support. The father is an enforcer for the mob, but instead of taking the normal superhero path of busting heads in order to fix things, Wonder Woman employs an almost completely non-violent approach to the problem. She simply walks into a meeting of the mob and declines to leave. The mob is paralyzed because they can't risk trying to kill a member of the Justice League, nor can they call the police (obviously). Meanwhile, Wonder Woman continually answers the phone, offering "helpfully" to take messages for the Mafia boss. This creates much consternation for him, as he fears his colleagues will believe he's selling people out to the superhero community. The mob boss, unsurprisingly, caves in and insists his employee pay the child support.

It is, in many ways, the perfect Wonder Woman scene: she takes care of a distinctly women's issue in a clever, non-violent way. And it's a glorious metaphor for feminism in general – upholding the virtue of persistence and the effectiveness of refusing invisibility as a tactic. In the long history of Wonder Woman, issue #81 is one of the high points. And while I admit to frequently disagreeing with her, Trina Robbins is spot-on when she praises it as such in the letter column of issue #85.

Unfortunately, issue #85 also marks an unpleasant turn for the comic in general as it introduces a new penciler – Mike Deodato. Initially he's just a guest artist, but after a four-issue gap he takes over with *Wonder Woman* #90 and remains for the last year of Messner-Loebs's tenure. Almost immediately, it all goes wrong.

It's impossible to explain what starts happening in *Wonder Woman* #90 without first explaining comic books in the 1990s in general. The early 1990s saw a speculator's bubble in comic books. People had noticed how classic Golden and Silver Age comic books dramatically appreciated in value over the years, leading to some farcically exaggerated news stories in which comic books were described as a better financial investment than stocks or bonds. Since the books that appreciated in value were typically either the first of their runs, introduced new characters, or killed off major ones, both Marvel and DC flooded the market with huge events of these sorts, using every gimmick imaginable to sell comics.

At DC, the two best-known of such events are the *Death of Superman* story arc from 1992-93, and the *Knightfall* arc in Batman from 1993-94. Both of these stories had similar plots: the main character, defeated by an unstoppable and brutal menace, is temporarily replaced by a new version. Both sold extremely well, and so inevitably the same thing had to happen to Wonder Woman. But it's also important to understand the underlying reason of this development. In the late 80s and early 90s, superhero comics became an increasingly artist-driven form. This led, in 1992, to a group of Marvel's most popular artists departing the company to form their own, called Image Comics. The name was in many ways telling – Image, at the beginning, featured superstar artists writing their own books, and they were triumphs of style over substance. But they sold like mad, so Marvel and DC rushed to imitate their style.

Unfortunately, the style itself was ludicrous. As with George Pérez, the Image creators tended to write what they liked to draw, but where he liked intricate panel layouts packed with expressive characters, they liked sophomoric displays of overwrought masculinity. Male characters were reliably steroid-ridden blocks of muscle, typically adorned with some combination of cybernetic implants, massive guns, large amounts of decorative battle armor, and skulls. Women tended to be at least forty-percent breast by volume. The most common pose for them is what's mockingly called "the brokeback" – a position in which women swivel in anatomically improbable ways so as to simultaneously display their breasts and buttocks for the (presumably male, as ever) viewer. This is what DC sought to emulate in hiring Mike Deodato.

On the face of it this seems a poor mix for Messner-Loebs's light-hearted humanism. But following the arrival of Paul Kupperberg as editor, Messner-Loebs set off on a storyline that's a clear copy of *Death of Superman* and *Knightfall*. In it, Themyscira is finally restored, home to both the Amazons and the Bana-Mighdallian, a splinter tribe of the

Amazons created by Pérez. Upon returning to Themyscira, Diana's confronted by an erratic Hippolyta, who declares a new contest to select Themyscira's ambassador to Man's World. Diana is defeated by Artemis, one of the Bana-Mighdallian, who accordingly becomes the new Wonder Woman.

Artemis is in many ways the archetype of the Image-style character. She's a bigger-breasted "badass" version of Wonder Woman, armed with a bow and arrow, and almost permanently contorted into the brokeback pose. Her most visually defining characteristic is a grotesquely long ponytail (considerably longer than floor-length) that defies all laws of physics with its routine curls and mid-air pirouettes. Like any Image-style character, she's far more ruthless and violent than Diana. At one point she belittles a battered spouse for not fighting back, and declares that it would be better for her children to "starve than have a mother who is a parasite and a coward."

But there's something odd about Messner-Loebs's dabbling in the style of the 1990s, which is that even after replacing Wonder Woman he's still more interested in Diana than Artemis, who doesn't even appear in every issue. On top of that, Artemis is played as a somewhat more comedic figure than one might expect. She repeatedly saves the day for various causes by fighting gratuitously over-the-top villains. For instance, a battered women's shelter is attacked by a hulking brute who declares, "All these women have deserted their husbands! They've violated natural law – they must be punished! So says... The Chauvinist!" The Chauvinist is an almost spherical mass of muscle sporting bracelets with massive spikes and an alarmingly large set of chains wrapped around his chest and shoulders. Artemis eventually defeats him, much as she's able to defeat The Exploiter, who runs an illegal sweatshop, and Involute the Conqueror, who pillages the rainforest.

Figure 9: Artemis in a classic "brokeback" position confronting a typical Image-style villain in *Wonder Woman* #97 (1995), art by Mike Deodato, copyright DC Comics, used under the principle of fair use.

Eventually it's revealed that these fights were staged by a PR firm (with an unwitting Artemis) to distract from the real issues on the theory that once the fighting was over the media would stop paying attention. For instance, after the big fight against The Chauvinist, the battered women's shelter is quietly bulldozed. So the ludicrous approach Artemis embodied, of extreme violence against over-the-top villains, was exactly as ineffectual and ill-advised as it superficially appeared, while the concrete, material investment in the real world promoted by Messner-Loebs before he was sandbagged with Deodato was still the only real way forward.

Interestingly, right as he begins the Artemis story, Messner-Loebs brings back a phrase that had been absent from Wonder Woman comics for decades: "loving submission," which Hippolyta uses several times in relation to Diana. Of course, the return of "loving submission" evokes the Marston era and its bondage themes. But by 1994, when the Artemis storyline began, those themes had already taken on a markedly different tone. The pornography and fetish scenes were considerably better known and organized than they were in the 1940s, if not completely mainstream. 1995, the year the Artemis storyline ended, saw the publication of *Screw the Roses, Send Me the Thorns*, one of the first well-known books on BDSM. And it's clear that the Image style of depicting female characters was heavily influenced by pornography (to the extent it drew any influence from human anatomy at all).

In practical terms, this posed a real problem for Wonder Woman. When Marston invoked bondage themes in the 1940s, he did so without the context of a larger community; the existence of bondage and discipline as a fetish was known, but there wasn't the wide-scale mainstream access to explicit fetish pornography that existed in the 1990s thanks to the rapidly growing Internet. Marston drew upon bondage themes that were intensely sexual, but they weren't inherently connected to the extreme misogyny that characterizes most of the pornography industry. So when these themes were brought back into the foreground by Messner-Loebs, they took an altogether more sinister tone.

The problem is that there's always been an erotic element to Wonder Woman, and the 1990s only highlighted it by foregrounding a fetish-based sexuality. It can't simply be taken out, nor can it be consistently ignored. While it's clear that Messner-Loebs finds the implications of this troubling, he never makes the move that would alleviate the problem: allowing Wonder Woman's sexuality to exist for her own sake.

This failure is, in the end, the crux of what goes wrong for Messner-Loebs's resistance to the dominant style of comics in the 1990s. For all that his Wonder Woman struggles against it, in the end it's a doomed struggle. For one thing, it's clear that Deodato is nowhere near the same page as Messner-Loebs. A subversive parody of the Image style can and has been done, but this isn't it. Deodato executes his style without a trace of irony, relegating Messner-Loebs's resistance to a couple of small touches that get overwhelmed in the mass of skulls and boobs. Sure enough, Messner-Loebs's final issue, *Wonder Woman* #100, is little more than a blood-soaked fight scene ending in Artemis's death.

The exploitative and fetishized depiction of women that characterizes the Image style isn't something that can be done halfway. Either you're depicting women in brokeback poses with massive breasts and butts, or you're giving them some sort of meaningful agency and self-identity. Messner-Loebs may have been aware of how awful the Image style was, but he didn't have (or, equally likely, was editorially discouraged from expressing) a meaningful alternative. In the end, acknowledging that something is ridiculous while still doing it straightforwardly just isn't enough. Ironic distance is not equivalent to dissent.

Messner-Loebs was a lone and largely silent voice of resistance against the inevitable. By 1995 almost all traces of the charming and noble style he'd first brought to the book were gone. Only a few months after he departed, DC released

The Wonder Woman Gallery, a comic consisting of various portraits of Wonder Woman. Out of thirty-two drawings, twelve feature the heavily sexualized brokeback position, including an appalling one by Jim Balent where Wonder Woman is attacked by skeletons that grope at her breasts and one that bites at her thighs. It's clear that DC had finally settled on a direction for Wonder Woman: she was a piece of meat.

A Golden Thread: An Unofficial Critical History of Wonder Woman

Chapter 18: The Second Wilderness (1995-2002)

The chain of writers following William Messner-Loebs form a period not unlike the tail-end of Wonder Woman's original series. The character changes hands every few years, is wholly reinvented each time, and ranges from disastrous to good, but never to great. The first of these writers, John Byrne, at least looked promising. Byrne was one of Marvel's biggest stars, poached by DC to oversee the post-*Crisis* relaunch of *Superman*. But by 1995, as the boom and subsequent bust of the 1990s comic industry hit, Byrne felt increasingly like a creator past his peak. This was reflected in the basic marketing and description of his run on Wonder Woman, pitched as Byrne doing the one major superhero he'd never done before – which is to say, he was doing his last choice of the major superheroes for the sake of checking something off his bucket list.

    On top of this, Byrne is an easy creator to criticize, which is only partially based on the quality of his work. He is infamously outspoken, pugnacious and willing to savage other creators. But there's a larger problem: what Byrne creates often conflicts with what adamantly declares in interviews and on his website. For instance, he criticizes the tendency of "new writers and/or editors thinking being assigned to a title or character is a mandate to blow everything up and start from scratch." But his first issue of *Wonder Woman* moves her from Boston to the fictional Gateway City with no explanation whatsoever for the change, jettisons the supporting cast that Pérez and Messner-Loebs had spent a hundred issues building, and ends with Wonder Woman becoming the earthbound Goddess of Truth.

Similarly, Byrne criticizes what he deems "Superboy syndrome." Starting from the premise that it's impossible to enjoy serialized fiction unless you actively pretend that the main characters may not survive, Byrne complains that Superboy stories – i.e. stories about a teenaged Clark Kent – lack any tension because the audience knows that Superboy will live to become Superman. And yet Byrne's *Wonder Woman* has an entire four-issue arc where Hippolyta travels back in time to be Wonder Woman during World War II, all narrated in flashback, so there's no chance at all that anything bad will happen to her.

Byrne's complaints about Superboy syndrome reveal a larger issue with his work: he thinks taking superheroes seriously is important in the first place. Such was the case with his Superman revamp. He removed "silly" aspects like Krypto the Superdog and a wealth of odd ideas like multicolored Kryptonite, and he restricted Superman's powers. The result was a version of Superman that could only be taken seriously, the square-jawed rock of blandness that the character is so frequently dismissed as being. It's not that his work is without humor – he wrote an extremely well-regarded and hilarious run on Marvel's *She-Hulk* – but he reserves humor for peripheral characters. When it comes to a character like Wonder Woman, he's exceedingly serious.

Worse than taking Wonder Woman seriously is the fact that Byrne takes her the wrong sort of seriously. Messner-Loebs dealt with very serious issues in the Taco Whiz plot, even as the actual comic was hilarious. But Byrne's run is centered almost entirely on the fantastic and imaginary aspects of the DC universe. This is clear from the first moment of the book as he moves the setting from Boston – a setting that made Wonder Woman one of the few DC heroes

A Golden Thread: An Unofficial Critical History of Wonder Woman

to exist in a real-world city – to the fictional Gateway City, akin to Gotham City or Metropolis.

This focus entirely on the fictional is frustrating, especially for Wonder Woman, who's defined in many ways by how she combines mythological and material concerns. But Byrne takes the matter even further. He abandons not just the real world, but much of the mythic world as well. Yes, the gods and goddesses of Pérez's run appear, but not until Byrne establishes unequivocally that all of the various real-world pantheons were really created by the New Gods, a set of cosmic entities invented by Jack Kirby in the 1970s.

The impact of this new model on the basic concept of Wonder Woman is significant. Much of the conceptual strength of Pérez's run came from the way in which Wonder Woman was not a traditional superhero but a mediator between gods and humans. Now that the gods stand revealed as mere derivatives of superheroes, any independence Wonder Woman had from standard superhero narratives is lost.

This is at the heart of Byrne's approach, taking the character entirely in the terms of comic book fandom. His main priority is to get Wonder Woman to fit smoothly with the rest of DC Comics, and any part of the character that doesn't define her in those terms is suspect and subject to elimination. The only issue in which Byrne puts any real effort into establishing something unique about her is *Wonder Woman* #125, in which the Justice League heroes praise Wonder Woman at her bedside (she's hospitalized in a coma). Though all of them pay their respects, nobody ever articulates a reason why she's special. Tellingly, the next issue (which features a striking pseudo-newspaper cover with the headline "A World Without Wonder Woman?") mostly ties into the Byrne-written crossover event "Genesis" that focuses on the New Gods and Darkseid. Even when dying, Wonder Woman is little more than a guest star in her own book.

It is worth pointing out the depth of irony here. Byrne spoke in interviews about wanting to restore Wonder Woman to her place as one of DC Comics' "Big Three" alongside Superman and Batman. This is, of course, a reference to the old "one of three continually published characters" chestnut. But in the 1990s it wasn't even true anymore. Unlike *Action Comics*, *Superman*, *Detective Comics*, and *Batman*, *Wonder Woman* did have a significant gap in publication, taking nearly a year off after *Crisis on Infinite Earths* before restarting as a new series. The image of her as one of the big three was, by 1995, pure nostalgia. The trouble with this sort of nostalgia is that the longed-for past being revived isn't defined by nostalgia or traditionalism. Wonder Woman didn't survive the 1940s by being just like all the other superheroes that got cancelled. She survived because she wasn't like other superheroes.

For all of Byrne's protestations about the tendency of DC to "de-unique" their characters (the neologism is entirely his), he oversaw a bizarre profusion of Wonder Woman clones. When he came onto the book Wonder Woman had at best one clone, and that was Donna Troy, whose origin had very little to do with Wonder Woman at that point. During his run, Artemis was brought back from the dead – a decision that admittedly wasn't Byrne's, but nevertheless meant that Wonder Woman had two clone versions. Given that, the decision to introduce a new Wonder Girl in Cassie Sandsmark is strange. (Indeed, Cassie Sandsmark is a strange decision in general; she's not particularly distinct from Vanessa Kapatelis, one of Pérez's supporting characters.) Even worse, Diana is stripped of being the first Wonder Woman when Byrne has Hippolyta take on the Wonder Woman mantle by traveling back to World War II to restore the existence of a Golden Age version. As if that weren't enough, he wipes out Donna Troy's origin story in favor of making her a literal clone of Diana.

The result is that Wonder Woman herself becomes one of five versions of the character, and for a significant portion of Byrne's run, Diana is the most peripheral of them. After killing her, Byrne resurrects her as the Goddess of Truth, elevated to the Greek pantheon proper. The death and resurrection features a truly bizarre scene where a morgue technician shouts in horror as Wonder Woman's body bag sits up: "She can't be!! I had her brain in my hands fer cripes sake!!" The sheer casualness with which the event is treated is astonishing – her death and resurrection happen in the same issue, as Byrne doesn't even try to get a cliffhanger out of the event after leaving her in a coma for several months. But even when "elevated" to the Goddess of Truth she remains peripheral. Being a goddess limits her participation in the material world, leaving her myriad clones to carry most of the plot; her status within the Greek pantheon is also marginal, since she isn't an actual ancient Greek god.

This is a logical extension of turning Wonder Woman into a side of meat – she's become nothing more than something to stare at, and has very little narrative relevance. No, she won't get cancelled again because she's too important to DC Comics, but that means little when she's become an unthreatening shell of a character almost wholly incapable of doing anything interesting or subversive.

It's not surprising, then, that the next writer tapped was the profoundly unheralded Eric Luke. Luke isn't a bad writer – it's just that his brief twenty-issue run of *Wonder Woman* (the shortest of any of the regular writers on Wonder Woman's second series) had little influence and were the high point of his career, making it easy to treat them as a footnote in Wonder Woman's history. This is somewhat unfortunate. He quickly did away with Byrne's worst excesses, and had several clever ideas of his own, most notably the Wonderdome, an expansion of the famed invisible plane into a giant floating home for Wonder Woman from which she metes out justice.

In this regard the comic is more in tune with the zeitgeist than it gets credit for. The debut of the Wonderdome resembles one of the most acclaimed comic series of 1999, *The Authority*, by Warren Ellis and Bryan Hitch. *The Authority* is about a team of superheroes, unsubtly based on the Justice League, who are openly proactive about saving and reforming the world. However, the Authority is deeply (and deliberately) problematic; for all their good intentions, their overall impact isn't actually a good thing. Bolstered by Ellis's gift for science-fiction storytelling of the "five minutes in the future" variety, *The Authority* was a delightfully provocative comic.

Given the acclaim *The Authority* got, Luke deserves credit for getting many of the ideas first with *Wonder Woman* #142, in which Wonder Woman intervenes directly in a conflict in the Middle East. (The countries involved are deliberately left vague, but it's still a decidedly real-world conflict.) The degree to which Wonder Woman represents outside intervention in the conflict is heavily stressed, with her arrival described as a moment where "thunder breaks open the sky." Unable to stop the fighting on the front lines, she kidnaps the leaders of the two unnamed countries and attempts to force a negotiation of peace. Instead they fight, so Wonder Woman binds them with her lasso, at which point the mutual understanding of "the terrible details of their sordid little lives" causes them to reconcile. Wonder Woman declares victory and withdraws to the Wonderdome, where she drinks a glass of wine and watches the news – and sees an extremist suicide bomber kill both leaders, sending the countries back into war. It's a stirringly bleak comic.

There are, of course, problems. The use of two nameless Middle Eastern states falls into a deeply unfortunate pattern of American genre fiction that treats the Middle East uncritically as a land of uncontrollable violence and barbarous extremism. The entire intervention and its consequences are predicated on the idea that "those people" can never stop fighting, making the story less about the problem of superheroes imposing their will on the world and more about an Islamophobic belief that the Middle East will always be at war.

At the end of Luke's run, he revisits the Middle Eastern conflict and Wonder Woman's attempt to stop it directly, but this time the Wonderdome is truly a part of the story, transforming itself into a series of embassies across the planet that will facilitate honest communication between leaders. On the one hand this closely resembles her failed strategy from *Wonder Woman* #142, but there's a crucial difference: the embassies are explicitly part of the world, integrated into its cityscapes; Wonder Woman doesn't just deliver moral authority from on high. It isn't perfect, but it's the best image the comic has seen since Deodato's arrival.

Luke was followed by Phil Jimenez, who oversaw the most nostalgic run of Wonder Woman to date. An unabashed fan of the character, Jimenez described working on *Wonder Woman* as his dream job. Virtually every major period of Wonder Woman's history is paid homage at least once in his twenty-four issues. This broad embrace of Wonder Woman's history, somewhat ironically, comes at the expense of a clear vision of the character. This isn't necessarily a bad thing – not every run on a comic book needs to have an overall philosophical take on its main characters, and Jimenez's run is at least as good as Luke's, with considerably more focus on character development. But it does pose a problem in talking about the Jimenez era in the general case.

That's not to say that generalizations can't be made about Jimenez's time. Perhaps the biggest and most obvious one to make is that Jimenez owes a tremendous debt to George Pérez. Jimenez employs a very similar drawing style as Pérez: both love pages comprised of smaller panels and large casts; both draw similar facial structures and use similar poses for their characters. Jimenez's style is a bit rougher – he imports several of the less excessive techniques of the Image style, most notably the use of cross-hatching to add moodier, deeper shadows to the work. But for the most part he straightforwardly updates Pérez's 80s style for the late 90s and beyond.

But Jimenez's debt to Pérez extends beyond the art. He focuses on similar parts of Wonder Woman's history, bringing the Greek gods back into a similar role as they played in the Pérez era, and recasting Wonder Woman as an ambassador and not just a superhero. Although he displays considerable nostalgia for the entirety of Wonder Woman's history, it is consistently the Pérez era that he returns to the most. Indeed, Pérez even returned to co-write a two-issue arc featuring a civil war on Paradise Island.

Jimenez's overt fondness for the Pérez era extends into making implicit critiques of past eras, most particularly the decision over the Byrne and Luke eras (though to a meaningful extent in the Messner-Loebs era as well) of marginalizing Pérez's supporting cast. Jimenez wrote a cutting storyline in which Vanessa Kapatelis, who had been completely absent from the book for years besides a one-off issue in the Byrne era (that was itself an almost complete recycling of a Messner-Loebs story), is revealed as the latest iteration of the Silver Swan, a villain introduced by Roy Thomas and Gene Colan back in 1982. Vanessa's motivation for becoming the Silver Swan stems from her resentment over being abandoned when Wonder Woman left Boston. In other words, Jimenez has Vanessa Kapatelis go bad because she got harshly and needlessly written out of the book and replaced with another character. It's one of the sharpest swipes at a comic writer by another in the history of the series.

This is not the only aspect of Jimenez's nostalgia that's critical of the past. Jimenez cleans up one of Byrne's more unfortunate decisions, namely when he made Hippolyta the Golden Age Wonder Woman, which relegated Diana to a lesser echo of the "real" character (i.e. the original vision). Because Hippolyta is also a queen with dominion over Diana, the situation unambiguously weakened Diana's position in the comics.

But through a combination of external fortune and his own good ideas, Jimenez became the rare writer whose work on a character was helped by a company-wide crossover, namely the 2001 event *Our Worlds at War*. In Jimenez's account, DC Editorial drew up a list of characters to die in the event, and Hippolyta was put on it. Jimenez had no choice in the matter. Although Jimenez was not in favor of it, it's hard to argue seriously that the decision didn't work to his benefit.

It's clear that the Diana/Hippolyta relationship was one Jimenez wanted to address. Prior to Hippolyta's death in *Wonder Woman* #172, Jimenez had been telling a story in which Diana expressed her frustration at Hippolyta's continued insistence on serving as Wonder Woman, viewing it as an abrogation of her duties as Queen of the Amazons – and with the rather cutting observation that Hippolyta's service as Wonder Woman was intended as a punishment for manipulating events so that Artemis would die in Diana's place. Hippolyta was being positioned not as a superior Wonder Woman, but one whose time was past, who refused to yield to the future. Regardless of Jimenez's intentions, her death furthered that.

The marginalization and death of Hippolyta frees Jimenez up to play with the larger galaxy of Wonder Woman material, and he litters his run with bits from a variety of eras. Perhaps the most obvious example of this is his revival of Diana's method of changing into her costume by twirling around, which comes from the Lynda Carter series. This provides an interesting but essential insight into the nature of Jimenez's nostalgia, which is more for images than specific storytelling ideas. Given that he's an artist first, it would be churlish to make this a complaint about superficiality.

Jimenez's other major innovation is Trevor Barnes, Wonder Woman's new love interest. Wonder Woman has had love interests before, but since Pérez's relaunch she's been almost entirely asexual. This was never something she was supposed to be. Barnes, thankfully, is a compelling character. He isn't cowed by Wonder Woman, and has no interest in exerting any sort of dominance over her. He's exactly what a romantic partner for Wonder Woman should be.

Unfortunately, the move was tremendously unpopular. Jimenez's frequent suggestion that Wonder Woman was going to lose her virginity to Barnes never panned out, with

Barnes killed off in the six-issue Simonson fill-in arc immediately after Jimenez's departure. What's truly upsetting, however, is the seeming reason for Barnes's unpopularity: he was black. None of Wonder Woman's white love interests ever attracted the level of vituperation that Barnes did, and Jimenez has bluntly accused comics fandom of racism on this point. If it weren't for the sorry state of comics fans regarding Barnes, Jimenez's goal of adding another dimension to Wonder Woman's character would have better allowed her to embody human experience while doing it in a strongly feminist way.

In this spirit, it's worth taking a particular look at *Wonder Woman* #170, one of the most acclaimed issues of Jimenez's run (and, along with the death of Hippolyta in issue #172, his favorite of his tenure). Lois Lane shadows Wonder Woman for a "Day in the Life" feature, a basic setup with a lot to like – Lane is portrayed as a hyper-competent journalist, and her narration, in the form of notes for her article, is sharp and insightful. Jimenez has the good sense to let her cross lines that the series is, under normal circumstances, unwilling to cross. Lane expresses frustration at Wonder Woman, both on the personal level of being mildly jealous of her relationship with Superman, and on the broader level of her excessive earnestness. This makes Lane an extremely compelling character, and anchors *Wonder Woman* #170 with two supremely strong female leads.

Also impressive is the scope of the comic, which is part of the point, showing the breadth of things Wonder Woman deals with in a day: being domestic with Etta Candy and Steve Trevor; addressing the UN; tending to a Rwandan refugee camp; teaching self defense to Indonesian prostitutes; playing basketball with inner-city Atlanta youth; eating at a greasy spoon; doing a television interview; taking a shift on the Justice League watchtower, and so on. It's a whirlwind tour of the various contexts in which Wonder Woman makes sense as a character, and compellingly shows the strength of the concept.

But perhaps the most interesting thing about *Wonder Woman* #170 is the final scene, in which Wonder Woman and Lois Lane shoot pool at a seedy pool hall and discuss the day. Seeking to wrap up her interview, Lois asks Wonder Woman how it is that she "owns her contradictions" – a question that begs to be read in the context of the aforementioned whirlwind of diverse perspectives on and settings for the character. Wonder Woman's answer is that the lasso of truth keeps her from lying, including self-deception. Lois Lane's final comment sums up the focus of her story: "Wonder Woman is a mirror... a mirror of human truth. She reflects the contradictions of the world – of the person staring at her – takes them onto herself... and gives you truth, love, respect in turn." However much his run and this entire period lacks focus, this is, in many ways, one of the greatest single-line descriptions of the character in her history.

Chapter 19: Greg Rucka (2002-05)

Greg Rucka's *Wonder Woman* run was an oddly delayed thing. Jimenez's tenure had originally been announced as a one-year fill-in before Rucka took over. Instead it stretched to two years, followed by a six-issue run under Walter Simonson. When Rucka came on in 2003 it was after two-and-a-half years of anticipation.

In the midst of this delay Rucka produced a single ninety-page hardcover graphic novel with art by J.G. Jones entitled *Wonder Woman: The Hiketeia*. It centers on an ancient Greek ritual called Hiketeia, in which someone begs for the protection of another by pledging complete and utter supplication to that person. As Rucka puts it, "To grant Hiketeia is to accept complete responsibility for the supplicant. Through debasement in ritual – the prostration on the ground, the bowing of the head, in all of these things the supplicant denies his own worth and honor in the face of your own. There is but a single power that remains. Only he can end the obligation. He must leave of his own accord."

Although "hiketeia" was a social and religious institution of ancient Greece, the way Rucka plays with the concept comes straight out of the contemporary BDSM scene. This is not a remotely strained interpretation. The bondage themes of Wonder Woman are so well known as to be infamous, and Rucka has dealt explicitly with the BDSM community in two other works: a 2002 miniseries starring Marvel's Black

Widow, and his 1997 novel *Finder*. There is no plausible way to suggest that Rucka did not know exactly what he was doing when he reintroduced the theme of supplication to Wonder Woman in 2002.

Equally, however, this is not the same conception of bondage that existed in 1941 when Marston created the character. Certainly bondage existed in 1941, and documentation of internal controversies over Wonder Woman at DC Comics shows they were well aware of it. But by 2002 an active and quasi-open BDSM community had come into being. (BDSM is a combination of the acronyms BD, for bondage and discipline; DS, for domination and submission; and SM, for sadism and masochism.)

This shift towards a community-based vision of BDSM meant that instead of just being a sexual fetish, it'd become a social structure with relatively clear-cut norms. Protocols within the community codify appropriate interactions between submissives and dominants. Broadly normalized symbols of submission exist, most obviously the wearing of a collar. This is significant. Wearing a largely symbolic artifact is a ritualized way of demonstrating submission, and is very much akin to what Rucka describes with "the prostration on the ground, the bowing of the head" (also adopted by the BDSM community).

Similarly, to say that only the supplicant can end the obligation mirrors another aspect of the social norms of BDSM in which the submissive has what is called a "safe word" – a word they can say to immediately halt a sexual scene, should things go too far. (It's worth remarking upon the significance of the word "scene" within the community to describe a given piece of "play" – itself a revealing word. Both further highlight the ritualized aspects of sex within the BDSM community.) This is both an absolute power – ignoring someone's safe word is considered one of the most appalling and unacceptable things that can be done in a scene – and the only substantive power the submissive has. Again, the parallels to Rucka's description of the Hiketeia are clear.

By centering a story on this vow of supplication and protection, Rucka goes back to the iconography of the 1940s while approaching the concepts as they exist in 2002. In some ways it's astonishing that no one has done this before, but the sexual politics of the early Wonder Woman comics are, as this book has repeatedly observed, something DC is monumentally uncomfortable with and prone to frantically erasing. But by 2002, at long last, the circumstances were right. Comics for mature audiences were taken more seriously, thanks to the work of former Wonder Woman editor Karen Berger in creating the Vertigo imprint at DC, along with scattered other developments. Most of the brightest lights in mainstream comics were coming from that direction. The main superhero industry had been nearly wiped out in the speculation bust of the late 1990s, and only those books that found new homes outside the sputtering market of superhero fans made any impact.

One such market was female fans. Somewhat ironically, Wonder Woman is not a great place to explore contemporary female superhero fandom. To look at that you'd want to look at Batman fandom in the early 21st century, which was a hotbed of feminist and queer approaches supported by some truly innovative and boundary-pushing comics. One of the major writers of Batman in this period was Greg Rucka, who quickly made strong, female characters one of the defining traits of his comic book work. Putting him on *Wonder Woman* was a no-brainer.

This dynamic gave Rucka an unusual level of freedom with the character, particularly in a prestige book like *The Hiketeia*. For the first time since DC needed the prestige and reputability of William Moulton Marston more than he needed them, Wonder Woman had a writer who could get away with touching the third rail of the character and who was actually interested in doing so. While I would never suggest that it's a good thing this aspect of the character has been shoved under the rug for over a half-century at this point, the very fact that these themes haven't had much of a chance to evolve only heightens the power of Rucka's work.

The Hiketeia basks in this power. It's structured as a classical tragedy, upon which Wonder Woman's narration unequivocally reflects: "Greek tragedy is always a story of the insoluble. The conflict of personal desire versus the demands of society." The demands of society, in this case, are represented by the Hiketeia itself, and thus tied inexorably to the ideas of submission. This too is made explicit through narration: "We are slaves to laws."

Danielle Wellys is the young girl who pledges Hiketeia to Wonder Woman in order to gain her protection. The reason Wellys requires protection is simple enough – she's hunted down and murdered four people, and now Batman is after her. But what's significant is why she killed these four people: they got her sister Melody addicted to drugs, used her to shoot pornography, and left her to die of an overdose. This section is six pages long, a non-trivial portion of a ninety-page graphic novel. It's two pages longer, in fact, than the narration about law and ritual that introduces the idea of Hiketeia.

Such length indicates that it's a major part of the story, and yet it features characters who died before the book starts – save for one, Wellys's final victim, who dies in the course of a three-page sequence early on after a grand total of four words of dialogue. Instead, its importance is thematic. It's stressed again and again how Wellys's sister was controlled, used, and objectified by the people Wellys has murdered. The narration is cutting: "Time for another humiliation. Time for another control. They shame you. They take your worth. They steal your soul... You're an appliance now. You're a television. And there's nothing left. And when you die, cops make jokes... because you're just another junkie whore." This sets up another form of sexualized control to contrast with the notions of submission and control implicit in the Hiketeia.

Not only does the story of Melody Wellys demonstrate the way in which what happened to her is, if not overtly legal, at least something that exists within the scope of laws and society – equally, it's important in the way it motivates Danielle Wellys. Her anger at her sister's degradation is palpable, and Wonder Woman implies she'd likely respond the same way Danielle does if it were Cassie or Donna on the receiving end.

Batman, within this context, becomes an interesting figure. It's impossible to separate Rucka's writing of Batman here from the extended run he'd already done on the character. While there's not much depth to Batman as he's portrayed in *The Hiketeia*, a fair bit of context is imported from Rucka's previous work. First of all, Rucka's Batman is never, under any circumstances, going to abandon his pursuit of Danielle Wellys. Second, however, and more significant, is that Rucka's Batman is always driven by his own personal obsessions and demons. In other words, even though Batman is on the side of law and order, the nature of what he does falls firmly on the personal desire side of the ledger, not the demands-of-society one. So both he and Danielle Wellys are similar characters – driven by righteous obsessions. The difference is that Wellys kills people and Batman doesn't.

It falls to Wonder Woman in this story to represent the demands of society. Her personal desire is almost entirely elided – the only exception is where she weighs in to empathize with Wellys's anger. Her focus is on the duties of her job as ambassador, and the duties imposed by Hiketeia. And yet Wonder Woman is clearly the most powerful character in the story, with both Danielle and, later on, Batman pledging Hiketeia to her. Batman's motives in this are altogether strategic, but the scene is nevertheless stunning, with Batman on the ground, head underneath Wonder Woman's boot, and then kneeling before her as he pledges his submission.

So Wonder Woman is positioned as the adjudicator of how social demands ought to govern the competing personal

Figure 10: J.G. Jones's cover to *Wonder Woman: The Hiketeia* (2002), copyright DC Comics, used under the principle of fair use.

obsessions of Batman and Wellys. Of course *The Hiketeia* is, as previously mentioned, a tragedy, and so unsurprisingly her adjudication goes poorly. Wellys kills herself to avoid capture by Batman (which would in turn force Batman and Wonder Woman into an unceasing conflict over her) and in the process releases Wonder Woman from her oath.

This is not a criticism of Wonder Woman. Classically, tragedies are stories about great men (always a man, of course) brought down. Typically this downfall is described in terms of a tragic flaw, but it's more accurate, especially in modern tragedy, to say that the fall is due to the hero's virtues being the wrong virtues for the situation. Regardless, the structure of a tragedy means that it's not a critique of the tragic hero. The fact that Wonder Woman fails in this story doesn't mean that Rucka is siding against the character.

The crux of this tragedy comes in the two competing forms of sexuality that exist within the story's construct of society. Diana is the ambassador to a world in which notions of sex and power work like they did for Melody Wellys, but Diana herself embodies the notion of sex and power implicit in the Hiketeia, and, in turn, implicit in Marston's original comics. The reason she can't break through and find some way of mediating the impasse between the personal desires of Danielle and Batman is, ultimately, that the relationship between women and power that Wonder Woman embodies isn't one that's prevalent in the world.

In this regard, *The Hiketeia* is an elegy for the world Marston envisioned. It's a tragedy about the fact that Wonder Woman's strength isn't the mainstream image of female sexuality – that the idea of submission to her and to her agenda isn't considered the feminine ideal. *The Hiketeia* takes up Marston's ideas some sixty years after their debut and is horrified to find how many ways in which they've failed. Its central tragedy is that Marston's utopia never arrived.

Having offered this scathing diagnosis, Rucka moved on to his run proper, in which he attempts to articulate his own compelling vision for the character. The standard description

A Golden Thread: An Unofficial Critical History of Wonder Woman

as it started was that it was going to be Wonder Woman meets *The West Wing*, at the time an acclaimed television show by Aaron Sorkin about a fictitious Presidency. As with most descriptions that amount only to a list of superficial similarities, this description misses a lot. Greg Rucka is comfortable writing procedurals, and so his run on *Wonder Woman* takes on many aspects of a Themysciran Embassy procedural, but in this regard he draws more on his history writing detective stories than he draws on *The West Wing*.

The difference, however, is that *The West Wing*, as reverential as it is towards its fictitious President, remains fundamentally about the ensemble of public servants who work in the White House, all figures of intense nobility and virtue. In Rucka's *Wonder Woman* none of the Embassy staff, good and noble characters as they are, come anywhere close to being main characters or contenders for the moral center of the story. That role is unequivocally and unambiguously reserved for Wonder Woman herself.

This is made clear from Rucka's first issue, *Wonder Woman* #195, which parallels the story of Jonah McCarthy working his first day at the Themysciran Embassy (thus giving a convenient reason to actively introduce the entire cast) with a story of Wonder Woman arresting an African dictator on behalf of the UN. This latter story, however, is told with very little focus on Wonder Woman herself – instead we see the reactions of the people given the unfortunate job of trying to stop her.

The result is that our initial perspective of Wonder Woman is very much an outsider's – she doesn't fully appear until the penultimate page of the comic. Instead we get the embassy staff describing their relationship with Diana, Jonah reacting to his new circumstances, and people with fighter jets and guns being thrashed by an unseen force. Wonder Woman is thus presented at a distance from the viewer. Furthermore, the dialogue stresses the ways in which Wonder Woman is a figure of awe. One of the issues the embassy workers face is a lawsuit (filed by a criminal who Wonder

Woman captured) that claims, "Diana by her nature compels a self-incriminatory answer from whoever she questions." Wonder Woman is so striking and imposing that just by her presence alone she forces people to obey her.

Clearly, Rucka draws on Marston's conception of the character, but the issues familiar from *The Hiketeia* show up once again. Rucka writes for a world where Marston's vision of female supremacy failed – one where the strong woman whose very nature compels men to submit to her not only isn't the mainstream conception of feminine beauty, it's not even remotely acceptable. From his first issue we can see how he proposes to tackle this – by portraying Wonder Woman as someone who is, in fact, the Marstonian ideal and who does, in fact, inspire exactly the reaction Marston believed would occur.

The other thing to observe about Rucka's first issue is how it reworks Eric Luke's *Wonder Woman* #142 – the issue where Wonder Woman intervenes in a Middle Eastern conflict. Both Luke and Rucka deal with the issue of superheroes and real-world problems, and specifically with Wonder Woman involving herself in political and military conflicts outside of the United States. The shift from the Middle East to Africa is straightforward enough post-9/11. But the real change is the nature of Wonder Woman's intervention. Luke has Wonder Woman act unilaterally, imposing her view on the world via the Wonderdome; Rucka's Wonder Woman acts in tandem with the United Nations.

The difference is substantial. Rucka positions Wonder Woman as someone thoroughly integrated in the existing structures of power within the world. This is paralleled with his use of the Embassy characters – instead of having a sentient shape-changing piece of alien technology as her only ally, he gives her a large human staff (plus one minotaur). Rucka's Wonder Woman, in other words, isn't just a return of Marston's vision, but firmly embeds that vision into the very world that has, in practice, rejected it.

Having established Wonder Woman as a functional Marstonian ideal, Rucka now works through the consequences. What would actually happen if someone who embodied Marston's vision of femininity actually existed in the world? Rucka's answer, unsurprisingly, is that it would be massively controversial.

To this end, Rucka's first storyline concerns a seemingly low-scale occasion where Wonder Woman publishes a book of her philosophical and political views, and quickly finds herself under a public relations attack. Rucka, to his credit, does not attempt some ill-fated push towards an "unbiased" perspective that tries to position Wonder Woman outside of existing political controversies: her book unabashedly endorses progressive politics, and her critics are unambiguously allied with the political right. This is, as we've previously seen, appropriate – Wonder Woman's history is deeply intertwined with progressive causes, such that portraying her as anything other than a political liberal would be difficult to justify.

It's not an easy needle to thread. Rucka sides with his Marstonian protagonist, ideologically speaking, and yet takes a realistic position that acknowledges Marston lost that battle. This requires the adjudication of two contradictory narrative absolutes. The Marstonian Wonder Woman is a character who, by definition, always inspires a sort of loving submission, but fealty to social realism requires a world in which this position has a rough road and continually fails to fully assert itself.

Another way of looking at this is as a resolution to the long-standing conflict between Marston's "strong woman" feminism and the I Ching era's "real women" feminism. As we've already established, much of the supposed conflict between these two models was always based on a misunderstanding. Marston, after all, had no illusions that the world he lived in was one in which women dominated. The sexist status quo was an ever-present issue in his Wonder Woman stories. The only reason Wonder Woman and socially realist feminism ever came into conflict was the idea that superheroes, because of their power, pose a problem of authoritarianism.

In this regard, Rucka returns to Marston's approach of portraying Wonder Woman as a figure of inspiration who cannot meaningfully hope to change the entire world, not because her ideas are flawed, but because the idea of one person single-handedly transforming global culture into a homogenous viewpoint can't be taken seriously in the first place. And so Wonder Woman and her allies, when they're finally able to confront her critics, simply wipe the floor with them. Even her assistant, Peter Garibaldi, is able to run rings around her most trenchant critic in a television interview. When the major villain of Rucka's run, Veronica Cale (about whom more in a moment), plots a large-scale PR blitz against Wonder Woman, Diana stops it in its tracks, in part because one of the people tasked with developing a strategy against her is appalled by the idea and chooses to leak their playbook to the Themysciran Embassy.

For all of this, Rucka is rather muted about the potential impact Wonder Woman can actually have. In the third issue of his run, *Wonder Woman* #197, amidst the brewing backlash against her book, Wonder Woman does a Q&A session at a bookstore during which she's asked no questions about her writings – instead, people want to know about her love life and the invisible plane. In other words, for all her provocative nature it's ultimately the most superficial aspects of her character that people latch onto, and there's not a lot she can do about this. The irony positively drips.

The same issue also features a sequence in which Wonder Woman and the Flash rush to deal with a forest fire. Wonder Woman is insistent on managing the fire – keeping it from reaching people's houses but allowing it to burn through the forest, while the Flash wants to extinguish the entire blaze. What's more important than Wonder Woman's position on forest ecology is the way she frames it. Yes, at this point it's a mainstream belief that destructive fires are a necessary portion of a forest's growth cycle, but Wonder Woman doesn't explain her position in terms of scientific research – instead, it's an absolute position of nature: "Death is necessary, Flash. It is part of life, and if we say life is a blessing, we must say that death is a blessing, as well." This reiterates another aspect of Marston's take on the character, namely that Wonder Woman herself repeatedly submitted to loving authority, but Rucka ties it into Pérez's notion of Gaea. Wonder Woman, for all her strength, is still subject to the existing order of the world. More than that, Wonder Woman's strength derives from being in harmony with this order.

This helps explain how Rucka's major villain for Wonder Woman, Veronica Cale, is meant to function within the narrative. Veronica Cale's high-concept description is simple: she's Wonder Woman's Lex Luthor. These days the standard take on Lex Luthor is that he's jealous of the fact that Superman's power trivializes his own successes. Cale is given essentially the same story, as introduced in *Wonder Woman* #202. She grew up poor, raised by her mother, and her father was both abusive and absent. She's a genius, and after blackmailing money out of her rich father she went to school and became a successful businesswoman. And she hates Wonder Woman because, as she puts it, "I am the American success story… I am rags-to-riches, I am everything the Wonder Woman pretends to be. And the difference is that I earned it."

What's key about this is Cale's fundamental misunderstanding of Wonder Woman. She complains that Wonder Woman sets an unobtainable ideal that people will never manage to emulate, because no one can "be a super-powered super-model, just like her." The giveaway is the suggestion that Wonder Woman's nobility is in some way connected to her physical appearance. In fact, Rucka's Wonder Woman opposes her own over-sexualization: she had her representatives aggressively shoot down a proposed book cover featuring a semi-nude depiction of her. More broadly, the idea that Wonder Woman would even remotely derive strength from an unobtainable body image cuts against all of the progressive feminism around which she's built.

Cale misunderstands the nature of Wonder Woman's strength, for she assumes that the model of female success is capitalist triumph – that success is equivalent to power in the world. The only way she can imagine emulating Wonder Woman is by acquiring a comparable degree of power – which, as she's observed, is impossible. Thus it's hypocritical for Wonder Woman to play the role model, whereas Cale's success can, in theory, be achieved by anybody. In Marston's terminology, Cale mistakes Wonder Woman's power as being equivalent to masculine dominance, when in fact her real strength is her ability to inspire submission, which doesn't come from any notion of potency, but rather, extending from Pérez's work on the character, from a larger sense of harmony with the world.

But the introduction of Veronica Cale does raise an interesting question of its own: what kind of person is like Wonder Woman? Having shown the marginal victories that Wonder Woman can hope to win, most days, and having raised the question of what it means to emulate Wonder Woman, Rucka moves into the second act of his run. Where the first act treated Wonder Woman with some distance, and understanding what she does in the world, the second act is a marked shift towards dealing with Diana's interiority.

This act consists of two major plot arcs, both of which culminate in moments that address this theme. The first concerns an attack by Medusa. This is already a substantive shift from his earlier stories, where the two major villains – Veronica Cale and Doctor Psycho – deal with the theme of Wonder Woman's interactions with the general public, Cale being a mundane source of media manipulation and Doctor Psycho being a more fantastic version of the same concept. But Medusa is a proper supernatural threat, a creature of legend. Rucka does much to play up the horror of the character, slowly building her storyline over several issues so as to create a sense of looming dread. He also lingers extensively on her power, reminding the audience that not only is her threat intensely brutal (she can kill someone instantly) but she also has the particularly disturbing and macabre ability to compel people to look at her.

After building her up, Rucka has Medusa attack the Themysciran Embassy, where she kills one of Peter Garibaldi's sons, and challenges Wonder Woman to a duel to the death. This is a shocking moment – Garibaldi was a major supporting character, and killing the young child of a major character is unusual. Kids are usually safe, so the moment echoes as a particularly egregious failure on Diana's part. It immediately pulls the reader into a position of empathy for Diana as we see her genuine horror and agony at failing to save the boy. After fifteen issues of distance from Wonder Woman, we suddenly see her weeping. It's a jarring, chilling moment – even in *The Hiketeia* Rucka didn't go so far as to have Wonder Woman in tears.

As a result, when Wonder Woman has to face down Medusa in mortal combat in the next issue (*Wonder Woman* #210) the stakes are particularly high. She's at one of the lowest points we've ever seen her, and Medusa has been built into a massive enemy. Rucka makes the very smart choice to pull back the camera and show Wonder Woman from the same detached distance as his first issue. Instead of being inside Diana's head as she fights, we see it through the eyes of people around the world watching it on television. When the fight builds to its climax – Wonder Woman resists Medusa's gaze by blinding herself, then decapitates her foe – the reader is allowed to be awed at Diana's resilience and the lengths to which she'll go in order to do what she has to do. It's a concrete demonstration of the practical implications of her strength: the willingness to do something as extreme as this.

Rucka continues in this vein for several issues, taking time to establish that Diana is still an effective superhero despite her blindness. In a memorable story, the Justice League has to decide whether to keep her as a member, which culminates in a fight where the blind Wonder Woman holds her own against Batman before deflecting a bullet fired by Superman. All told, Rucka spends four issues with the status quo of Wonder Woman's blindness before embarking on a three-issue arc where she descends into the Underworld to rescue Hermes, by the request of Athena.

This is the second major arc in a row in which Wonder Woman confronts a mythological threat instead of a mundane one. Veronica Cale is still present in these issues, but pushed to the background, conspiring with Circe in preparation for a future (never realized) storyline. The threats here are magical ones – and in the three-issue gap between the two arcs she faces a third mythological threat, as well as the Cheetah, one of her more supernatural villains. But this doesn't mark a turn away from any sort of material focus. After starting his run by positioning Wonder Woman as an absolute pillar of feminine strength in an indifferent world, Rucka portrays her against a backdrop of mythological threats so that the material nature of her strength is brought into relief.

It's not a surprise that Wonder Woman triumphs in the Underworld and rescues Hermes, but that's not what's interesting. In exchange for descending into the Underworld, Athena offers Wonder Woman "her heart's desire," which Rucka spends three issues suggesting is her sight. But at the end of the arc, in issue #217, it turns out that her actual wish is the resurrection of Garibaldi's son – she forsakes the opportunity to see again. Athena restores her vision anyway, but once more we see what defines Wonder Woman: a willingness to take extreme action, including drastic self-sacrifice, for the greater good.

This is not a hugely original concept – indeed, there's something aggressively old-fashioned about it. On a basic level, Wonder Woman is a strong and inspirational figure because she does impressive and heroic things. It's not radical. It's what Wonder Woman did from day one. But equally, it had been decades since we last saw this Wonder

Woman – the inspirational figure who represented our best hopes and best instincts. Rucka managed to dust her off and put her smack in the middle of the present day.

But from day two, Wonder Woman found herself frustratingly and infuriatingly subverted by the larger corporate concerns of DC Comics. Having executed an almost flawless re-creation of the original vision of Wonder Woman, Rucka's run ran smack into a re-creation of what came next.

Chapter 20: *Infinite Crisis* (2005-07)

It's not quite fair to say Rucka's time on *Wonder Woman* was derailed by DC's 2005-06 event *Infinite Crisis*. Rucka, after all, was one of the major architects of the buildup to *Infinite Crisis* and one of the main people to work out DC's new direction following the event. Nevertheless, it's difficult to describe the event as anything other than a major disruption of his work. The first and most immediate consequence was that his plot threads were moved to the back burner to accommodate a nine-issue stretch that set up *Infinite Crisis*.

These nine issues aren't bad, but they display an oddly disjointed quality absent from the rest of Rucka's run, mostly because they're interwoven with another book's pace. *Infinite Crisis* was set to start in October of 2005. The six months prior were filled by four concurrent miniseries that set up various aspects of the plot, with a new issue from one of the four series coming out every week. (For our purposes the most important of these is *The OMAC Project,* a conspiracy thriller written by Rucka.) On top of that, in March of 2006, synchronized with the release of *Infinite Crisis* #5, there was a line-wide soft reboot in which every title jumped a year forward in its characters' lives – so every book had to at least partially resolve its plots by February of 2006.

In practical terms, the major effect of this forced anyone writing a tie-in (in this case, Rucka) to pace their stories not according to the needs of the story itself, but to another story entirely. Wonder Woman's major event in the buildup to *Infinite Crisis* had to take place in issue #219 simply because that's the issue that came out between the publication of *The OMAC Project* #3 and #4, which is what *Wonder Woman* was tying into. Similarly, all of Rucka's plots had to be wrapped up by issue #226 simply because that was the February issue. Even though Rucka was writing *The OMAC Project*, the pacing on these final nine issues remains idiosyncratic at best. There are two major plot beats in these nine issues, but *Infinite Crisis* forced one to get far more time than it needed, while the other got short shrift.

The first big event, in *Wonder Woman* #219, comes when Wonder Woman discovers that a man widely considered a hero, Maxwell Lord, has been controlling Superman's mind, using him to attack Batman. Wonder Woman, unable to stop a rampaging Superman, finally determines that the only possible solution is to kill Maxwell Lord, and she snaps his neck. Most discussions of this story focus on its ethical dimensions, which is far from the most interesting angle. Almost no practical ethical system outside of superhero comics holds such an absolutist position as to aver that it's wrong to kill someone to prevent the destruction that would be wrought by what amounts to an evil Superman.

What's most interesting is how the event casts Wonder Woman as a distinctly different character from her two counterparts in DC's "trinity." Both Superman and Batman are appalled at her actions. This makes sense – Batman and Superman are abstracted fantasies about what perfect men would be like. Batman is supposed to represent the smartest and most capable man imaginable, while Superman is the strongest and most powerful. Their stance against killing is part and parcel of that perfection, a position that exists largely to show that Batman is so capable, and Superman so powerful, that neither of them need ever kill.

Wonder Woman, however, is very different. She's still idealistically constructed, but her central fantasy is based on her practical capacity to affect people. Whereas Batman and

Superman can take the unrealistic position of never killing anybody, ever, for any reason, Wonder Woman can't adopt a position that far from human morality without fundamentally undermining who she is as a character. She's always been defined in part by her involvement in material human concerns, so she's the only one of the three characters who can take what would be, in any remotely real-world analogue, an uncontroversial course of action.

Not only is this vision of Wonder Woman wholly consistent with Rucka's tenure on the character, it largely depends on the work he's already done with her. Rucka's return to the Marstonian paradigm of Wonder Woman as a figure of practical inspiration, his rooting her in real, material concerns, and his development of her intense heroism in the face of vast and mythic situations are the exact character traits that make Wonder Woman so well-suited to this role in the story. This speaks to Rucka's care for character development in his tenure on the book – compare it, if nothing else, to Wonder Woman's primarily symbolic role in *Crisis on Infinite Earths*.

Unfortunately, the schedule of *Infinite Crisis* meant that the killing of Maxwell Lord only got a few issues to breathe. Following out of *Wonder Woman* #219, the plot returned to *The OMAC Project*, where quasi-robotic soldiers seek revenge on Wonder Woman for killing Maxwell Lord and, eventually attack Paradise Island as part of the lead-in to *Infinite Crisis* proper. Due to the timing of these larger series, not only was Rucka stuck with three issues of *Wonder Woman* where all that could happen were endless robot attacks, he also had no time afterwards to resolve any of his plot arcs before the One Year Later jump. Wonder Woman ends up bidding a hasty goodbye to her entire Embassy staff (since there's no longer a Themyscira for her to represent as ambassador) and with only more issue to work with, leaving no space for Wonder Woman to actually do anything in the larger narrative, Rucka serves up a bland retrospective of Wonder Woman's relationship with Superman.

The title of his penultimate issue, *Wonder Woman* #225, is quite suggestive: "Nothing Finished, Only Abandoned." While the bulk of the DC line simply jumped forward a year, several titles, including *Wonder Woman*, ended and restarted with a new number one, and as part of the relaunch DC decided to replace Rucka on *Wonder Woman* with Allan Heinberg, a well-regarded television writer. This decision, it should be stressed, had nothing to do with Rucka being done with the book. His title for issue #225 is a none-too-veiled commentary on the fact that he was prematurely removed. His plots remained wholly unresolved – Veronica Cale, for instance, was pushed to the background to make way for *Infinite Crisis* and then left abandoned by future writers (at Rucka's request).

The logic behind rebooting Wonder Woman after the Infinite Crisis wasn't based on what was going on in the books, but wholly on the fact that it was one of the titles to end and restart around *Crisis on Infinite Earths*, which *Infinite Crisis* was overtly modeled on.

In this regard, it follows its predecessor better than intended. Like *Crisis on Infinite Earths*, *Infinite Crisis* pays lip service to the idea that Wonder Woman's on equal footing with Superman (and, this time around, Batman, who was largely absent from the previous Crisis). Like its namesake, *Infinite Crisis* largely short-changes Wonder Woman compared to the other two parts of DC's trinity. After a big showdown conversation with Batman and Superman in the first issue, Wonder Woman disappears to defend Themyscira from OMAC robots for two issues and doesn't even appear in the fourth installment.

It's in the fifth issue that she finally gets something resembling a major scene, as she comes face-to-face with the pre-Crisis Earth-2 version of herself. The Earth-2 Wonder Woman explains that at the end of *Crisis on Infinite Earths* she was spared "for this very moment," and she uses the last of her life to tell the post-Crisis Wonder Woman that she should stop "trying to be so perfect. You've been a princess, a goddess, an ambassador and a warrior. But the one thing you haven't been in a very long time is human." She's then instructed to go help Superman.

As grotesque as this may sound, it's actually a step forward for Wonder Woman in terms of big DC events. The fact that Wonder Woman gets a substantive scene interacting with her pre-Crisis self is a real and material acknowledgment of her importance to the story, and more than she got in *Crisis on Infinite Earths*. But this does not escape the fact that Wonder Woman's major role – a role for which the Earth-2 Wonder Woman was preserved at the end of the original *Crisis* – is to go help Superman. Even at her most triumphant moment in a story about the fundamental nature of the DC Universe, she's good for nothing more than standing by a man.

Let's also take a moment and talk about the absurd suggestion that Wonder Woman's fatal flaw is her failure to be human – a suggestion made worse in interviews when Phil Jimenez, the primary artist for *Infinite Crisis*, suggested the Earth-2 version was somehow more human than the post-Crisis one. Certainly the post-Crisis Wonder Woman is written in part around the idea that she's an outsider in Man's World, but so was the Earth-2 version, who, as designed by Marston (and Marston's version is clearly the one invoked, with Jimenez drawing the panel where she recaps her origins in Harry Peter's style) was always an outsider imposing Amazon values on the world.

But more to the point, it's farcical to claim that Rucka's Wonder Woman, who just before *Infinite Crisis* accepted blindness to restore the life of her friend's child, somehow lacks empathy with humanity. The idea that Wonder Woman needs to be "more human" in the wake of a run that went to great lengths to reground her in the material world borders on the offensive, and suggests a deep-lying failure to understand Rucka's work.

I bring this up because it's illustrative of the relationship between DC Comics, a corporate entity peddling a broad commercial product, and the feminist politics of Wonder Woman. Clearly, DC wasn't consciously hostile to what Rucka was doing on the title – not only is there no evidence they objected to the content of any of his issues, he was tapped to help write their big crossover event. He continued working for the company for several years after his stint on Wonder Woman, and his work remained consistently progressive. Rucka was only taken off the book because DC wanted to do a soft relaunch of the book after *Infinite Crisis,* just as they had following *Crisis on Infinite Earths,* and they wanted to use a "big" writer from television to do it.

Indeed, none of DC's regressive moves with Wonder Woman have seemed like conscious reactions against the leftist politics of the book. Samuel Delaney's storyline wasn't cut off because it was going to deal with abortion, but out of a misguided belief that Gloria Steinem's take on the book was accurate. The Artemis storyline wasn't a reaction against Messner-Loebs's Taco Whiz plot, but because Deodoto's art style was selling books at the time. Even the original regressive turn in Wonder Woman, Robert Kanigher's tenure, was not based on a decision to abandon Marston's goals, but rather because Marston died; nobody tried to fire him prior to that.

Nevertheless, it's clear that in practice DC is hostile to the progressive politics of Wonder Woman. Crucially, however, this hostility is purely incidental. It's not like DC consciously targets Wonder Woman's progressive politics for censorship, nor does it do anything to promote them. This is sadly fitting. Misogyny, after all, rarely comes wrapped in convenient black-hatted villains. (Indeed, this is exactly what Messner-Loebs attempted to parody in the Artemis arc.) For the most part it manifests through the erasure of women's stories from the larger cultural conversation. That DC so often steamrolls interesting developments in Wonder Woman through a conspicuous blindness to their very existence illustrates how this works in the real world.

This explains the general lack of concern DC had with the launch of a third *Wonder Woman* series in 2006. After getting the first two issues out, the title ground to a halt. Allan Heinberg was a busy television writer and he simply couldn't keep up with the scripts. Issue #3 was delayed by four months, issue #5 by three, and Heinberg's story still hadn't wrapped by then. By the time it was finished, in the *Wonder Woman* annual for November 2007, Heinberg had written only five issues over the course of fifteen months.

Needless to say, these delays did little to help the book. Heinberg's reinvention of the character had no momentum and sales wilted rapidly. Worse, with the conclusion of his story pushed so far back, his take on Wonder Woman ended up having next to no impact. (Indeed, in one regard it's nearly impossible to square the end of Heinberg's plot with the storyline that came next, as we'll see shortly.) On top of that, it just wasn't that big of a reboot. Heinberg teased the possibility that maybe Donna Troy would permanently replace Diana as Wonder Woman, but ultimately it was Diana who kept the mantle. The resulting new series had little reason to exist – there were no major changes to the premise.

However, this is not to say that it was bad. On the contrary, there's much to enjoy about Heinberg's short stint. Terry and Rachel Dodsons' art is delightful – their style combines a cheesecake aesthetic with a slightly cartoony look that lends Wonder Woman some eroticism without turning her into a sex object. Their work isn't devoid of brokeback poses and bizarre moments of oversexualizing female characters, but there's a playful innocence that takes the edge off of the worst of it, while retaining a nostalgic fondness for the sexuality of vintage Wonder Woman.

Heinberg's story is itself a mixed bag, long on spectacle and short on content. In addition to introducing a new status quo for Wonder Woman and teasing the possibility of Donna Troy as a replacement, the story slightly revamps the rogue's

A Golden Thread: An Unofficial Critical History of Wonder Woman

Figure 11: Terry and Rachel Dodson's cheesecake yet cartoony art style on the cover of *Wonder Woman* #3 (2006), copyright DC Comics, used under the principle of fair use.

gallery, plays out an argument between Wonder Woman and Wonder Girl, tries to deal with the fallout from killing Max Lord, and crams in a huge number of guest stars to boot. It's a bit much for five issues, and no aspect of the story really gets enough weight to make a significant impact, with the most spectacular ones getting the lion's share of attention – Heinberg gives the Dodsons plenty of splash pages to draw iconic shots of big villains. Their debut issue, for instance, has seven splash pages out of twenty-two in total. The result is a comic that looks pretty and is full of big moments, but lacks the space to deal with anything other than people punching each other.

On the other hand, Heinberg is a skilled television writer with plenty of experience in prime time soap operas that juggle large numbers of plots in a single story. None of the plot threads have room to breathe, but Heinberg is good enough to keep them all feeling like they're part of the same story. The problem is that the glue holding them together is somewhat superficial. Heinberg's arc is called "Who is Wonder Woman?" (nodding to a pair of famous storylines entitled "Who is Donna Troy?" and "Who is Wonder Girl?"), and this points to its major theme – Wonder Woman trying to figure out who she is. A cynical critic might point out that if Wonder Woman doesn't even know who she is then it's a bit hard to expect a readership to care.

But there's a larger issue here. Wonder Woman's uncertainty regarding her own self-identity does indeed suture together the new rogue's gallery (thus giving us a way to define Wonder Woman in contrast), her extended family (allowing definition by analogy), the guest stars (to define the character in comparison with the rest of the DC Universe), and the Max Lord plot (which is not only the highest profile Wonder Woman story in several years, it's what this revamp is explicitly defined in opposition to). Unfortunately, this means that the story is defined more by her lack of identity than by any actual answer. When the entire story is focused by design on the question of who Wonder Woman is, then by

A Golden Thread: An Unofficial Critical History of Wonder Woman

necessity the most immediate answer is, "Someone who has a bit of a hazy definition."

The resolution comes with Wonder Woman and Circe having a heart-to-heart about how they both want to be human. Wonder Woman mopes, "I'm not even a real person. I'm a golem. A clay statue brought to life. I have no idea who or what I am. All I know is I'm alone." Circe points out that her friends are all fighting for her outside and that she's not alone. It is, frankly, difficult to take even remotely seriously.

Although the focus on making Wonder Woman human follows from *Infinite Crisis*, it also provides an opportunity for Heinberg to do something unusual. *Wonder Woman*, like any superhero comic, has been quite nostalgic for years. But this nostalgia has been limited in key ways – only a few specific parts of the Marston era can allowably be referenced directly, for instance, and almost no overt references to the I Ching era have appeared since it ended. So it's quite a surprise when Heinberg ends his first issue with a splash page of Wonder Woman, her first appearance all issue, dressed in the white catsuit associated with the I Ching era and identified as Diana Prince. On top of that, she's depowered at this point in time and there's a passing reference to her training with I Ching, who appears briefly on a computer screen.

What is interesting about this is that the I Ching era was all but officially abandoned and denounced by DC, with Gloria Steinem's criticism allowed to stand unchallenged. This poses some interesting problems. As off-base as Gloria Steinem's criticism actually was, the fact that DC caved to it so decisively means that her version of events is far better known than the actual content of the comics, so returning to the iconography of the I Ching era isn't completely straightforward. Having previously accepted Steinem's criticism of the book, there's a degree to which a return to the I Ching iconography feels a bit like an anti-feminist backlash.

On the other hand, there's something to be said for returning to the unfinished business of the I Ching era. Its central idea is still relevant and sensible: connecting Wonder

Woman to the material world. More importantly, while the iconography of the I Ching era finally makes a return, in the long term the concept doesn't – Wonder Woman is briefly depowered, but at the end of Heinberg's story she's her usual superpowered self, albeit with the tiny wrinkle (essentially ignored after Heinberg establishes it) that she only has superpowers when dressed as Wonder Woman, and not in her human identity. Ultimately, it's merely the iconography that's reappropriated, not the actual controversial concept. Still, it's hard to read the intent as anything other than a long overdue reappraisal of the era. (It's telling that just a few months after Heinberg's storyline ended, DC finally reprinted the I Ching era as a series of trade paperbacks, further reflecting a willingness to claim the era without shame.)

Still, even if the intentions of the move were sound, there's no getting around the superficiality at the root of the story. For all the focus on Wonder Woman being human now, and the restoration of her "Diana Prince" secret identity, there's not a lot to do with the idea. In the I Ching era itself Diana worked an intelligible job that fit in smoothly with the world of her readers: she owned a clothing boutique. Even if most of her readers were too young and probably not upper-middle class enough to own a small business in New York, this sort of job at least makes sense. But Heinberg's Diana Prince is a secret agent for the Department of Metahuman Affairs, and her partner is a shapeshifter named Nemesis. This is, to say the least, not a version of "being a human being" that exists outside of comic books, and it undermines the supposed point of the exercise considerably.

Still, for all its flaws, Heinberg's arc provides a usable foundation for the character, paling only if one insists on comparing it to Greg Rucka's run. It's difficult not to do that, as one replaced the other, but spared of the comparison we can at least admit that it works fairly well. However, given the delays in publication, the "Who is Wonder Woman?" arc never got the chance to be the foundation. Instead, after a fill-in issue by Will Pfeifer, the comic plowed into one of the worst storylines in the history of the character: the *Amazons Attack!* crossover.

To give an idea of how disastrous it was, let's start by noting that the actual *Amazons Attack!* series was outsold by Wonder Woman. In fact, every tie-in (the series crossed over into *Supergirl*, *Teen Titans*, and *Catwoman*) to *Amazons Attack!* save for three issues of *Catwoman* outsold the actual series, and *Catwoman* was less than a year away from cancellation at the time, so its low sales are hardly surprising. This is staggering. In the normal order of things a crossover event is a company's best-selling book, and it gooses the sales of what it ties into. *Amazons Attack!* was admittedly a small-scale event, but for it to fall below *Wonder Woman* itself in sales meant that the event was so uninspiring that the people reading *Wonder Woman* didn't go to read a Wonder Woman-centered miniseries that *Wonder Woman* tied into for over six months.

That the storyline was uninspiring is not a huge surprise. Coming off the languorous scheduling Heinberg's run, *Amazons Attack!* seemed abrupt, getting only two issues of setup in *Wonder Woman*. Its concept is a complete U-turn. Hippolyta and the Amazons return out of the blue, in a form quite unlike anything we've seen before: they suddenly and aggressively attack the United States. The setup casts the goddess Circe as the villain who manipulates the Amazons to launch their attack, which is simply bizarre in contrast to the conclusion of Heinberg's arc, where Circe and Wonder Woman have their heart-to-heart. It's understandable – Will Pfeifer, who wrote *Amazons Attack!*, didn't have the end of that story. Such fallout from Heinberg's tardiness exacerbated the problems of the relaunch, and made it increasingly difficult to articulate what it was about in the first place.

This, however, is nothing compared to the bizarre problem of making the Amazons psychotic killers who casually slaughter millions of Americans on minimal pretext. Pfeifer tries to blunt this, having some of the Amazons question Hippolyta's methods and eventually revealing they were being externally manipulated, but when those are stacked against the Amazons literally setting fire to the entire state of Kansas there's not much room to negotiate. To claim the Amazons are sympathetic is a stretch when they've knocked down the Washington Monument and commented on the castration metaphor of this act.

In essence, *Amazons Attack!* is based on the most appalling and base paranoias of feminism as anti-male and anti-American, recasting the Amazons from an inspirational culture to a caricatured nightmare. It rips away a huge part of Wonder Woman's central concept, and when paired with Heinberg's "becoming more human" angle, this new version of Wonder Woman becomes a complete renunciation of Marston's original vision. The Amazon culture she hails from is shown to be depraved and evil, and her heroism comes entirely from forsaking her role as an inspirational feminist figure and embracing patriarchal culture wholesale.

Amazons Attack! further undermines Wonder Woman by having the Greek gods be casually defeated thanks to an impersonation by Granny Goodness, a minor figure from Jack Kirby's Fourth World mythology. To have her completely defeat the Greek pantheon single-handedly marginalizes them even more than John Byrne's efforts to make the Fourth World mythology the defining cosmology of the DC Universe. It further erases Wonder Woman's distinct characterization, turning her into as generic a figure as possible. And it's difficult to read this as anything other than the point of the exercise, given that bringing the Amazons back after their departure from the world at the end of

Rucka's run just to make them irredeemably evil before destroying them again only serves as a moral repudiation of the Amazons. On top of that, the story ends with a banal if well-intentioned speech by Athena about how everyone has failed in the course of this conflict, how war is folly, and how politicians infringed on civil rights. But only a few pages later it turns out that Athena is really Granny Goodness, which casts suspicion on the entire speech, rendering the larger morality virtually incoherent.

Not only is *Amazons Attack!* morally bankrupt and functionally incoherent, it marks a startling lack of basic common sense. While *Amazons Attack!* was running, Jodi Picoult was writing a five-issue arc for *Wonder Woman*. As Picoult is an enormously popular and best-selling author with a known fondness for comic books, this was, broadly speaking, a brilliant move. Her audience dwarfs *Wonder Woman's*, and is largely female, unlike the main superhero demographic. But instead of using this opportunity to try to bring in new readers, DC squandered Picoult on tie-ins to a terrible crossover event. Picoult's work is actually quite good, and she does some very interesting stuff with the Wonder Woman/Hippolyta relationship, but for a potential new reader it's a disaster. Because her storyline is so intertwined with leading up to and then tying into *Amazons Attack!*, DC didn't even get something that could easily be sold as a trade paperback. It's a bewildering waste of an opportunity, vying with the sacking of Samuel Delaney in sheer stupidity.

The post-*Infinite Crisis* relaunch of *Wonder Woman* ended up with almost the exact opposite effect of the post-*Crisis on Infinite Earths* one. Where Pérez's relaunch brought needed coherence to the character and built a strong foundation that could still be used twenty years later, the Heinberg/*Amazons Attack!* relaunch left an incoherent mess drained of almost everything that made the character interesting to begin with. In less than two years the character was taken from one of the best positions she'd ever been in to one of the worst. Even by the standards of DC's penchant for shooting themselves in the foot with Wonder Woman, this era is impressive.

Chapter 21: Gail Simone (2008-10)

Gail Simone's arrival on *Wonder Woman* was, for unsurprising reasons, a big deal. As she herself has pointed out, it's not as though she was the first female writer on *Wonder Woman,* nor the first ongoing one – in the 1980s, Mindy Newell was signed on for just that (before the events surrounding *Crisis on Infinite Earths* and her clashes with the editor put a swift end to it) and in practice she was an ongoing co-writer with George Pérez post-*Crisis*. And, of course, the uncredited contributions of Olive Byrne and Elizabeth Holloway Marston in the early days of the character can't be ignored, even though it's hard to pin down the specific details of their work.

Nevertheless, Simone's entrance marked the first time a woman took over the book and had a prolonged period of being the sole credited writer. As such, she received a tremendous amount of good will – a lot of people understandably wanted her to succeed. The fact that there'd been no long-term female writer on *Wonder Woman* for nearly seventy years after her creation was by any measure appalling. Gail Simone, by far the most successful female writer in superhero comics at the time, was the obvious choice.

If anything, in fact, she was too obvious a choice – a fact Simone reflected on in interviews, admitting that for a while she avoided taking on *Wonder Woman* out of a fear that it would result in getting her pigeon-holed as a writer of female books. (This isn't entirely unreasonable – comics writer Christopher Priest essentially departed the industry in protest over the degree to which he could, as he put it, write any superhero he wanted as long as they're black.) So it wasn't until she decided that she was ready to depart *Birds of Prey*, a book that featured an all-female team headlined by Black Canary and Barbara Gordon as the disabled Oracle, that she was willing to take on another female-led book.

The degree to which Simone ran the risk of becoming stereotyped as a "girl books" writer stems in part from the fact that she'd already established herself as an outspoken feminist critic of the comics. Simone entered the industry on the basis of her fan criticism, starting with her website *Women in Refrigerators*, which catalogued the myriad ways in which mostly male superhero writers mistreated and marginalized their female characters. Simone parlayed that into a regular column for the website *Comic Book Resources*, which led to a gig writing comics for Bongo Comics based on *The Simpsons* and, in turn, to wider success outside the humor market. But her early work as an outspoken critic of misogyny in superhero comics remained powerful, and the growing presence of feminist critiques within fandom quickly came to see Gail Simone as one of their own who'd broken into the mainstream.

So her *Wonder Woman* run was, for a certain section of fans, tremendously exciting. From a wider perspective the impact was a bit more muted – sales jumped a healthy nine percent when she came onto the book, but given the shambolic state of affairs left in the wake of *Amazons Attack!* it would have been astonishing had they not. More troubling is that her second issue immediately shed nearly twice as many readers as her first had gained. By the end of her run, *Wonder Woman* languished at less than half the sales from when she'd started, and her final issue was only the fourth best-selling female-fronted book DC was putting out. (To be fair, two of those were first issues of new comics, and *Wonder*

Woman's sales were broadly in line the more successful of DC's female-fronted books.)

While raw sales are obviously a poor measure of the quality of a *Wonder Woman* run, these numbers indicate the degree to which the investment in Simone writing it narrowly targeted a specific circle of fandom. Gail Simone was the great feminist hope for *Wonder Woman*, coming to the character in her hour of need like King Arthur returning to Britain. Given that Simone also ended up being an island of stability between the upheavals of *Infinite Crisis* and *Amazons Attack!* and the upheavals to follow, it's not a huge surprise that, among Wonder Woman fans, Simone is untouchable in much the same way as Pérez and Rucka.

That said, Simone's tenure is more problematic than her supporters are inclined to admit. But this fact shouldn't be taken to say that Simone was not a massive improvement over the disastrous *Amazons Attack!* nor that she doesn't have some genuinely original and worthwhile things to say about Wonder Woman. In many ways her biggest innovation is that she brings a real and deep sense of humor to her. This isn't surprising, given Simone's history in humor writing, but it's remarkable for Wonder Woman, a character who's typically been straight-laced.

The humor adds a new sort of humanity to Wonder Woman as a character. For instance, in *Wonder Woman* #18, upon being taken to an alien planet whose military she had once defeated, she discovers they've honored her by building a statue in her likeness. The statue, however, is heavily distorted, depicting her as a troll-like alien. As the statue is presented to her, one of the aliens explains, "Our sculptors felt they had to pretty you up a bit. No offense is meant. I know you can't help your hideous appearance." Wonder Woman reflects, "I like to believe I don't list vanity among my faults... but there's something very disconcerting about that, I'll admit it. I wish I'd brought my cell phone. I think Donna would find this endlessly hilarious."

This exchange is interesting in several regards. It tackles a very big problem within Wonder Woman, which is that she's somewhat incapable of taking on something like body-image issues (which are at the root of the joke here). After all, the entire idea of Wonder Woman suggests a woman who's above the petty sexism of body issues, and it's difficult even to have her display empathy with regards to it given that she's consistently depicted as a sexual ideal. About the only thing Wonder Woman could do with an issue along these lines is spout bland platitudes about loving yourself that would be indistinguishable from every other bland and largely ineffectual attempt to give people without supermodel physiques a consolation prize (as opposed to actually depicting alternative body types as attractive on a regular basis).

But Simone, with this scene, finds a way to have her cake and eat it too. The basic situation is absurd enough that Wonder Woman doesn't actually have to confront the question of body image in a direct fashion. She's obviously confronting an analogous issue, but Simone doesn't have to present the ludicrous idea that Wonder Woman might think she's unattractive. Indeed, the entire joke is predicated on the fact that the statue is wildly grotesque. More importantly, by confronting the issue with humor Simone can give Wonder Woman a perspective that simultaneously concedes the point – she's a little disturbed by this attack on her attractiveness – and having her instantaneously rise above it, showing it to be ridiculous. As a result, even though Wonder Woman's on an alien planet it has a relevance and materialism previous eras of Wonder Woman had to stretch themselves to achieve.

This comedic approach to Wonder Woman's humanity is also key to the way in which Simone is able to slay another sacred cow, tackling the question of the character's love life for the first time since Phil Jimenez (and only the second time since pre-*Crisis* Steve Trevor, unless for some reason you desperately want to count John Byrne's definitive "no way in hell" on the subject of the Superman/Wonder Woman romance). That this remains a major issue for Wonder Woman is one of the more frustrating things about the character – another way in which she's meticulously cut off from embodying real human experience. Nevertheless, the idea of Wonder Woman having any sort of sexuality remains taboo. Let's be clear about this: it's not that Wonder Woman is sexualized, which she's obviously been for years, with considerably less controversy than is warranted. Nor is it that writers are portraying her having sex in the comics – it's not as though there's any remotely explicit content with Wonder Woman's love interests, any more than marrying Lois Lane meant a bunch of sex scenes for Superman.

No, the objection that persists around Wonder Woman having a romantic interest in anybody is rooted in the objection to her having any sort of romantic or sexual desire. Admittedly, given the many decades in which her love for Steve Trevor provided an endless litany of appallingly sexist moments, there's real merit to resisting the idea that every story about a female protagonist ought to be about her finding a boyfriend, and the degree to which post-*Crisis* Wonder Woman stories avoid that is something to praise. However, turning Wonder Woman into a sexless character swings the pendulum too far in the opposite direction.

Regardless, the issue is a minefield, and once again Simone deftly uses humor to work around it. She has Wonder Woman court her partner in the Department of Metahuman Affairs, Thomas Tresser, aka Nemesis, framing the plot with comedy. For instance, Diana first approaches Tresser about her interest in him while he's in the hospital following the events of *Amazons Attack!*, engaging in what she describes as a traditional Amazon courtship ritual. Tresser, for his part, asks about the courting rituals of his culture, and Wonder Woman, with a slightly over-serious expression on her face, intones, "I don't know how to bowl, Tom. But I could learn, if it's important." In a similarly light touch, when Tresser realizes that Wonder Woman's people are all women, Wonder Woman jokes, "Aren't you the observant one," and when asked if it still counts with a male, she says, "We'll adapt, somehow."

As with the alien statue, humor makes it easier for Simone to get away with tackling a relatively controversial subject with the character. By having the scene play out with jokes regarding the awkwardness of courtship, Simone folds the controversy over whether Wonder Woman should have romantic partners into the story itself. Yes, it's awkward to have a romantically active Wonder Woman, but the comic knows that, and that makes it easier to get away with. A broader look at the Diana/Thomas romance shows that a large number of scenes advancing the plotline pull comedy out of awkwardness, like in the issue where Tresser has to go to Themyscira to meet Hippolyta for the first time. The result is the most successful attempt at romance for Wonder Woman to date –something even Marston wasn't able to do.

Unfortunately, in later issues the romance goes off the rails in a manner that's symptomatic of the larger problems with Simone's run. It's revealed that Wonder Woman doesn't really love Tresser: her interest in him was purely out of her desire for a mate, motivated by wanting to preserve Amazon culture. This is deeply unfortunate. Having raised the controversial point of Wonder Woman having romantic attraction, to close the door on it because she's only interested in preserving her people sets the issue back even further – it suggests she's emotionally incapable of having a relationship, a horrible outcome that removes her from any sort of reflection of actual human beings, the large majority of whom do, in fact, have romantic interest in other people.

At the root of this is Simone's basic conception of the character, which is fundamentally based on the idea that the Amazons are a warrior culture, a conception that mitigates involvement with the material concerns of everyday life. In an interview before she took on the character she expressed her view that this was the defining aspect of Wonder Woman in the DC Universe: "When a giant robot attacks Metropolis, send Superman. An alien attack? Get Green Lantern. When a car is hijacked by an escaped loony, turn on the bat signal, by all means. But if an *army* shows up on your doorstep, that's when you call in Wonder Woman."

It's telling that the three heroes Simone mentions prior to Wonder Woman were, in 2007, the three biggest-selling heroes in DC's stable, which returns to the age-old question of justifying Wonder Woman's position as an anchor of the DC Universe. But the answer Simone gives here is largely arbitrary. Yes, Wonder Woman has some experience repelling armies, but typically they're alien armies, making the contrast with Green Lantern specious at best. More to the point, the claim that her history is defined by fighting off armies is ludicrous. That's just not what she's been throughout her history.

This gets at a larger problem with the basic question of Wonder Woman's role in the DC Universe, which is that it tacitly mandates that we define her primarily in terms of male superheroes. "What is Wonder Woman's role in the DC Universe?" is a deeply loaded question given she's their only A-list female superhero. It suggests that Wonder Woman can't be her own thing, but has to fit into a role defined by the male characters around her. Tackling this in a story like *Infinite Crisis*, where the entire point is to define everyone's role in the DC Universe, is one thing; meta-commentary on superheroes, particularly in showcase events, is common. It's quite another to endlessly flail about with this in her own series, years later.

Out of desperation to come up with a succinct answer to an unnecessary question, Simone's Wonder Woman ends up being less than her original concept. This is the same problem that plagued the year following Simone, as J. Michael Straczynski executed a year-long arc obsessed, once again, with the question of who Wonder Woman is. (In this case it was further harmed by his leaving the book after a few months, leading DC to have another writer tie up his plots off an outline that was apparently somewhere between sketchy and non-existent.)

But for Simone there's an even larger problem: militarism is just a lousy way to define Wonder Woman. This is exemplified in the centerpiece of her time on the book, an eight-issue epic called "Rise of the Olympian." The plot of this arc focuses on a seemingly unstoppable enemy named Genocide, crafted in the future from the body of a great warrior who, in a revelation that surprised no one, turns out to have been Wonder Woman. The eight issues consist almost entirely of fight scenes and Zeus's efforts to create a new all-male race to replace the Amazons. It's an overbearing storyline where almost all of the tension consists of Wonder Woman vowing repeatedly to destroy Genocide, before deciding at the last moment to have mercy on an inhuman killing machine made from her own desecrated corpse.

In the midst of all of this is a vaguely feminist message based around Zeus's attempt to replace the Amazons with men, something he justifies by saying he wanted to give Wonder Woman the freedom to become a wife and mother. There's a nice barb in Wonder Woman's furious response, and the incident is a pretty solid swipe at the idea that women inherently want to be stay-at-home mothers, their careers an unwanted distraction. There's also a pair of fun two-issue stories, in which Wonder Woman teams up with Black Canary and Power Girl. They clearly have a feminist slant, but tip into the very problem Simone was ostensibly concerned with – making Wonder Woman into the "girl" book. But in the end, Simone's run would have been improved had she been willing to engage the feminist premises of Wonder Woman more often. For the most part, her run reduces *Wonder Woman* to a generic superhero book with little to say. In an effort to be definitive about Wonder Woman's nature in contrast with the rest of the DC Universe, Simone trades in a key part of what actually makes her interesting.

What's disappointing about this is that so much of Simone's tenure is very, very good. Other than having a vaguely neoconservative tinge, the stories aren't ethically problematic by any measure. There's a wonderful zaniness to

Wonder Woman that's been almost completely absent since the days of the Glop. In her first issue, Simone introduces a tribe of talking warrior gorillas who camp out in Diana's apartment and pass judgment on her visitors while hiding in the bathroom. This is absolutely wonderful, and after reading it it's genuinely difficult to go back to comics where the protagonists don't have warrior gorilla roommates. She also plucks freely from Wonder Woman's history, from restoring Etta Candy to a major role in the comic (and Steve Trevor to a smaller one), to referencing Reformation Island and Taco Whiz (though Simone is less than enamored with that plot element). It's very easy to love Simone's Wonder Woman, especially taken on its own.

But in the larger context of the character's history, at times it's hard to like. It's unfair to criticize it too harshly; it's no worse than many of the other quite good periods in Wonder Woman's history, like the Luke or Jimenez years, and after the year-and-a-half disaster following *Infinite Crisis* it's a welcome return to form. To condemn it for its faults strays distressingly close to holding Simone to a higher standard simply because she's the first major female writer of *Wonder Woman*. But equally, if it matters that she's the first major female writer, then it matters that she do a good job with the character. Unfortunately, in her drive to make *Wonder Woman* something other than "the girl book" she ended up making it something that isn't quite Wonder Woman either, but rather a tiny fraction of what the concept and character can be.

A Golden Thread: An Unofficial Critical History of Wonder Woman

Chapter 22: Movies and TV Projects

It was largely inevitable that the boom in superhero movies, beginning with *X-Men* in the year 2000, would eventually impact Wonder Woman. If anything, the biggest surprise is how little impact it's had – Wonder Woman is by far the most prominent superhero not to have a major film in the last decade. That's not to say there haven't been efforts – following the Christopher Nolan reboot of the Batman franchise and Brian Singer's less successful Superman reboot, Joss Whedon was hired to oversee Wonder Woman. This project never came to fruition – the studio didn't see eye-to-eye with Whedon regarding the script – but the overall climate of superhero adaptations led to making new Wonder Woman material for a non-comics audience. The two most prominent examples are the 2009 animated film *Wonder Woman*, and David E. Kelley's unsuccessful 2011 pilot for a television series.

The 2009 *Wonder Woman* animated film has its roots in the long run of animated television shows based on the DC Universe that ran from 1992 to 2006. These shows, typically referred to as the DC Animated Universe, were overseen by Bruce Timm, who moved on to individual direct-to-DVD animated films, the fourth of these being *Wonder Woman*. In the DC Animated Universe television shows, Wonder Woman was compelling if often underdeveloped. Most distinctively, a romantic subplot is introduced between her and Batman, although Batman declines to act on it. (As he puts it, "You're a princess from a society of immortal warriors. I'm a rich kid with issues.") However, the basic idea of suggesting a romantic entanglement for Wonder Woman with someone other than Superman – and who is in many regards Superman's opposite – is refreshing.

The 2009 film is not part of the Animated Universe, and has a subtly different take on Wonder Woman. The Animated Universe version has a bit more humor; the film is vocally ambivalent about the world. But these differences are ones of degree. The Animated Universe is, if not overtly for kids, at least broadly intended as an all-ages franchise. The film, on the other hand, is PG-13, and the first cut was deemed violent enough to be rated R. The two characters are also presented at different points in their lives. The film is an origin story featuring Diana's first few days in Man's World, whereas the animated series features a Wonder Woman who's made numerous friends in the superhero community. It's not surprising that the latter is a bit more light-hearted.

More broadly, the differences between the two takes on the character result from their starkly different approaches. In *Justice League Unlimited* Wonder Woman is part of an ensemble of DC heroes, and even when she's the focus of a story there's only so much role she can have in shaping the tone of the series, but in the film version her world is the basis for organizing the entire story. Drawing from Zack Snyder's then-popular adaptation of Frank Miller's *300*, *Wonder Woman* is drenched in sword-and-sandal violence. Huge swaths of the film consist of elaborate fight scenes, and it goes out of its way to show the Amazons as fierce, brutal warriors. In many ways this goes too far – it's difficult to see any reason why the Amazons should be treated any differently than Ares, aside from the fact that the Amazons are clearly marked as the heroes and Ares as the villain. Nonetheless, it's a striking choice that goes a long way towards making the Amazons compelling and modern.

A Golden Thread: An Unofficial Critical History of Wonder Woman

Even though this take on the Amazons is contrary to a lot of what Wonder Woman has stood for in the past, at least superficially, it's clear that the film isn't criticizing it. The film's default position is that Wonder Woman and the Amazons are cool. It derives considerable humor from Wonder Woman's martial instincts. In what's probably the film's best scene, Wonder Woman encounters a young girl who isn't allowed to play pirates with a group of boys because, as she puts it, they need someone to rescue. Wonder Woman gives the girl a brief sword-fighting lesson, and sends her off to "unleash hell." It's a great comic beat, but more to the point it's a moment where the audience is expected to firmly side with Wonder Woman's somewhat brutal worldview.

The comparison with *300* isn't just superficial. Wonder Woman has always had roots in Greek myth. So when a high-profile comic-inspired movie about a quasi-mythic Greece hits it big, it would be strange if it didn't have an impact on Wonder Woman. Finding a way to have Wonder Woman sensibly extend from a *300*-style take on Greek culture is just a basic part of writing Wonder Woman to respond to popular culture. But it's here that the film falters. Ultimately, the violent take on the Amazons is unconsidered. There's no meaningful commentary on their militancy, and the closest thing there is to one, as we'll see, is enormously problematic.

Much of this stems from the way in which the film aggressively tackles feminist issues. Throughout the film Wonder Woman has an aggressive suspicion of men, including Steve Trevor, which is played in a multi-layered and heavily ironic way. On the one hand, there's sympathy for Wonder Woman by default, as she's the titular superhero. On top of that, Steve Trevor, who's in most of the scenes that invoke misogyny and feminism, is unambiguously portrayed as a sexist pig; he makes comments about Wonder Woman's breasts, and generally objectifies and demeans her.

But on the other hand, Trevor's voice is provided by Nathan Fillion, popular among geek audiences for his portrayal of Malcolm Reynolds in Joss Whedon's *Firefly*. Fillion has made something of a career out of playing lovable rogues with a healthy dollop of sexism, made palatable with enough ironic self-awareness that one can readily separate the actor from the role. Even as a voice actor he's immediately identifiable, and this complicates the reading of Steve Trevor. Still, the film holds to the standard romantic comedy playbook of misunderstandings that are resolved with the eventual triumphant kiss, as in the obligatory scene where Steve confronts Diana with her faults in response to her constant complaints about him and men.

The prevalence of these themes in the script can be narrowed down to one of its co-writers, Michael Jelenic. We know this because the other writer, Gail Simone, has said in an interview that these themes were not present in her initial drafts, that she found them off-putting, and that the film's feminism was "very first wave." Given that she also describes it as "very 70s," it's probably safe to assume she meant "second wave," and that her critique is based on the perception of the second wave as anti-male. But this obscures the fact that there isn't a practical sense of feminism that's not at least partially anti-male. Men make twenty-three cents more on the dollar than women, men are responsible for the overwhelming majority of rapes and sexual assaults, and men have social privileges that are systematically and categorically denied to women – so yes, they have to be treated with a measure of suspicion, categorically. That's a consequence of group-based systemic discrimination.

In that regard, the movie misses a huge point by having Steve's big rant about Diana's cultural failings include a line about men holding doors for women, and how that's not sexist. Because even though holding a door for someone is a courtesy, not discrimination, that's not the objection feminism raises against such chivalry. The objection is that the broader cultural assumption that men ought to hold doors for women (and not vice versa) is a symptom of a larger and more deeply entrenched form of discrimination

A Golden Thread: An Unofficial Critical History of Wonder Woman

and bias. The film ends up staking out overt opposition to this viewpoint, which is deeply problematic.

The most unfortunate moment, however, comes when Hippolyta confronts Persephone, an Amazon who's betrayed her sisters to free Ares, with whom she's fallen in love. As Persephone dies at Hippolyta's hand, she explains that she wanted a life with romance and children, and says, "The Amazons are warriors, but we are women too." Because, apparently, the true definition of femininity is based on making babies. With that line the film's attempt to juggle feminism and the martial conception of the Amazons comes crashing down.

This is unfortunate, because the film comes close to working. The material involving Steve Trevor is phenomenal, and Fillion does a very good job of lacing Trevor with enough irony to function. A scene in which Trevor accidentally gets his foot caught in Wonder Woman's lasso and admits that his masculine bravado is just a front to cover up his insecurities is particularly brilliant. But he's the only part of the film sufficiently steeped in irony to work. The rest of it plays the *300*-esque violence too straight to be undermined when it needs to be, and ends up falling far short of the feminism it seems to be aiming for. Even though Simone's critique misses the target, it's not that far afield. The problem isn't that the film's feminism is second wave, it's that the film ultimately serves as another entrant in the ongoing culture war against the second wave long after it had become a historical relic. The real problem is that the film thinks feminism still has the second wave's problems, and it fights the wrong war as a result.

In this regard, David E. Kelley's *Wonder Woman* pilot is considerably more promising. Unfortunately, as mentioned, the pilot was unsuccessful, and no series was picked up. It was almost universally panned, and this was the case even before it was shot. Given that it's never seen a legitimate release, it's difficult to believe that most of the subsequent criticism was based on actually seeing it, either. The backlash against the project began almost as soon as it was announced. Some of this no doubt came from the inherent strangeness of the project. David E. Kelley has had a long career in television, and is best known for quirky legal dramedies like *Boston Legal* and *Ally McBeal*, the latter to which his *Wonder Woman* was typically compared. His past credits include no examples of science fiction, fantasy, or even, save for the script for *Lake Placid* and ten episodes of a detective show called *Snoops*, anything remotely close to the action-adventure genre. To say that he was not an intuitive choice to create a new *Wonder Woman* series is an exercise in understatement.

On top of that, Wonder Woman became a cultural flashpoint as various factions laid claim to the project. A fair number of fans still nursed a grudge at the derailment of Joss Whedon's Wonder Woman movie, not unreasonably. Given that Whedon has since made the third highest-grossing film ever for DC's competitors with *The Avengers*, sacking him from a Wonder Woman movie has to go down as a dumb move even by the standards of Hollywood. But even before that, the number of people who wanted to see the creator of *Buffy the Vampire Slayer* (likely the most famous female lead in sci-fi/fantasy) tackle Wonder Woman was substantial. The movie's cancellation was always going to poison the well for the next big Wonder Woman project.

Many of those who were so disappointed by the abandonment of Whedon's project belonged to the feminist fandom circles we talked about last chapter. They found much to be alarmed by in the script, with a scene where Wonder Woman in her Diana Prince identity gorges on ice cream at a girl's-night sleepover coming in for particular criticism. The objection was that this was sexist and trivialized Wonder Woman. This is at least in the general realm of reasonableness, although one need only remember the I Ching era to see the limits of this line of thought.

And then there was typical comics audience of (mostly male) fans whose sole interest was in discussing how attractive Adrianne Palicki looked in the Wonder Woman costume, how the costume could be more revealing, and what actresses they would prefer to see playing the role. (These proposals usually consisted of models with little to no acting experience, with the occasional porn star thrown in for good measure.) This was when they weren't complaining about how boring Wonder Woman was, and how nobody should even try to make a movie or television show about her in the first place.

With so much hostile ink spilled before the pilot was even finished, it's not a huge surprise that NBC declined to pick it up. Going into production with a series that was already getting such bad press would have been absurd. While from an aesthetic point-of-view the objections of those whose interest in Wonder Woman extends primarily to her chest and legs can be safely dismissed, from a television production standpoint bad press is bad press. It's the feminist objections that are thornier, because in this regard the uncomfortable parallels to the Gloria Steinem controversy flare up even more brightly. We're back to the most basic problem Steinem had: criticism based on a sketchy understanding of the actual text.

In hindsight, now that the Kelley pilot has leaked onto the Internet, we can make some more substantive judgments. Kelley's basic conceit is that Wonder Woman has two alter-egos. The first is a non-secret identity: Diana Themyscira, head of Themyscira Industries, which licenses Wonder Woman's image for action figures and the like. The second is Diana Prince, an ordinary woman who lives alone with a cat. The core trick of Kelley's approach is to move back and forth among these identities, contrasting the confidence of an Amazon with a fairly straightforward chick-lit character.

The ice cream sleepover that was the focus of so much condemnation isn't even in the final version of the script. But while that specific scene is gone, the approach it suggested is not. The pilot still has a scene in which Wonder Woman munches potato chips and watches *The Notebook* while nursing a bad breakup. But here the advance criticism of

Kelley's approach runs into the other major problem that Steinem's critique did. One can't seriously argue that chick-lit is not a part of a lot of women's lives, or that there aren't a lot of women who have, in fact, watched *The Notebook*. This is a part of women's culture in America in 2011. So the question becomes whether the material experience of actual women is legitimate ground for Wonder Woman to cover. And the answer, as it always has been, is yes. This is not equivalent to the disastrous "Who's Afraid of Diana Prince?" pilot in which Wonder Woman's strength is actively belittled and demeaned, where she's portrayed as a delusional and unattractive woman. Kelley's Wonder Woman is without a doubt a strong and powerful character. It's just that she's equally without a doubt a character in the tradition of *Bridget Jones's Diary*.

These are difficult to balance, but here Kelley's skill in writing television comes into play. He's done shows with quirky characters that flit between intense drama and absurd comedy, and very quickly he demonstrates that he can move nimbly back and forth between the chick lit perspective on Wonder Woman and the austere Amazonian superheroine. His major tool in accomplishing this switch is the same one that animated much of the Lynda Carter series: camp. In this regard it's not far from Gail Simone's use of humor to get away with confronting things that Wonder Woman comics usually have to avoid. The show recognizes the absurdity of Wonder Woman and her costume, and plays everything just straight enough to allow the humor of the concept to emerge organically.

Beyond that, Kelley pulls off the masterstroke of casting Adrianne Palicki as Wonder Woman. She's not a great actress, and looks a little uncomfortable in the role, but in this regard she's much like Lynda Carter. Her delivery may lack subtlety and nuanced expression, but she has a solid consistency that sells each component of the character with equal legitimacy. She's just awkward enough to let the audience in on the joke, and that helps make the whole thing work. She may not be an actress who is perfect in any role, but she's ideal for this one.

This isn't to say that the pilot is perfect. It's not. It's got all the moving parts to navigate between its two genres, but they don't quite work; it lacks an element that clearly connects the chick-lit and the superhero genres. There are possibilities, most notably Steve Trevor, employed this time as the now-married ex-boyfriend Diana left to take on the Wonder Woman mantle, who's come back into Diana's life as a Justice Department liaison. But nothing in the pilot makes the connection strongly enough to justify the show's conceptual high-wire act.

There are also moments of real promise, where the structure allows for a meta-commentary on Wonder Woman and what she does. The highlight of the pilot is when Diana rejects a design for an action figure on the grounds that its breasts are excessively large, a moment that provides more incisive and vindicating commentary on Wonder Woman's larger social role than the last five DC-prompted reinventions of the character combined. This also provides the occasion for a monologue that serves in many ways as the pilot's mission statement, as Wonder Woman snaps at her employees, "Of course Wonder Woman isn't vulgar. Wonder Woman is perfect. Perfect tits, perfect ass, perfect teeth. I mean, look at these teeth. She always does everything right. I mean, God forbid she make a mistake. It's not like we should expect the world to accept her being human." This exposes the central conflict Kelley is interested in, and the major potential of his approach: the tension between the feminist ideal and the material human reality, and the way in which we expect our activists and champions to be perfect instead of human. It's a good theme, and one that's spot on for what Wonder Woman should be used for.

Unfortunately, because fans of various stripes got noisy on the Internet without actually seeing it, the pilot was a non-starter. To be fair, it's far from certain that the show would have taken off. Camp is a tough sell in 2011, and the daringness of the show's approach is the sort of thing that could fall flat with viewers who refuse to take the show on its own terms. The same viewers who insisted blindly that Wonder Woman must never pig out on ice cream are, admittedly, unlikely to be mollified by a postmodern genre fusion that relies on giving equal validity to multiple contradictory aspects of the character. And even with an audience who didn't insist that an action-adventure show had to be played straight, the fact remains that Kelley hadn't gotten all the kinks out of the approach by the pilot. In the best case, the show would have improved over its first and (hopefully) second season. In the worst case, Kelley was never going to get it to work.

Regardless, Kelley's approach to Wonder Woman is one of the most interesting ones to surface in the last decade, and it's better than almost everything in the comics since the mid-nineties. Its status as a legendary failure is wholly undeserved. Like the I Ching era its fortunes seem to mirror, it has obvious flaws, but they are smaller and subtler than its critics insist. And like the I Ching era, its biggest legacy seems to be set as a negative example, when in fact it should be a model for the future. Sadly, the odds of that are slim to none.

Chapter 23: Brian Azzarello (2011-13)

As mentioned previously, Gail Simone's run on Wonder Woman was followed by a brief and unheralded stint by J. Michael Straczynski. But in September of 2011, DC Comics launched yet another attempt to revamp their entire line, this time called the New 52. As such attempts go, this was more ambitious than usual: they cancelled every book they were publishing in August (even ongoing titles from 1930s and 1940s such as *Action Comics*, *Detective Comics*, *Batman*, and *Superman*) and replaced them with fifty-two brand-new issues the following month, all starting at #1, and all with a fresh continuity.

Wonder Woman's relaunch was eventful. The announced creative team of Brian Azzarello and Cliff Chiang clearly had talent, but Azzarello was a wild card to say the least. He's highly acclaimed, but primarily associated with noir crime comics, a far cry from most takes on Wonder Woman. His statements in interviews only made things more curious, as he boldly declared his take on Wonder Woman would be as a horror comic. There was also a bit of a stir over Wonder Woman's costume: at the apparent behest of DC Comics' newly installed co-publisher Dan DiDio, the preview art for *Wonder Woman* was repeatedly changed back and forth between her wearing briefs or wearing slacks. (They eventually settled on no slacks.)

Once the book started, Azzarello quickly proved adept at getting people talking. He got some national headlines with his retcon of Wonder Woman's origins – the "made from clay" story was a lie to protect Diana from Hera's wrath, for she was in fact the biologically conceived child of Zeus and Hippolyta. A few issues later, there came the revelation that the Amazons were not, strictly speaking, exclusively female; they conceived children by storming boats and raping the men, with any male offspring sold into slavery under the god Hephaestus.

It's difficult to find much good to say about either of these plot twists. The first led to a desperately unfortunate scene in which Hippolyta is reduced to "the other woman" pleading for Hera's forgiveness. While a defense could be mustered on the grounds that it's an interesting and novel take on the material realities of female life, it would be a feeble defense at best. However much one might wish that Wonder Woman would have more engagement with sex and sexuality, the sight of Hippolyta begging Hera to forgive her for having an affair with her husband is just painful.

The other plot twist is indefensible. The Amazons have been rendered fallible and morally questionable in the past, but never to this extent. Azzarello makes the Amazons a culture based on rape and androcide. This is a massive blow to the basic idea of Wonder Woman. Instead of coming from a fundamentally noble culture to help improve man's world, she comes from a bunch of murderous psychopaths. Given how often the Amazons have been explicitly tied to a feminist idealism, this comes dangerously close to a wholesale rejection of Wonder Woman's entire history of idealism.

As with past eras of Wonder Woman that had such outwardly horrifying plot developments, the problems with Azzarello's run are mitigated by the overall quality of the work. It's exciting, it's atmospheric, and it's just well done. Azzarello refocuses on the Greek mythology angle of the character, revamping the entire pantheon and giving them starkly non-human traits. Hermes is portrayed as pale, unusually thin, and with oversized, jet-black eyes. Apollo has obsidian skin and burning eyes. More strikingly, Hades is a young boy with candles burning on top of his head, the wax running down his face. And Poseidon is simply a gigantic tentacle-laden fish. The effect is to have the mythological components of Wonder Woman's world seem strange and alien.

Not even in Pérez's tenure was the mythic aspect of Wonder Woman like this. It's magical, not in the cliché sense of being entrancing and beautiful, but in the sense of being properly mysterious and otherworldly. Under Azzarello, the mythological aspects of Wonder Woman become genuinely wondrous again. He makes the smart decision to separate Wonder Woman from the rest of the DC Universe until the last panel of his twelfth issue, introducing the New Gods after only he's wrapped up his first plot arc. This lets the strange world he's built take center stage. And even after he introduces the New Gods, he mainly just uses a single character, Orion. This is fitting – Orion, like Wonder Woman, is an explicitly martial figure with roots in two very different worlds.

As much as some of his revelations about the character grate, on the whole it's a compelling take. Instead of getting involved in the "Who is Wonder Woman?" debate that's plagued the character since at least *Infinite Crisis*, and has derailed other eras more than once before, Azzarello finds a new perspective on the character and just takes off with it. It's easy to like on those grounds, if for no other reason than it's been a long, long time since anyone had a take on Wonder Woman this unconcerned with defining her in the context of the larger DC Universe (a task left to Geoff Johns, the post-New 52 writer of *Justice League of America*). The idea of a *Wonder Woman* run in which Wonder Woman is defined entirely on her own terms is genuinely refreshing. Two years in, the book's only guest star has been Orion, who isn't appearing in any other books at present.

It is, of course, a mug's game to predict where Wonder Woman will go from here. But in just two years, Azzarello's run has already done something few others could manage: add something new to Wonder Woman's core box of tricks. Unsettling supernatural horror is now one of the arrows in Wonder Woman's quiver, so to speak. It's all but inevitable that future writers will talk about wanting to get back to the Azzarello days, just as people inevitably want to get back to Pérez or Marston. It is these things, not the troubling changes to Wonder Woman's origin, may or may not endure. Almost certainly, Hippolyta and the Amazons will be retconned again – their track record on that front is extraordinary.

In spite of some of Azzarello's poorer decisions, bits of Wonder Woman's existing legacy have already crept in, whether inadvertently or out of conscious effort; Azzarello's a good enough writer to make the latter plausible. The revelation of Wonder Woman's true parentage, for instance, comes with a page that (tastefully) depicts Zeus and Hippolyta's coupling, in which it's made clear that Hippolyta was on top, and that Zeus's "absolute control" was "given up." This reaches back to the earliest days of Wonder Woman, with Hippolyta taking the classic Marstonian role of inspiring men – even the father of the gods himself – into submission.

Similarly, even though the retcon of the Amazons is horrifying in its implications, there's a nice moment in its wake that reaches back to the deep past of Wonder Woman. Enraged at the discovery, Wonder Woman tries to free the male Amazons from Hephaestus's slavery. But after successfully binding Hephaestus and beginning an inspirational speech about freedom and being warriors, she's interrupted by the male Amazons who ask her to release their "master." They explain that Hephaestus saved their lives, that "he wanted us and he raised us... here we are artists... and we are happy." Hephaestus explains that he saw his own origins reflected in the abandonment of the male Amazons, and that letting them die was "something I could never allow."

Confronted with this, Wonder Woman is stunned into silence. Rightly so, as in effect she's confronted with her own original premise. The male Amazons' argument is indistinguishable from a claim that they are happy through submission to loving authority. Seventy years later, the utopian concepts of Marston still worm their way into the story. And seventy years later, Wonder Woman is still unable to quite confront them, let alone embody them.

But Azzarello's take on the character exists within the larger context of DC's New 52 initiative, and in the face of that the bright spots that exist are hard to celebrate. The New 52 has been roundly and rightly pilloried for its stunning lack of female characters and creators. Several prominent DC characters were outright removed from the continuity – almost all of them female. Perhaps most astonishingly, at an October 2013 panel at New York Comic Con executives at DC actively bristled at all questions involving the diversity (or lack thereof) in their comics while rewarding fans who asked banal questions about how to break into comics by giving them prizes like e-readers and limited edition lithographs. At one point a fan asked how a character could breathe in their helmet, prompting John Cunningham, the panel moderator, to specifically praise this as the sort of question he liked, as opposed to ones he complained about such as why DC keeps killing off all its characters that aren't straight white men.

Elsewhere, J.H. Williams III and W. Hayden Blackman, the Eisner-winning creative team on *Batwoman* (who wrote a fantastic arc of that book guest-starring Wonder Woman), were forced off the book because they wanted to write a plot where Batwoman married her partner, Detective Maggie Sawyer. And, of course, there's the fact that Wonder Woman conspicuously fails to get a movie adaptation even as superhero movies become increasingly common and popular. The stated reason is always the same: the character is too hard to get to work right. (How one squares this away with seventy-two years of continual publication remains murky.)

Against all of this, the fact that *Wonder Woman* has had some cool images of the Greek gods does not exactly stack up.

But as we've seen, Wonder Woman winds her way back and forth from good periods to bad, as do comics in general. Yes, the New 52 era is a particularly low point for DC. Then again, so were twenty years of Robert Kanigher, the ill-conceived intervention of Gloria Steinem, the post-Linda Carter period, and John Byrne to boot. The problems are significant, but, at least in terms of Wonder Woman, they are new ones. Which is where we started: progress is making new mistakes. The Azzarello run is making them. In the dire context of the New 52, that counts for a lot.

More to the point, one hardly needs to speculate about the future of Wonder Woman. Over seventy-two years of her history have elapsed with the same patterns. She will endure, simultaneously unable to fulfill her own utopian promise and unable to abandon it, and the tension between those two demands will continue to produce moments, both appalling and inspiring, that on the whole turn into this thing we call progress.

In the end, this is almost perfect for Marston's creation. Marston's utopia, as imagined, was almost farcically naive. But equally, as we saw, it was never meant to be a final state of affairs, some fixed configuration of female dominance and male submission. Marston's utopia was always a messy one that had to be continually worked towards. So too with his great creation – a messy character whose greatness often comes not from what she is at any given moment, but from the endless process of working towards what she could be.

About the Author

Philip Sandifer is the author of *The Last War in Albion*, an ongoing blog-based history of British comics, as well as four volumes and counting of *TARDIS Eruditorum*, a critical history of *Doctor Who*. He lives in Connecticut and is frequently climbed on by his cats.

He blogs at philipsandifer.com.

Made in the USA
Lexington, KY
03 November 2013